MANAGING PRIMARY SCHOOLS IN THE 1990s

Christopher Day is Reader in Educational Management and Head of the In-Service Unit in the School of Education, University of Nottingham. Before moving to his present post, he worked in primary and secondary schools, initial teacher training and as an LEA adviser. He has worked extensively in in-service teacher development and consultancy. As part of his in-service commitments, he directs regional and national management courses for heads and senior staff of primary schools. Among his publications are *Appraisal and Professional Development in Primary Schools* (Open University Press, 1987) and *Insight into Teachers' Thinking and Practice* (Falmer Press, 1990).

Patrick Whitaker is currently Director of the Educational Management Development Unit in the School of Education, University of Nottingham. He has a background of teaching and headship in primary schools and was General Adviser in Derbyshire until August 1989. His publications include *The Primary Head* (Heinemann, 1983) and *Appraisal and Professional Development in Primary Schools*. (Open University Press, 1987).

David Johnston has spent twenty-five years associated with primary schools and, at present, is Deputy Chief Education Officer in Manchester, having previously worked as a senior inspector in Manchester and as a general adviser for primary education in Derbyshire. He has been a head of two primary schools in Sheffield, and throughout his career has taken a keen interest in the management role of the head, especially as it relates to how all the people associated with a primary school can work together effectively.

MANAGING PRIMARY SCHOOLS IN THE 1990's

A Professional Development Approach

Second Edition

Christopher Day,
Patrick Whitaker
and
David Johnson

P·C·P
Paul Chapman
Publishing Ltd

Copyright © 1990 by Christopher Day, Patrick Whitaker and David Johnston

All rights reserved

Paul Chapman Publishing Ltd
144 Liverpool Road
London
N1 1LA

No part of this publication may be reproduced, stored in a retrieval system, or transmitted, in any form or by any means, electronic, mechanical, photocopying, recording or otherwise, without the prior permission of Paul Chapman Publishing Ltd.

British Library Cataloguing in Publication Data
Day, Christopher
 Managing primary schools in the 1990s: a professional development approach. –2nd ed.
 1. Great Britain. Primary schools. Management.
 I. Title II. Whitaker, Patrick III. Johnston, David, *1944–*
 372.1200941

ISBN 1-85396-110-8

Typeset by Setrite Typesetters Limited, Hong Kong

Printed by Athenaeum Press Ltd, Newcastle upon Tyne

B C D E F G   5 4 3

CONTENTS

Preface ix

1 LEADERSHIP AND CONSULTANCY: AN ACTION-CENTRED PERSPECTIVE 1
  Action-centred leadership 9
  Leadership or consultancy 14
  Professional relationships and motivation 16
  Intervention: constraints, purposes and processes 20
  Leading the team 24
  Principles of consultancy-leadership 27
  Conclusion 31
2 ROLES AND RESPONSIBILITIES 32
  Constraints and possibilities 35
  Traditional assumptions 36
  Leadership 39
  The functional approach 42
  Developmental approach 48
  In practice 53
3 THE SELECTION OF STAFF 56
  A vacancy becomes available 56
  Assessing the needs 57
  Providing information for candidates 61
  Visits and visiting 65
  References and confidential reports 69
  Interviewing 71
  Induction 80
4 DEVELOPING PROFESSIONAL AWARENESS AND EXPERTISE 81
  Keeping everyone informed 82

	Systems of communication	83
	Staff meetings	83
	Encouraging participation	85
	Non-verbal communication	87
	Keeping ideas flowing	89
	Active listening	90
	Establishing priorities and procedures	91
	The effective management of time	92
	Managing teachers effectively	98
	Handling staff complaints	99
	Dealing with cliques	101
	Feedback	102
	Reviewing teacher progress	103
	Delegating responsibility	105
	Needs and motivation of staff	107
5	INNOVATION AND CHANGE: THE HUMAN FACTOR	113
	Professional learning	114
	Promoting change	116
	Resistance to change	117
	Force-field analysis	123
	The management task	126
	Leadership roles	130
	Affective relationships	132
	The helping process: entitlements, contracting and action planning	133
6	MANAGING THE CURRICULUM	136
	A working model	137
	Planning	138
	School philosophy and values	141
	The learning process	144
	Knowledge about teaching and learning	147
	A practical approach to curriculum management	151
7	REVIEW, DEVELOPMENT AND APPRAISAL	162
	Contexts of appraisal	162
	Accountability	165
	Review, development and appraisal	167
	Key elements	169
	Classroom observation	172
	The appraisal interview	172
	Teacher autonomy	175
	Whole-school review	178

	Managing the process	185
	Classroom-based self-appraisal	186
	Self-review procedures	188
	Classroom monitoring techniques	191
	Providing moral and intellectual support through 'critical friendship'	193
8	DEVELOPING RELATIONSHIPS WITH PARENTS AND GOVERNORS	197
	The role of the primary head	198
	Relationships with parents: some initial considerations	199
	Action strategies for developing relationships with parents	201
	Relationships with governors	208
	Keeping governors informed	210

References and bibliography	214
Author Index	221
Subject Index	223

PREFACE

Those of us who queued up for a copy of the Plowden Report in 1967 (Central Advisory Council for Education (England)) may be saddened (or inspired) by what has happened since. There is no denying the changes, however – and those changes have to be managed in a way that allows the provision of quality learning for the child to continue to be the prime feature of the school.
British primary schools are relatively small and – whatever the current fashion for curriculum subjects, leadership of key areas or core responsibilities – for the most part the integration of learning and the matching of levels, times and ideas to the needs of the child will still be paramount. Mercifully, the tone of this much-needed book clearly fits that prime set of concerns. This *is* a volume about management, about responsibilities, about leadership but, central to the authors' concerns, are those of quality primary education. The themes may be of the moment ('action-centred perspectives', 'innovation and change') but the leitmotiv will be secure and familiar to all concerned with effective primary schooling. Of course, the authors see the book as about the work of the school, but throughout they are concerned to emphasize that such work takes place with real children and with real adults. These are not individuals to be manipulated: these are people concerned with the processes, the feelings, the rules, roles and relations. It is this that keeps the humanity of the process to the fore and, to my mind, makes the book readable and educational.
A great deal has been written about leadership over the years, from the concerns of princes and generals to the more recent preoccupations with

industrial and commercial patterns. Inevitably, the theories sometimes conflict and the language of leadership has become replete with jargon — some of it quite dehumanizing and inappropriate to educational concerns. In this area, too, the book steers a kindly course. The jargon is minimal and the processes of action and concern made explicit. Few could avoid recognizing that the authors have been concerned to make things accessible to the reader and, drawing on much English (and some north American) work, syntheses and explanations are offered in words that make it clear that the goals of British primary education are still the same.

In a recent book (Friesen, 1987) it is pointed out that, throughout the short history of schooling, there have been constant calls for changes in objectives, content or teaching approval. We should not be surprised at this. The school contains the nation's youth. What more prized possession can there be? Headteachers, who (by definition) are bound to have some experience of the educational enterprise, will have already seen much change or demand for it. As Ansoff said, we live in an age of paradox, ambiguity and risk. We can therefore expect schools to reflect uncertainty and major shifts in emphasis from time to time. Such shifts and changes are the very stuff of the educational pendulum. Whilst Britain moves into a period of tight central control of the curriculum and more assessment than has been seen for many years, other countries are actively moving away from control and assessment towards more holistic and individually shaped curricula. No doubt it will always be the same, since there are cogent arguments to support many different approaches. Yet, if a school is to survive as a caring, educational unit, it has to provide security for the children and its teachers. Above all, that is the prime responsibility of its leader. From collegiality to communication, it is easy to get it wrong. From local management of schools to school discipline, schooling is, as Maritain (1960) once said, always at the crossroads.

What, the reader may ask, has all this to do with the subject of this book? 'Everything', is the reply, for here is a book written by lovers of primary education, by practitioners mindful of the need to manage primary schools as professional, accountable and yet essentially *educational* institutions. This is an account and a compendium blending theory with practice, research with prescription. It recognizes that school teaching is one of the 'caring professions' and seeks to examine how a school may best be run and evaluated. At the same time, it is concerned to show that a good primary school is a humanizing, warm and supportive place where the quality of relationships between children, parents and teachers is of vital importance.

Preface

The other side of the picture perhaps needs emphasis too. Warmth is not enough, and haphazard learning is not likely to encourage systematic understanding or the growth of persistence and self-responsibility. Schools have a dual role — to serve society and to serve the individual. Each role must be sustained, examined, developed and assigned equal value. When the rhetoric of accountability and utility dies down, the balance of this dual role is still the collective responsibility of the DES, the LEAs, the headteachers and individual class teachers. To this end, the enhancement of the teaching profession lies not only in its collective levels of control, supply and qualification, but also in the serious study of the mechanisms of institutionalized education with a view to making these amenable to identification, understanding and possible agreement. In this way intuition and ideology are replaced by a proper combination of theory and practice. Whilst primary education may never have been short of imagination, it has never been short of ideology either; and frequently the latter has been confused with theory.

It is particularly important that small institutions dealing with the difficult-to-quantify 'production' of enlightened, considerate, reflective human beings should not be confused with large commercial establishments. It is seductive to attempt to translate 'line-management', 'productive workforce' and similar concepts straight into Merryfields Primary School! In the past the collective wisdom concerning management of secondary schools (with their staffs of ten times the size of that of the average primary school) has too often been added to commercial experience and then offered as a curious admixture to primary heads. In more recent years, experienced practitioners have begun to rectify the glib translations and omissions of such packages. They have recognized the uniqueness of the British primary school, its smallness, its polymathic concerns, its less rigid classification and framing, its majority of female staff. They have been at pains to emphasize that, whilst there are identifiable skills necessary in staff selection, there are also anxious parents leaving their 4-year-olds for the first time — and known ways of alleviating that anxiety.

Leadership is a recurrent theme throughout this book — a leadership that recognizes the unique and independent traditions inherent in teaching; leadership that stresses there is a delicate balance between maximizing institutional health and preserving that of the individual teacher. Changes in the patterns of recruitment, and relative stasis in career opportunities, combine with other, wider social and political forces to make the role of leader somewhat more difficult than that implied in the old notices of legendary fame: 'Headteacher — do not disturb', 'Parents not allowed into the school without prior permission', and so on. To run a school is not quite as simple as some industrial barons would have us believe. Schools are not there merely to mould, certificate and grade, they are concerned with human development, with the welfare of a nation. Moreover, schooling occurs in a very public arena. Everyone is an expert; we have all been to school. No shortage of advice is offered. The delicate balance between individual and societal needs is paralleled in that balance inherent in a curriculum that must provide for an unknown future and the dynamics of change as well as for a firm basis of cultural 'roots' and past experience. Thus, the headteacher has many balancing acts to perform. He or she has to articulate and clarify ambiguities of social expectation to both parent and LEA. He or she must consult, modify and (perhaps) inspire those to whom 'the daily round, the common task' can at times seem pointless and undramatic.

Overall, I remain convinced that Britain is extremely lucky to have such an expert, such a caring, such a democratic and such a hard-working teaching profession. Teachers deserve wholehearted support and interest. We should remember that they are frequently neglected, derided and (seemingly) deliberately misunderstood. Only when the leader has experience of the routines of such institutions of their peer pressures, happiness, insolence, surprise, resentment, noise and anxiety, and only when that leader manages from a certain sure basis of empathy and expertise can the professionalism emerge that takes a school forward into the future.

Most air-pilots will be familiar with the five basic manuals on how to do it. The goals are not quick side-slips or barrel-rolls. The overall concerns are with the management of a smooth, level, safe and enjoyable flight. To soar like a bird has been, for many years, one of humankind's outstanding ambitions; to educate in happiness and to instil a love for learning is even more fundamental. Here, then, is a useful pilot's manual. It explores the familiar ground, from Machiavelli to the Education Reform Act, from the business of staff selection to working with governors. It does this in a direct, commanding and simple way that, to my mind, does no offence to the basic principles of education but rather *enables* the leader to emphasize and enhance them:

> The development of confidence in one's own genuine powers – however limited these may be – is the first essential of personal growth, and such confidence is rooted in an attitude to the world which finds it a good place, and the people in it worthy of trust and love. Given the right start, children want to grow up; they want to learn to use their own bodies skilfully, to

create in clay, paint, dance and music; they want to learn to read, write and count, to explore the world around them, to master ideas and to help one another.

(Morris, 1972)

Philip Gammage
University of Nottingham
1990

1
LEADERSHIP AND CONSULTANCY: AN ACTION-CENTRED PERSPECTIVE

This chapter considers the headteacher first and foremost as a leader of adults with responsibility for ensuring opportunities for staff development that are related both to individual and to school needs. These will be of different kinds at different times since staff, like children, will be at different stages of development, and schools will have to respond at different times to externally generated demands. The complexity of leadership and consultancy roles is recognized and the chapter offers practical assistance in planning and reflecting on the task of leadership in which the head acknowledges that staff have an active part to play in their own learning and, thus, the management of the school.

Leaders in the 1990s operate in a context of increasingly detailed answerability to parents, governors, LEAs and the DES for the quality of education in their schools. The late 1980s brought major legislation – the culmination of Callaghan's (1976) Ruskin speech calling for more accountability – that resulted in a great number of externally imposed innovations. All of these have had to be 'managed'. Leaders in the 1990s must ensure that their schools have annually reviewed, publicly available school-development plans, systematic teacher appraisal, a school-marketing policy, efficient monitoring and assessment procedures for the National Curriculum – and all this whilst managing 'directed time', professional development days and a 'real' school budget. It is not just that headteachers and others need to possess a wider range of skills and qualities than those of the 1980s, but also that they will be called upon to apply them more frequently, and in more complex and stressful situations, not least in their own schools amongst staff whose morale is not always as high. Yet in the ever-increasing number of texts concerned with management, the most neglected area is often the process of managing. There seems to be an assumption that once aims, objectives and means of assessment have been clarified all that has to be done is to follow a series of prescribed steps or to complete a checklist; or, at another extreme, that leaders (or managers) must already possess the necessary qualities and skills or they would not be leaders! Those who have experienced leadership roles will know that prescribed checklists for action are fallible and that opportunities for teachers to develop management skills are even now few and far between.

Management style is the biggest single factor in making quality improvements in school. It will be the headteacher who ensures collegiality internally – so necessary a thing if progression and continuity within and beyond the National Curriculum are to be achieved. It will be he or she who ensures that the staff gain skills of communication and collaboration needed for working more closely with parents and governors. This kind of facilitating leadership places an emphasis upon 'consultation, team-work and participation' identified long ago as contributing to effective leadership (DES, 1977a). In 1983, the DES reiterated their view of the importance of effective leadership:

> Head teachers, and other senior staff with management responsibilities within the schools, are of crucial importance. Only if they are effective managers of their teaching staffs and have the material resources available to them, as well as possessing the qualities needed for educational leadership, can schools offer their pupils the quality of education which they have a right to expect.

Yet effective leadership is the result of a complex interaction between style, prevailing staffroom learning cultures, uses and perceptions of power and authority, and individual and group relationships as applied to particular tasks. After all, since Plowden (Central Advisory Council for Education (England), 1967), an increasing number of teachers who are not heads or deputies have become 'leaders' within curriculum and pastoral areas of school life. Indeed, ILEA's *Improving Primary Schools* (1985) recommended that 'Primary school teachers, except possibly in their probationary year, should take responsibility for advising the rest of the staff on major aspects of the curriculum or associated matters, for example assessment'. This is now enshrined in legislation (DES, 1988).

ILEA's junior-school project's (1986) findings confirmed the move from a concept of the headteacher as leader to a concept of the head as 'leader among leaders', who works to facilitate leadership and encourage it among the whole staff. Three of the twelve key factors in effective schooling concerned leadership:

Purposeful leadership of the staff by the headteacher
'Purposeful leadership' occurred where the headteacher understood the needs of the school and was actively involved in the school's work, without exerting total control over the rest of the staff. In effective schools, headteachers were involved in curriculum discussions and influenced the content of guidelines drawn up within the school, without taking total control. They also influenced teaching strategies of teachers, but only selectively, where they judged it necessary...a systematic policy of record keeping was important. With regard to in-service training, those heads exhibiting purposeful leadership did not allow teachers total freedom to attend any course: attendance was encouraged for a good reason....Thus, effective headteachers were sufficiently involved in, and knowledgeable about, what went on in the classrooms and about progress of individual pupils. They were more able to feel confident about their teaching staff and did not need to intervene constantly. At the same time, however, they were not afraid to assert their leadership where appropriate.

The involvement of the deputy head
Where the head generally involved the deputy in policy decisions, it was beneficial to the pupils....
Thus it appeared that a certain amount of delegation by the headteacher, and a sharing of responsibilities, promoted effectiveness.

The involvement of teachers
In successful schools, the teachers were involved in curriculum planning and played a major role in developing their own curriculum guidelines. As with the deputy head, teacher involvement in decisions concerning which class they were to teach, was important. Similarly, consultation with teachers about decisions on spending was important. It appears that schools in which teachers were consulted on issues affecting school policy, as well as those affecting them directly, were more likely to be successful.

(*Ibid.*)

In an article focusing on primary-school leadership, Southworth (1988) asserts that whilst research into leadership generally supports the notion that leadership is an important factor in determining organizational effectiveness and that leaders, therefore, can make a positive difference to the effectiveness of an organization, few studies have focused on primary-school effectiveness. He cites ILEA's junior-school project (1986) (to which we have already referred) as one 'notable exception', ILEA's committee on primary education report (1985) and a study by Coulson (1986) as others.

The Primary School Staff Relationships (PSSR) project (Nias,

Southworth and Yeomans, 1989) indicated that the heads of schools that offered a 'positive' model of such relationships *lived* the beliefs underlying 'their' schools' culture. Thus, these heads were able to operate at two different levels: a high level of abstraction (e.g. defining their beliefs about the social and moral purposes of education) and at the level of their day-to-day actions, even those at the most mundane and detailed level (Southworth, 1988). From his review of literature on effective leadership, Southworth (1990) derived a list of characteristics of an effective headteacher. *An effective headteacher*

- emphasizes the centrality of teaching and learning: via his/her teaching commitment; persistent interest in the children's work and development; through attention to teachers' plans, practice, reflections and evaluations.
- ensures that there are explicit curriculum aims, guidelines and pupil record keeping systems and that all of these are utilized by teachers and other staff in order to establish some consistency, continuity and coherence.
- acts as an exemplar: regularly teaches; leads assemblies; works long and hard for the school.
- ensures that the teachers have some non-contact time.
- sets high expectations for self, children and staff.
- encourages and develops others to lead and accept positions of responsibility.
- involves the deputy head in policy decision-making; head and deputy operate as partners.
- involves teachers (and sometimes others) in curriculum planning and school organization; generally (but not necessarily always) adopts a consultative approach to decision-making.
- is conscious of the school's and individual teacher's needs with regard to teacher attendance on in-service training courses; is aware of own professional development needs.
- is considerate towards staff: offers psychological support; takes an interest in staff as people; is willing (on occasions) to help reconcile and make allowance for personal/professional role conflicts (health problems, domestic crises, clash of evening commitments).
- constantly enquires into many aspects of the school as an organization: tours the school before, during and after school; visits staff in their classroom and work places; perceives the school from different perspectives; observes and listens; manages 'by wandering about'.
- develops and sustains a whole school perspective insofar as there is a shared and agreed vision of effective practice which is adopted by and becomes the staff's collective mission.
- nurtures and maintains a school culture which is inclusive of the school's staff and which facilitates professional and social collaboration.
- is personally tolerant of ambiguity.

- ensures that the school has an explicit and understood development plan: has a sense of direction; anticipates future developments.
- involves parents and governors in the work and life of the school; is an effective communicator of the school's successes and challenges, presents a positive image of the school, staff and children.

Leadership is not confined to head or deputy. Clearly, the effective leader will also be at times a member of the group, and it may be that 'the ultimate test of heads' leadership is the effectiveness of their membership − that they perform a valued function for and within the group' (Yeomans, 1986). An interesting elaboration of this view emerged from the PSSR project (Nias, 1987b). One of its members gave four examples of how effective heads worked:

> First, these primary heads devoted time nearly each day, certainly every week, to touring the school. They walked the corridors, visited all areas of the school, met and talked with colleagues and co-workers. If they were free from teaching duties they did this during the school day, if they were a teaching head they did it either when released from teaching or before and after school.
> Literally, the heads were out and about and, in common with many other managers, they were, as Peters and Austin say, doing MBWA − Managing By Wandering About!
> Second, MBWA embraced a range of key skills. The heads in the PSSR project, for example, were constantly listening to the school. Their tours allowed them to hear how colleagues thought the school was doing, to talk about successes and difficulties, to share problems and anticipate developments.
> In a sense the heads were not so much monitoring the school as enquiring into the school: How are we doing? What are we thinking? What do we need to be doing? The heads were forever finding out about their schools. MBWA thus involves curiosity, the capacity to listen, and the ability to seek out or anticipate challenges before they become problems which ambush one.
> Third, the heads were also skilled negotiators. They met staff face-to-face and, moreover, they met staff very frequently. They kept times between seeing staff to a minimum. Consequently, it did not take long to up-date one another, nor was there much time for difficulties to develop, let alone fester and infect other parts of the school.
> Simultaneously, if they suspected there was someone who was unhappy, discomforted or displeased their tours not only kept them in-touch but also created opportunities for the 'problem' to be aired, and shared and provided a context whereby the two could resolve, say, some disagreement, on a one-to-one basis.
> Fourth, all of these activities enabled the heads to manage the school as an organism rather than as an organization. Whether it was cause or effect I do not know but the heads' close and constant involvement with people, their

problems, aspirations, successes and *feelings* certainly made it impossible for them to remain insensitive to the emotional side of the school in terms of the staff and the children.

These heads did not regard their schools as mechanisms controlled by lines of command and driven purely by instructions and systems. Rather, they accepted that their schools were densely populated places loaded with feelings and values.

(Southworth, 1988)

It is clear that the preferred management culture for effective schooling — paradoxically given more emphasis by the introduction of a National Curriculum — is *interdependence* rather than dependence or independence. Jennifer Nias (1987a), in another paper outlining the 'culture of collaboration' that characterized some of the schools in the PSSR project, claimed that:

To work effectively together, people must share three understandings about their work (that is, in schools, about education). They must agree on what they are trying to achieve (aims and purposes), on how to achieve it (so, they must hold similar beliefs about cause and effect) and on how hard they will work and to what standard. Teachers are aware of the need for agreement on these dimensions.

Research in America identified two categories of schools as 'learning enriched' and 'learning impoverished'. The characteristics of 'learning enriched' schools were

- Collaborative goals at the building level
- Minimum uncertainty
- Positive attitudes of teachers
- Principals supported teachers and removed barriers for them
- Principals fostered collaboration as opposed to competition.

(Rosenholtz, 1989)

Characteristics of 'learning impoverished' schools were

- No clear goals or shared values
- Teachers rarely talked to one another
- Teacher perceived the school to be routine
- Norms of self-reliance flourished, as did isolation.

(*Ibid.*)

It is clear from these researches that headteachers must be people-centred as well as task-centred and that they must be skilled in managing uncertainty themselves so that they can assist others. They must be able to mediate in situations of conflict or potential conflict, and they must be able to manage themselves.

A study by Alan Coulson (1986) suggested that good headteachers have

- clear goals
- are capable of making these goals operational
- a high degree of personal security
- can tolerate a high degree of ambiguity
- are proactive in confronting internal and external demands
- are sensitive to the dynamics of power
- take an analytical approach to problem solving
- behave in ways which allow them to fulfil the demands of the job without being swamped by them.

(Quoted in Dean, 1987)

Yet above all, headteachers must be able to create and sustain a climate in which there is room for planned personal, professional and institutional growth and development – and this means being able to manage the individual, the team and the task.

Before proceeding further, it is necessary to define the notion of leadership that underpins this chapter and that is implicit in the book as a whole. Leadership here is defined as 'consultancy'. This enables us to think in terms of roles rather than 'positions'; and this in turn has the immediate effect of focusing on people and purposes. The objective of this chapter, therefore, is to explore how all those (including headteachers) who wish to influence others might do so most effectively. Emphasis will be laid on particular processes of consultancy by leaders rather than on the particular, strict, occupational role different leaders might hold. In this way both the needs of leaders in 'managing' and the needs of staff who are being 'managed' will be considered.

> By the consulting process, I mean any form of providing help on the content process, or structure of a task or series of tasks, where the consultant is not actually responsible for doing the task itself (anything a person, group or organization is trying to do) but is helping those who are. The two critical aspects are that help is being given, and that the helper is not directly responsible within the system (a group, organization or family) for what is being produced. Using this definition, consulting is a function, not an occupational role per se.
>
> (Steele, 1975)

The consultant (be he or she head, deputy, allowance holder or LEA adviser/inspector) can only be *indirectly* responsible for the teaching in the classroom, for he or she is dealing with adults with their own perceptions of their responsibilities. Adults, like children, cannot be developed – they can only be given opportunities to develop. This is a crucial principle, for it points the way to the consultant's role in the process of curriculum and staff development. In essence, he or she cannot enforce change, only promote it.

It must be stated at the outset that the leader's job is first and foremost to influence others in order to ensure maximum efficiency and effectiveness of the teaching–learning process. In the case of primary-school headteachers, the people they must influence are the staff, the children, the parents, the school governors and the LEA. Although each of these groups will influence the headteacher, only he or she is in a position to have an overview that takes into account each of the needs expressed but that is more than their sum. This is expected of a leader and is variously called a policy, an ideal, a set of aspirations or a vision for the school the head holds and is expected to communicate to all the interest groups that make up a school community. Figure 1.1 is a simple representation of the head at the centre of a very complex communications network.

The network is complex because between groups and within each group there will be expectations, demands and abilities that may conflict. The head will need to identify and balance these interests before decisions are made, wherever possible taking into account the different influences at work and the consequences of accepting one at the expense of another. How effectively and efficiently this network operates depends on the head's ability to receive and interpret signals accurately, to ensure communication within and between groups and to influence one or more of the groups. The head is regarded by all groups as the focal point of school life – with the possible exception of the pupils, who may regard their class teacher in this way. Indeed, a useful analogy may be drawn here for, like the class teacher, the head has to ensure that his or her 'audience' feels secure (through good organization and an environment conducive to learning); feels able to contribute (to their own learning and, hence, feeling of self-worth); feels able to communicate (through the building of satisfactory working/professional relationships); and feels a sense of continuity, progression and achievement (through the head's ability to monitor and assess progress). So it is the way in which the head intervenes in the lives of these groups that is crucial to his or her success in influencing them.

There may be fears among headteachers that changes in structural relationships both externally and internally (which have been caused by the increased powers of governors, the introduction of the local financial management of schools, increased parental choice over school selection, the implementation and monitoring of the National Curriculum and teacher

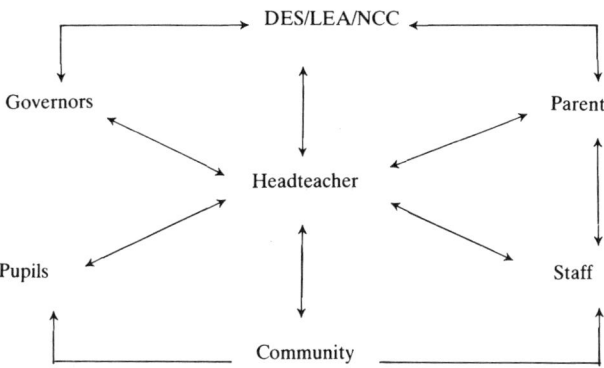

Figure 1.1 The head at the centre of the communications network

appraisal) will *of necessity* cause their role to become more administrative and less professional. Given that the abiding functions of leaders in schools will remain the achievement of task, individual and group maintenance and development and 'boundary' management, the roles of *leading professional and chief executive* (or professional-as-administrator – Hughes, 1988) will need to continue to be combined. In this sense, heads of primary schools will become more like their secondary-school counterparts:

> The innovating head, it appears, relies partly on exerting influence on staff colleagues as a fellow professional; equally, however, he accepts his position as chief executive, and uses the organisational controls which are available to him to get things moving. Professional and executive considerations reinforce each other as complementary aspects of a coherent and unified strategy.
>
> (Hughes, 1976)

Many heads will continue to activate and integrate contrasting and potentially conflicting aspects of their total role successfully (*ibid.*). Figure 1.2 provides a summary of the primary head's managerial roles.

ACTION-CENTRED LEADERSHIP

Given that most learning about management will continue to take place 'on the job', it may be helpful to identify a number of categories that, despite overlap and interdependency, constitute the kinds of knowledge

Roles	Description	Representative activities
Chief executive roles		
Interpersonal		
Figurehead	Symbolic head, performing routine legal or social duties	Assembly; signing reports and authorizations
Leader/supervisor	Responsible for the motivation and coordination of subordinates' work	Embodied in virtually all managerial activities involving subordinates: classroom visits, discussions, etc.
Liaison	Maintenance of network of outside contacts	Correspondence; external committee work; links with LEA people and governors
Informational		
Monitor	Seeks and receives wide variety of information to develop understanding of organization and environment; emerges as nerve centre of internal and external information	Handling mail and contacts concerned primarily with receiving information (e.g. observational tours of school; LEA and government circulars and memoranda)
Disseminator	Transmits information to members of staff: some information factual, some involving interpretation and integration of diverse value positions from outsiders	Directing mail and other material to teachers for informational purposes; verbal contacts involving information flow to subordinates
Spokesperson	Transmits information to outsiders on school's plans, policies, actions, results, etc.: serves as education 'expert' to general public	Governors' meetings; handling contacts involving transmission of information to outsiders

Figure 1.2 Summary of the head's managerial roles (Source: Coulson, 1987)

Roles	Description	Representative activities
Decisional		
Entrepreneur	Searches school and its environment for opportunities to initiate change through 'improvement projects'	Reviews of curriculum and policy involving initiation of 'improvement projects'
Disturbance handler	Responsible for corrective action when school faces unexpected disturbances	*Ad hoc* coping with breakdown of school facilities, unwelcome visitors; discipline
Resources	Responsible for the allocation of school resources of all kinds – in effect the making or approval of all significant decisions	Distribution of human and material resources in accordance with head's 'philosophy' and scale of priorities; timetabling; budgeting
Negotiator	Representing the school at negotiations	Promoting or defending the interests of the school
Leading professional roles		
Goalsetter and evaluator	Determining the overall character of the school and overseeing progress towards this as a goal	Shaping curriculum and organization; formulating statements of aims (e.g. in-school prospectus); school self-evaluation
Curriculum coordinator and developer	Making final decisions on emphases to be given among curriculum subjects and materials	Keeping informed of curriculum developments; chairing meetings; allocating posts of responsibility for curriculum areas; choice and purchase of materials; classroom supervision of teachers
Teacher	The head's time in classrooms: personal teaching or working alongside teacher colleagues	Scheduled teaching of classes or groups; covering for absent teachers
Exemplar of professional values	Displaying behaviours valued by teachers and seen by them as exemplifying 'professionalism'	Willingness to teach; 'commitment' to school; reliability, efficiency, concern for children and teachers; solidarity with teachers' interests

necessary for leaders. These have been conceptualized as follows:

Knowledge of people   This will play an important part in interpersonal relationships and the decisions taken in initiating and responding to colleagues.

Situational knowledge   This is concerned with how managers interpret the information they receive about school life, how they assess its status and significance and how they communicate it.

Knowledge of educational practice   This covers the extent to which managers keep themselves informed about new and existing practices in teaching, learning, organization, staff development, external relationships, etc.

Conceptual knowledge   Usually at an implicit level, this is defined as 'that set of concepts, theories and ideas that a person has consciously stored in memory' that is an aid to 'analysing issues or problems, or debating policies and practices' (Eraut, 1988).

Process knowledge   This is commonly known as 'know-how'. It is partly a matter of knowing all the things one has to do and making sensible plans for doing them; and partly a matter of possessing and using practical, routinized skills.

Control knowledge   This covers

> self-awareness, and sensitivity; self-knowledge about one's strengths and weaknesses, the gap between what one says and what one does, and what one knows and does not know; self-management in such matters as the use of time, prioritisation and delegation; self-development in its broadest sense; and generalised intellectual skills like strategic thinking and policy analysis.
>
> (Eraut, 1988)

Anyone who has been involved in leadership will know that there can be enormous discrepancies between what has been called the logic of planning and the logic of action (Stake, 1967). In the action of managing even the best-laid plans may go astray.

Below is a fine example, from an industrial context, of the logic of rational planning for action-centred leadership. It is suggested that there are interrelated purposes for the action-centred leader – developing individuals, achieving the task and building the team – and it is implied that there are 'action points' for putting these purposes into practice (The Industrial Society, 1983):

1. Set the task of the team. Put it across with enthusiasm and remind people of it often.

2. Make leaders accountable for 4–15 people. Instruct them in leadership actions.
3. Plan the work, check its progress, design jobs and arrange work to encourage the commitment of individuals and the team.
4. Set individual targets after consulting. Discuss progress with each person regularly, but at least once a year.
5. Delegate decisions to individuals. If not, consult those affected before you decide.
6. Communicate the importance of everyone's job. Explain decisions to help people apply them. Brief the team together monthly on progress, policy, people and points of action.
7. Train and develop people, especially the young. Gain support for rules and procedures, set an example and 'have a go' at those who break them.
8. Where unions are recognized, encourage joining, attendance at meetings, standing for office and speaking up for what each person believes is in the interest of the organization and all who work in it.
9. Serve people in the team and care for their well-being. Improve working conditions and safety. Work alongside people. Deal with grievances promptly and attend social functions.
10. Monitor action. Learn from success and mistakes. Regularly walk round each person's place of work to observe, listen and praise.

These stages of action are clearly relevant to leaders in primary schools in their planning, but in considering their actions it is necessary to uncover the value system and attitudes upon which this planning and action is based.

McGregor (1960) proposed two perspectives on management. He devised a 'Theory X' and 'Theory Y' view of human enterprise. McGregor (*ibid.*) postulates that workers become passive as a result of Theory X. Theory X

> is a conventional management perspective, which views people as needing to be directed, controled and motivated, with their behavior moulded to fit the needs of the organization. It reflects paternalistic and mechanistic approaches to management, which emphasize man's need for external pressures to 'keep him in shape' and combat his natural laziness and irresponsibility. Like a donkey, man works best with a conditioning mixture of the carrot (bribes) and the stick (threats). In practice, Theory X is exemplified in individual incentive schemes, clocking on, emphasis on discipline, and promotion based on length of service.

Theory Y, on the other hand, conceives of humanity as active by nature. Everyone has the potential for development, the capacity for responsibility and the readiness to direct their behaviour towards the goals of the organization. This is the participative approach in which work is seen as potentially satisfying in itself, because it is as natural an activity as playing. People only become passive and uncooperative because of their experiences, and it is a manager's job to remove obstacles and release potential. In practice, Theory Y is exemplified by agreeing targets, good delegation and job enrichment.

This book, whilst recognizing that there are occasions for adopting a Theory X approach, asserts that more effective leadership will occur through the use of a Theory Y view of management. We argue, for example, that in the case of the checklists and prescribed steps associated with Theory X, no account is taken of the attitudes to development held by the people with whom you have to work, nor to their expectations, abilities, feelings and different processes of working. These will tend to get in the way of the appreciation of the 'grand plan' devised in the tranquillity of home or office. Theory X also implies that leaders or managers have acquired the necessary expertise to 'manage' adults. This is by no means necessarily so, since almost all headteachers and deputies will have spent most of their professional lives working with children, and not with the adults who now claim the major part of their time and attention.

LEADERSHIP OR CONSULTANCY

Many people have attempted to classify leadership styles and to suggest which are the most effective. The best-known styles have been dubbed 'authoritarian', 'democratic' and *'laissez-faire'* (Lippitt and White, 1943) and, while it is generally accepted that the last is the least effective, there has always been disagreement about which of the other two is the more effective. The argument is often shelved by putting the difference down to the personality of the individual! Meighan (1981) indentified styles of leadership by the class teacher that may usefully be applied to leadership of staff. He described two broad categories: authoritarian (where the pupils remain dependent on the teacher) and democratic (where pupils are interdependent with the teacher). Within each of these categories there were a number of orientations.

In Figures 1.3 and 1.4 we have substituted 'teacher' for the original 'pupil' and 'leader' for 'teacher'. Each of the 'authoritarian' styles (Figure

Leadership and Consultancy 15

Figure 1.3 Authoritarian styles – teachers remain dependent on leader (Source: Adapted from Meighan, 1981)

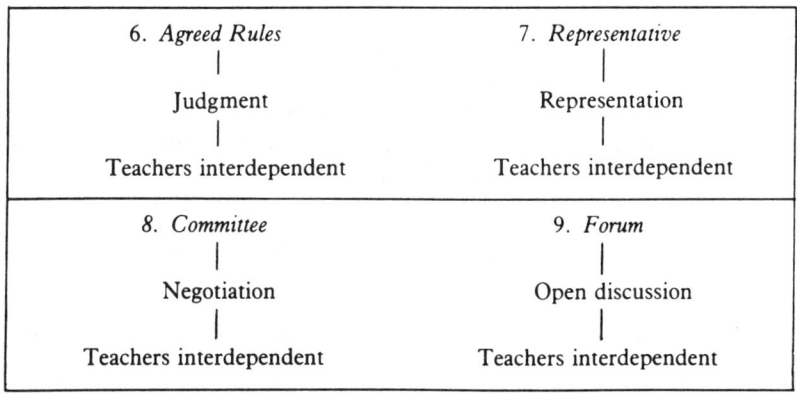

Figure 1.4 Democratic styles – teachers are interdependent with leader (Source: Adapted from Meighan, 1981)

1.3) is distinct, and each (with the exception of style 1) holds possibilities for movement towards the 'democratic' styles (Figure 1.4).

We are not seeking to make judgments on leadership effectiveness at this point. However, it is interesting to speculate on the possible cause-and-effect link between the authoritarian style of leadership and low self-expectations of teachers, who are rarely, if ever, called upon to participate in staff discussions on the shape of the curriculum or home–school policy, and who are not consulted about significant developments of any kind. Teachers in this position are unlikely to show initiative or feel confident in their own ability to engage in, for example, decision-making activities outside their own classrooms. In the first place they have had no practice, and, second, they may feel that it is not their responsibility. So it may be that the leader who consistently avoids involving others in planning and decision-making is actively teaching his or her staff to feel incompetent in these processes. Though working in a different context, Seligman (1975) indentified this as 'learned helplessness'.

PROFESSIONAL RELATIONSHIPS AND MOTIVATION

What most influences teachers in schools? Below are a number of vignettes provided by headteachers in answer to this question. Each has been selected because it provides an example of a different quality of leadership in action, and of how teachers were motivated by processes of social influence. In particular, each teacher was helped by the head in processes of internalization rather than in compliance or identification with authority or charisma. Change based on such compliance or identification is less likely to be long term than change that accords with or may be adapted to the person's own value system (Kelman, 1961).

Example 1: timing (knowing when to help and when to let staff get on)

In my first year of teaching I had a problem with teaching mathematics. I knew what I wanted to teach but my organization was letting me down and producing a negative effect with my class. My headteacher noticed this without me having to go to him, showing an awareness of things going on in school and an awareness of the problems confronting new teachers. He suggested that he took my class for mathematics for a period of three weeks while I stayed in the classroom and watched.

Form this I gained a good deal of knowledge about organization not only of mathematics but also of other subjects. His was a practical help which the situation needed initially and from then on he gave advice when asked for or when he felt it necessary.

Example 2: clear communication

The head in question was an excellent organizer. She knew what she wanted within the school and she made sure all the staff knew what was happening down to the last detail. This covered all aspects of school life, from organization of the curriculum to ordinary everyday events and the social life of the school. No member of staff likes to know they are being left in the dark; if they know what to expect they well respond positively.

Example 3: practical empathy

A few years ago I was teaching in a large primary school where three teachers were serving a probationary year. These were young female teachers, all with quiet personalities. On the staff at the time were some rather forceful characters. The three young teachers were afraid to enter the staffroom at playtime (and admitted this). The headteacher concerned dealt with this by having small weekly meetings with them to discuss their problems, and the progress they were making. (As deputy head I was also involved.) This was in addition to helping them individually in classrooms, or with lesson plans and evaluation. By being together, they felt more confident expressing opinions about their work. The sympathy shown by the head, by placing himself in their position, encouraged them to contribute in full staff meetings.

Example 4: leading by example

The headteacher was very enthusiastic about the countryside and 'environmental studies'. He inspired others. A Bird and Tree Festival was held annually at which an invited speaker talked to the children. A tree or shrub was planted in the school grounds. All the classes prepared for the day by studying some aspect of the environment and a prize was awarded for the best class project. There was music, dance, verse, writing and creative activities. The headteacher worked hard to build up to the day and he, throughout the year, kept the school garden attractive and productive of fruits, vegetables and flowers. The school benefited tremendously from the interest radiated by the headteacher without whom none of this would have taken place.

Example 5: supporting staff against external pressures

Several years ago, the school where I worked as a language consultant had a particularly obnoxious chairman of governors who thought a great deal of himself and very little of teachers. His manner towards teachers was hectoring and loud and he and I fell foul of each other during a course I was running in my own time. He made loud comments and suggestions and his presence and attitude were undermining my work.

The head arrived on the scene and summed it up. His choices were to support me and incur the displeasure and its consequences of the chairman, or to laugh it off and let me down.

He spoke very coldly to the man, saying, 'If you feel you can do this better, then please go ahead. That will give Mrs X the chance to go home and rest; she's done a full day's work already. Otherwise I'd suggest you leave the premises.'

He left, clearly furious. At the next governors' meeting the head tackled the man and gained the support of the other governors. A resolution was passed that *any* governor would only come to school after telephoning or by invitation and would never interfere with the work of the school.

The head had shown his integrity by supporting me, who would make little trouble for him, at the risk of offending someone who was likely to make a lot — and subsequently tried to.

Example 6: caring about personal and professional needs

The head for whom I worked the longest was a fatherly, old-fashioned gentlemanly style of headteacher. I willingly served on his staff and loyally supported almost everything he did. In analysing why this was so, I've decided that it was because he genuinely cared about me as a person. He expressed interest, not only in my professional work, but also in the members of my family and in all my out-of-school activities. He always had time to listen. This concern, which applied equally to all members of staff, caused me to feel valued, and I gave my very best in response.

If effective leadership means the ability to achieve such a response from members of staff, that was an instance of it. Not perhaps a very dramatic situation but an 'effective' one.

Example 7: setting standards

As a newly qualified teacher my head was seldom too busy to talk to me and would continue to discuss the matter in hand even when I was on playground duty, by doing the duty with me. He always displayed a sympathetic approach and was ready with encouragement and praise when he visited the classroom. If he thought I was doing something which didn't quite measure up to his requirements or standards, he would say so — but always in a friendly fashion. I never felt that I was being put down and I respected that. He wouldn't suffer fools gladly, but he did it in a pleasant fashion. He was rather of the 'old school' and valued scholarship and 'standards'. He urged me to continue my own education, night-school courses, etc., in order to become better qualified. Although formal himself he accepted that teachers would try new ideas and methods, which he tolerated rather than really enthused over. This head was respected in the community and was liked by parents, children and staff.

As a new teacher I appreciated his listening ear and his readiness to devote time to me. I respected his judgments and I found his advice to be wise and practical. I valued him greatly as a colleague and, later, as a friend.

Example 8: supporting change

When first appointed as a deputy head I wanted to introduce a new maths scheme throughout the school as one did not exist at that time. I was given the opportunity by the headteacher of first of all going round other classes to see what they were doing currently in maths (he took my class during these times). Next, staff meetings were arranged where I could talk about the new maths scheme to the head and the staff.

Once general approval had been gained and costings carried out, the head agreed that the scheme should be introduced. The head had encouraged me in this venture throughout by enabling me to see what was needed and by backing the need for change (and taking the final decision to introduce the new scheme).

These examples show how teachers were *motivated* by various leadership styles and strategies. The main purpose of intervention by the leader is motivation. The heads of the schools concerned intervened in various ways in the teacher's professional development, and this motivated them. In work concerned with questioning the teacher's self-image, the nature of professional relationships is of prime importance. For example, changing one's teaching style may involve a temporary 'burden of incompetence' (MacDonald, 1973), so that there will be a considerable need for psychological and moral support. Change must take into account such matters as anxiety, status and identity (Day, 1981). Successful development requires more than rational planning and action. It requires a knowledge of, and allowance for, the way people feel. This 'affective' area is rarely made explicit in preparation for developmental work, yet the attitudes of teachers to the head or other consultant who intervenes in their professional lives are clearly vital to the success of the intervention.

How is the leader who intervenes perceived? Is he or she an authority or a threat? A 'process helper' or a judge with alien values? The answers to these questions will depend largely on the interpersonal relationships formed with colleagues, and these will in turn be determined by how much the leader is seen to take into account personal individual factors in his or her management of people.

In a survey conducted with sixty headteachers, the most commonly cited qualities of a good head were in the 'affective' area of the work, in other words,

1. sympathy towards the ideas of others;
2. appreciation of others' points of view;
3. understanding of and concern for others;
4. compassion;
5. approachability by staff, parents and children;
6. the ability to deal with problems as they arise and 'still have a smile';
7. the ability to inspire trust and confidence;
8. tolerance, especially of opposing ideas;
9. tact;
10. willingness to praise, and be seen to praise;
11. humour;
12. the quality of being a good listener;
13. the ability to cope with opposition and unpopularity, as well as with support and encouragement;
14. the ability to know when to pressurize and when to stand off;
15. the capacity to be fair and just, and to be seen to be fair and just; and
16. the ability to lead, to guide, to cajole when necessary, to be loyal and supportive of the staff, and to maintain enthusiasm despite any problems.

Few who read this list will be surprised, yet we must ask, how do heads gain and refine these qualities? There are still relatively few training opportunities in the field of interpersonal skills and helping others to increase professional effectiveness.

INTERVENTION: CONSTRAINTS, PURPOSES AND PROCESSES

Most of the time, in working with children, teachers are not able to spend much time reflecting on why they do what they do. The main reasons for this are the number of children involved, and the time and energy available. Classroom decisions have to be made, and problems resolved, relatively quickly. Because of the nature of their work, teachers become socialized into acting in this way, with the theory that underlies each action almost always at an implicit level. (This may be part of the reason for teachers' common mistrust of 'theory' as they understand it, i.e. not related to practice.) Given that this is so, it would not be surprising if leaders who are or have been part of this apparently 'theoryless' environment, in which decisions are taken on the spot and solutions quickly found to 'cope' with emerging problems, behaved in a similar way in their work with other teachers. After all, they have rarely received any in-service preparation for their new roles. And yet, because the head will be dealing with fewer 'clients', and because often decisions about development or change do not need to be taken on the spot, the leader has more opportunity to reflect and evaluate.

Since much teaching behaviour is at an intuitive and implicit level (we all have a 'filter system' in order to cope with the masses of information with which we have to deal), from time to time teachers need the help of a colleague or 'critical friend' from outside in identifying both areas of strength and areas for improvement. Often the headteacher fulfils this role, by means of the following:

1. Taking an 'overview' of the needs of the school as a whole.
2. Observing and working alongside individual teachers.
3. Providing the means by which the practice of individuals and the school may be monitored and reviewed.
4. Ensuring commitment of staff through participation in decision-taking.

The headteacher who observes his or her teachers at work in their classrooms, who encourages them to discuss their work with each other and him or herself at regular meetings with groups and individuals, will soon get to know the various stages of professional development reached by each of the teachers. Thus, having established a context for the learning, the head will be in a position to plan for the most effective means of motivating through a series of purposeful intervention strategies – purposeful in the sense that his or her perceptions of institutional need, which may be in potential conflict with those of the staff, can be modified in the light of systematically collected evidence of perceived staff need. So desired results may be achieved by thinking of the intervention strategies not only in terms of the task, but also in terms of human motivation and learning factors. (A detailed discussion of these is contained in Chapter

4.) While these learning factors will be specific to the individual, there are general psychological needs that may be identified.

One way to help teachers is by identifying how and why they learn. It has been suggested that teachers are motivated to learn when they (rather than others) identify a need or problem. Havelock (1973) presented problem-solving as a rational process (Figure 1.5). It is clear from this model that identifying and solving problems is a complex business. For example, the initial disturbance may come from a self-generated or from an externally generated source (e.g. a new headteacher, a missive from the LEA, a visit by a colleague to the classroom or simply a knowledge that all is not well). The feeling of need that arises may or may not be strong enough to warrant a decision to act. Indeed, the teacher may feel unable or unworthy to do something about the need, until and unless it is diagnosed as a problem. Even if the need is diagnosed as a problem, teachers may be inhibited in their search for solutions by lack of time, energy, ability, resources or skills. Clearly, the leader has a responsibility to ensure that teachers do have opportunities to reflect on their work, as well as to help them in identifying problems by providing alternative perspectives on their work. (For problems in introducing new ideas, see Chapter 5.)

It should not be assumed, however, that *all* adults have a need to be self-directing at all times. Some teachers, like some children, may need to be 'told' things on occasion, or may expect that they should be told (a 'felt incompetence' formed by such factors as role, expectation, socialization or psychological needs – McGregor's 'Theory X'). Indeed, when teachers are participants in their own learning, problems may arise because their enquiry skills are either underdeveloped or undeveloped. The leader will need to take this into account. Among teachers, as among children, the need and ability to be self-directing will vary. 'Need', for example, depends upon factors such as cognitive and personality development, motivation, social development and role expectation.

The assumptions about professional learning and the nature of change that underpin the thinking expressed in this book are as follows:

1. Professional development is not something that can be forced, because it is the teacher who develops (active), and not the teacher who is developed (passive) (Eraut, 1977).
2. Change that is not internalized is likely to be distorted and temporary. Hence, power-coercive strategies or external initiatives that rely on authority rather than on encouraging development may seem to work,

Figure 1.5 Rational problem-solving model (Source: Havelock, 1973)

but usually result in 'token' changes at surface level only. The head will often be the one responsible for ensuring a transfer of ownership of an innovation from agencies outside the institution to those inside.
3. Change at deeper levels involves the modification of perceptions and attitudes, and this is unlikely to occur unless there is participation in the decision-making and planning of the in-service activity.
4. The leader's role is consultative and collaborative.

Many people have suggested that teachers in schools will work most happily and effectively in an environment to which they feel they belong (how many times do we hear the teacher talk of 'my class' and the head talk of 'my school'!), with which they can identify and in which they feel accepted and esteemed − not only by their pupils but also by colleagues and their heads. Perhaps the prime task of the consultant/leader concerned with motivating staff is to provide the right conditions for motivation.

LEADING THE TEAM

Like an individual, a team must be led in ways that take account of its stage of development as well as the purposes of the leader. The 'leader' needs to be able to

1. identify the team's stage of development;
2. be aware of the range of approaches available to him or her;
3. select the appropriate approach, according to the team's stage of development and the leader's purposes;
4. possess and be able to use the ability to put this approach into practice; and
5. monitor the effectiveness of the approach, and modify where necessary.

In the ideal and most effective model of leadership, the head's role is collaborative and he or she will operate according to principles of participation, negotiation, trust and responsibility. The more the head 'tells' (makes the decisions and announces them) or 'sells' (through persuasion) the more he or she will demonstrate his or her use of authority and the less will be the personal investment of colleagues in the enterprise. The more the head 'consults' (e.g. presents a problem, gets suggestions, makes decisions) or 'shares' (defines limits, asks group to make decisions), the greater will be the area of freedom felt by colleagues, and the stronger their investment. Whatever the question to be dealt with − whether it is to agree on a policy for staff development, or to review curriculum, or roles and responsibilities − it is crucial that the focus has been agreed through consultation so that all agree to commit themselves to the task in hand. The way in which this agreement occurs depends on the leadership roles adopted and the skills that can be applied.

In practice, the head who then operates any of the above models (with the possible exception of 'telling') will do so by means of talking, observing and listening. He or she will therefore need to possess and use a variety of skills necessary to the leading of effective discussion, and these will include the following:

1. Negotiating skills (contract-making).
2. Summarizing skills (to form links between different ideas, where appropriate).
3. Questioning skills (to open rather than close discussions).
4. Selection skills (of key points in arguments).
5. Focusing skills (to concentrate and clarify discussion points).
6. Synthesizing and evaluation skills (to 'sharpen' issues).
7. Timing skills (to know when, and when not, to intervene in discussion).
8. Listening skills (to listen actively in order to respond to what is really being said − the hidden agenda).
9. Non-verbal skills (to identify people's attitudes and feelings, through observing posture, gesture, facial expression, etc.).

To summarize, in meeting with colleagues, either individually or collectively, the leader will need to demonstrate his or her ability to

1. negotiate sympathetically;
2. listen (actively), note and act;
3. account for individual needs;
4. ensure continuity and support; and
5. send colleagues away with a sense of achievement.

Let us now consider four crucial factors in the process of management.

The Needs of the Individual and the Needs of the Institution

These needs may be different, and sometimes conflicting. Colleagues need to perceive the need for development (and thus change), and feel a responsibility for implementing and sharing in this. Individuals like to have responsibility and be trusted, but they also need to see benefits for themselves as well as for 'the school', for example. How may this be achieved? One way is by making social contracts with staff through negotiation. By these means, colleagues accept that they may, at times and in the interests of others, contribute part of their autonomy. For example, the development of particular schemes of work may have to wait until there has been an appraisal of classroom teaching approaches. This 'contract-making' is often linked with the agreement to set different kinds of objectives according to agreed priorities (see also Chapter 7).

Short-, Mid- and Long-Term Tasks

There may be some tasks better left until a later date because other tasks are more urgent, or because it is desirable for the staff to feel an immediate sense of achievement. So it is the head's responsibility to ensure that tasks are assigned different priorities. This is not to say that all three kinds of tasks are not being pursued at the same time, but simply that there is an agreement to place more emphasis at any given time on one rather than another.

Timing and Containable Time

Closely linked to these two factors is the concept of 'containable time'. Changes must be manageable, and the time and energy teachers have available to devote to change is limited. It is counterproductive to stretch people beyond their personal limits. Through initial contract-making, agreements can be reached concerning the amount of time to be spent on any given task or project. The knowledge that a meeting or other event will end at a given time will provide security for staff with other commitments.

A personal sense of timing is also important. Friday afternoon three or four weeks into term, or a wet and windy day that has unsettled the pupils in the school, may not be the best time to introduce a new idea!

Handling Confrontation

Inevitably tensions will occur from time to time, and the leader will be expected to handle them. There is no formula for success, but here are some notes drawn from the experiences of sixty deputy headteachers:

1. Provide support and guidance, i.e. identify the causes and try to eliminate or alleviate the problem through discussion/practical help and support.
2. Praise strengths and improvements.
3. Avoid open confrontation.
4. Offer positive 'professional' criticism.
5. Minimize feelings of being threatened.
6. Be prepared to accept modifications/compromise.
7. Avoid showing prejudice in open staff meetings if personal opinions are put forward.
8. Where you cannot handle confrontation, be willing to use arbitration.

To these may be added a ninth:

9. Know which battles to fight, which to avoid, and which to lose!

PRINCIPLES OF CONSULTANCY-LEADERSHIP

What qualities, then, do you need to possess in order to be an effective leader? First you have to recognize that you are involved in the management of human and physical resources. You have to help individuals to develop, while at the same time maintain the team. You must also ensure that the task, whatever it may be, is achieved. This will only happen if you can motivate and support others. *Management is getting things done with and by other people.* In order to do this well, you will need skills of planning and organization, in particular, identifying opportunities by being knowledgeable about the needs of staff and children, setting targets, the art of delegation and using your time to the best advantage; communication — formal and informal; assessment and evaluation — through monitoring, observing and synthesizing. Most important, then, are the skills of working with people. No amount of forward planning, careful budgeting or efficient administration can substitute for this.

One of the first principles-in-action for the consultant is participation by staff. This is based on the assumption that if people are involved in making the decisions that shape their activities, then they are likely to be more committed to their work. It is important to remember, though, that collectivity does not abolish the ultimate responsibility of the headteacher for the work of the school. The seven major areas of responsibility for the headteacher (each of which is dealt with in more detail in the other chapters) are as follows.

The School Climate or Ethos

It will be the head's policies regarding, for example, access to classrooms by parents, team-teaching, a policy of professional development that is school-focused, the use of reward and punishment systems, the collegiality of school decision-making, that will determine whether the school is perceived as 'open' or 'closed' by staff and parents.

Organizational Health – Teaching and Learning Processes

What does the way in which school and classrooms are organized 'say' about the school? Is there a predominance of class teaching or individual work? Are the classroom doors usually open or closed?

The Framework/Expectations
(Standards of Behaviour and Achievement)

What are the standards of the school? Is there a high level of commitment by staff and children to providing a stimulating environment for learning? Is there an effective monitoring system for children's work? Is there a regular monitoring of staff's work? Are there regular head–staff, staff–staff, staff–parent, head–parent consultations?

Routines (Morale)

Are there frameworks of routines for staff and children in school? Are the regularly organized staff seminars, appraisal interviews, meetings with parents, professional development opportunities valued?

Management of Relationships

Leadership is a process, not a style. Constraints upon the processes are likely to be brought about by a number of factors. Some are outside the leader's control, i.e. national and local education policy. Some, however, are within the power of the head to influence.

Self

It is essential to have a strong professional philosophy. However, forceful expression of this may inhibit staff (who may not be so strong, clear-thinking or forthright), alienate staff, or inhibit the leader from acting in a collegial/democratic/consultative way with staff. Instead, the leader may resort to 'devious' manipulation that may, in itself, be counter-productive. Another problem for the leader is his or her isolation by status. It is difficult to share one's weaknesses, for example, with the person who is to write your reference!

Staff

It is unlikely that all the staff of a school will teach in the same way. Indeed, it is questionable whether this should be so, except in the most general terms. However, it will be necessary to establish a unanimity of purpose for the school and to lead by example, avoiding the temptation to 'forcefeed'. The head should, therefore,

1. create opportunities to develop unanimity from early success in an easy, non-controversial area, and limit change to single manageable areas but initiate changes fairly rapidly after initial assessment of needs;
2. establish consensus on problems – their recognition, analysis and resolution. Changes in management structure, for example, require a consensus of opinion in favour if they are to work;
3. give more thought to the operation to maximize contributions from all – this means plenty of preparation. Summarize discussion and record by written précis, ensuring continuous feedback to participants;
4. ensure acceptance by all team members that they may at times contribute best by surrendering part of their own autonomy, e.g. by accepting house rules in discussion and holding back criticism or interruption until the appropriate time;
5. identify motivation factors of each member of the team as individuals;
6. be aware of possible insecurities of staff (it is possible you may be carried away by your own enthusiasm);
7. ensure a commitment to the process rather than to the product of development;

8. establish a communication system that ensures truthful, honest and open assessment and evaluation.

The Curriculum

The curriculum represents the knowledge the school regards as important that the students gain. It includes the National Curriculum but is more than the sum of its parts. In practice it is a mixture of tradition (the culture passed down by society), innovation (ideas developed by educationists) and basic-skills development (numeracy and literacy). The curriculum is now under public scrutiny and there is more public participation in its content. It is no longer enough to say that the head/leader must be aware of all major developments and ensure that the staff are aware of them. It is the effective management of the curriculum in relation to these developments that is vital, and this involves planning, monitoring and evaluating the content, the processes and the outcomes, and ensuring that all are communicated and understood by a variety of audiences.

Evaluation and Assessment

Whereas assessment of the pupils' work is an essential of every teacher's job, evaluation of the work of individual teachers and the school as a whole is a prime responsibility of the headteacher. The purposes and practices of evaluation are considered in detail in Chapter 7 but they run implicitly through all aspects of management practice. For example, evaluation will involve a regular review of

1. staff progress (see Chapters 3 and 4);
2. the effectiveness of internal and external communications (see Chapters 5 and 8);
3. the roles and responsibilities of staff (see Chapter 2); and
4. the curriculum (see Chapter 6).

How the head manages these evaluations determines his or her effectiveness.

CONCLUSION

This chapter has described a leader as one who provides environments that minimize constraints on learning, and where a variety of concrete experiences may be reflected upon, discussed, assimilated and accommodated; who involves others in identifying need rather than identifying need for them; who matches, wherever possible, the perceived needs of the individual with the needs of the school as he or she perceives them. In working towards these ends, the leader will in effect be providing staff with access to and support from senior management; regular discussion with other professionals involved in education and other contexts; periods outside their classroom (and schools) to reflect upon practice; external professional knowledge and skills; and opportunities to establish and develop agreed and purposeful frameworks for their own roles.

2
ROLES AND RESPONSIBILITIES

Management in primary schools, as in most organizations, is about getting things done. Managers should be judged by the outcomes they facilitate rather than by the quality of their plans and policies. This chapter will explore some of the implications of this principle, suggesting that the present method of operating management and leadership responsibilities in primary schools can inhibit effective management and stifle dynamic school development. The chapter builds on the assumption made in Chapter 1 that effective management is about teamwork and shared leadership, the working with and through all members of the staff group. As an alternative to the somewhat individualized approach to responsibility currently practised, two alternative models are offered, both of which provide the basis for a more cohesive team approach.

The present allowance structure within primary schools has developed over the years by a process of accretion. Large schools have benefited most, with the provision of B and sometimes C allowances as well as A. Small schools have been largely untouched by these developments although in recent years there have been attempts to provide some opportunity for heads in small schools to be relieved of some of their class responsibilities.

This piecemeal growth and recent decline have meant that schools have used allowances in a somewhat haphazard way. Although such reporting committees as Bullock (DES, 1975) and Cockcroft (DES, 1982) have urged the designation of teachers as curriculum consultants in language and mathematics, there has been no concerted attempt to offer to schools a management-structure plan. Some schools have developed a structure of posts linked to a cohesive staff-development programme, but generally speaking the pattern is inconsistent.

The key change made by the *School Teachers' Pay and Conditions of Employment Order* in 1987 was to promote previous scale-1 teachers to join their scale-2 colleagues on the main professional grade. By contract, members of this designated group now carry management responsibilities beyond their class-teaching duties. This creates new management possibilities with all teachers in effect becoming co-managers of the school, and those with incentive allowances being expected to accept responsibilities over and above their main-grade colleagues. The pay and conditions order laid down four criteria for incentive allowances:

1. Good classroom teaching.
2. Responsibilities over and above the main professional grade.
3. Shortage subjects.
4. Difficulties in filling a post.

It is with the second category that we are concerned, as this criterion presents the best potential for establishing an effective co-management structure.

One of the factors that has contributed to this haphazard pattern is the assumption that once individual posts are designated they cannot be changed. It is true that teachers have protection from arbitrary changes to the terms and conditions of their contract, but there has never been a formal problem about change through mutual agreement. This tradition of immutability is now changing and many heads, working through participatory management, are involving teachers in the design of the staffing structure and in the redefining of roles and responsibilities.

Another factor, connected with the point made at the beginning of the chapter about managers being judged on performance, is that teachers themselves have tended to want to stay with those responsibilities with which they feel most safe – in other words, they see themselves as being judged on performance, and so are only happy with those responsibilities they are confident of being able to fulfil. This has inhibited the creative use of management responsibility to assist staff development. Posts have been associated with the idea of delivery rather than acquisition since teachers have been appointed for what they already are rather than for what they have the potential to become. Many curriculum-development projects and school-innovation programmes might have been more successful if the responsibilities relating to them had incorporated an element of staff development.

Staff mobility has also affected the issue. The tendency has been to replace like with like so that a teacher moving out of the school is replaced with another teacher who can carry the same or a very similar responsibility. The vacating of a post always creates an opportunity for reconsidering the structure and considering whether a programme of redefinition and reallocation can better help the staff as a team to respond to changing needs and circumstances.

One of the underlying beliefs that has helped to perpetuate the pattern of responsibilities has been that of balance and coverage. Heads often talk about needing a teacher to 'cover' a particular curriculum area and of wanting to spread the curriculum between the number of posts available. It is also the case that deputies, and heads themselves, are often left out of such an allocation.

All these factors have contributed to a system that has failed to serve the best interests of schools and of the teachers who work in them. They have tended to create a dividing element rather than a unifying one. By separating out responsibilities we are forcing teachers to work for the realization of their own individual goals rather than those of the school as a whole. What happens in practice is that responsibility holders have to try to influence each other in order to further their individual aims. The existence of many individual plans and many separate programmes is both confusing and divisive.

An improved management structure will be one that develops teamwork, facilitates group management and creates opportunities for leadership to emerge. It will also be one that utilizes and develops the personal and professional qualities of the staff. By linking the scale-post structure to a staff-development policy it will be possible to facilitate professional development through some form of job rotation and team responsibility.

In addition to these factors, it will also be necessary to develop a structure that has the flexibility to respond easily to new needs and changing circumstances. This suggests an underlying assumption that change in schools is a continuous process rather than a series of incidents or events. Regular curriculum and policy reviews will generate the awareness that will inform this process and provide the focus for teamwork and group management. The next part of this chapter examines the constraints that may prevent these conditions being achieved, and it looks at two models that attempt to overcome these and establish a truly collegial structure of roles and responsibilities.

CONSTRAINTS AND POSSIBILITIES

Our traditional pattern of roles and responsibilities in the primary school is locked within a system that regards a division of labour as essential. The head is seen as undertaking significantly different work from the class teacher, and between these two come a variety of roles, each with their different and distinct purposes. This pattern has been encouraged by the steady development in the pattern of allowances and responsibilities available in primary schools, and a belief that curriculum consultancy has the potential to improve the quality of learning inside classrooms. This pattern of curriculum specialization has not achieved what was hoped for it. Indeed, the HMI survey of primary schools, published in 1978, observed (DES, 1978)

> In a quarter of the schools in the survey teachers with positions of curricular organizational responsibility were having a noticeable influence on the quality of the work in the school as a whole. In the remaining schools there was little evidence that the influence of teachers with curricular responsibilities spread beyond the work of their own classes.

Although this revelation shocked many at the time of its publication, 25 per cent of teachers exercising influence beyond their own classrooms is a remarkable achievement given the limited time and opportunity they have to undertake such work. Within the education service there has been a determination to try to improve the skills and abilities of responsibility holders, mainly through in-service training. This is misguided. Carving up the curriculum into manageable chunks and distributing them to individual members of staff and asking them to go round influencing each other is no recipe either for improving the quality of pupil learning or for achieving a more effective management structure.

The kind of management structure more likely to be successful in meeting the challenges of the future is one that makes optimum use of the human resources at its disposal. This will not only require the skilful combining of individual strengths and abilities but a capacity to build group and partnership skills within the working team. Staff development is often regarded as a process relating to the individual's particular professional needs. In the school of tomorrow it should also include a consideration of the needs of the staff as a whole. Leadership needs to be seen as a key function of the group and not simply as the responsibility of a named individual. This need not diminish the role of the head. If anything it enhances it, creating new opportunities for working through and with a cohesive and committed team.

Such a structure is easier to conceive of than it is to achieve in practice, so it is important to be aware of the factors that currently work to inhibit the movement towards this more functional pattern. Foremost among these are the traditional assumptions affecting our work as teachers in an institutionalized education service.

TRADITIONAL ASSUMPTIONS

One of the reasons that teachers have found it so hard to respond to a more participatory style of school management is that such a model contradicts many of the established values of the schooling process. Teachers, like pupils, have been trained to follow and to occupy roles defined and structured for them by others. Within these prescribed roles of class teacher, deputy head or headteacher there is a tendency to be conditioned by the traditional orthodoxy displayed in the expectations that society has of its schools and its teachers. Many of the new generation of primary headteachers have gained their appointments because they have subscribed to an open and participatory managing style, only to find that they are faced by a staff who have not. The problem often lies not with the headteachers but with the staffs they are appointed to lead, who have not had the same opportunities to develop an awareness of new possibilities (see Chapter 5).

Education is plagued by mistake avoidance. Pupils are trained to believe that not only must they get it right but that they must also get it right first time. This ethic establishes itself early in the schooling process and becomes self-perpetuating. It has taken the computer to help us to realize that effective learning can be about getting it wrong first, and that the path to success need not be painful. The same ethic pervades the teaching profession, so that we have come to believe that there is one right way to do things and, rather than search for our own version of what that might be, we incline to the traditional, well-established and respected patterns where the possibility of censure and misfortune is at its least.

The last twenty or so years in education have witnessed a concern for curriculum development. This has emerged in the belief that if only we can get the design of what is taught in schools right most of the problems of education will be solved. This assumption has generated a view that the most desirable management activity in schools is changing things. Some heads seem to be preoccupied with the concept of the ultimate innovation. There is a belief that if change is approached systematically and painstakingly the school can be put on a sure footing that will support its activities for the foreseeable future. This is both to misunderstand the nature of change in schools and also to fail to appreciate that curriculum review can no longer be an occasional activity in schools but has to be a continual process. Instead of wanting our changes in school to be everlasting we need to see the challenge more as one of improving things for the time being. Curriculum development is now the process of responding to constant and accelerating change. The commitment is thus to the process of development rather than particular products.

Another traditional assumption that continues to inhibit progress towards a more participatory management process is the view teachers have of their own work. Succeeding generations of teachers continue to mould themselves on the image of the instructor, the formal vehicle through which traditional wisdom and knowledge are dispensed to the young. This has encouraged the view that teaching is about performing, about acting a part and fulfilling a role. The view that what a teacher teaches is what a pupil learns is hard to dislodge, and great importance is attached to techniques of control and persuasion. Our increasing understanding that learning is a capacity of the learner rather than a function of the teacher has been hard to get across to teachers in general. The support given by the Plowden Report (Central Advisory Council for Education (England), 1967) to this idea of teaching as a facilitation of the natural learning potential of the pupil continues unheeded, as HMI have pointed out in their compilation of published reports of primary schools. This view of teaching as a performing activity is reinforced by the teacher-assessing activities of tutors, heads, advisers and HMI (Gray and Coulson, 1982). The introduction of a system of teacher appraisal by the government could strengthen this tendency unless the new system is firmly set within a framework of professional development. Similary, the introduction of formal systems to assess pupil progress through the National Curriculum could well challenge the tendency away from teaching as instruction. Later (Chapter 7) we propose forms of appraisal for teachers and schools that are more in keeping with the notion of teachers as professionals.

In such circumstances it is understandable that teachers have become sensitive to comments about their teaching, even from their colleagues. Inevitably, curriculum development has become an activity to identify the content of teaching programmes. Considerations of classroom method and teaching style, because of their sensitivity, are left out, being regarded as matters of personal concern only to the individual teachers themselves. One of the reasons why curriculum development in primary schools has been so unsuccessful in recent years is that it has become largely a paper exercise – the preparation of guidelines and subject policies. How they are interpreted in practical terms in the classroom has been left to the discretion of the teacher. In the face of perceived threats from outside, schools and teachers have not been slow to develop a rhetoric of curriculum development. The introduction of the National Curriculum means that school-based development now becomes an exercise in the interpretation of objectives – not the establishing of them. This shifts the emphasis away from content towards process, and curriculum management will need to focus itself on pedagogy and classroom experience.

Professional development also is severely hampered by this performance view of teaching. If professional competence and expertise are to be extended there needs to be a climate in which the intensely practical aspects of classroom work are seen as an essential part of any curriculum-development activity. This will not be achieved if teachers, like the pupils they work with day by day, constantly see themselves as being judged and graded. A judgmental climate is not an easy one in which to talk freely and openly about 'how' and 'why' you teach as you do, or indeed to identify areas where you may need help and guidance. Many teachers have learnt to hide away their professional inadequacies and pretend they do not exist.

The National Curriculum reinforces a monolithic approach to the organization of learning that is sustained by three distinct pressures:

1. *Precepts* The 'musts' of the schooling system.
2. *Expectations* The 'oughts' and 'shoulds'.
3. *Situations* 'The way we do things here.'

These three sets of factors operate on schools and teachers to sustain established practices. They have combined to develop a belief that the schooling system needs to be solidly uniform throughout, allowing little scope for individuality or variation. Change continues to be problematical because schools, unlike manufacturing enterprises, have not had to adapt to survive. Their continued existence is assured.

It is against this background of traditional assumptions and new national prescriptions that we must consider how professional roles and responsibilities in schools can help to create the adaptability the future will increasingly demand. A new management paradigm is needed that will generate new assumptions, create new possibilities and establish new practices. Foremost among these new assumptions will need to be

1. an appreciation that teaching, like learning, is about creating a human environment in which it is safe to reach out and take risks; in which not getting things quite right the first time is regarded as a good way to learn and to discover;
2. a realization that change is a constant and ever-present feature of our lives, and that we do our pupils a disservice by sustaining a belief in the virtue of traditional orthodoxy;
3. a view of teaching as an activity of facilitation and not performance. A process of working alongside pupils in classrooms and finding, through the quality of our relationship with them, ever new ways to help them realize their amazing and ever-present potential; and
4. an understanding that management is an interactive process, a way of working together to achieve agreed aims through group cohesion rather than through attention to hierarchical separation and status differentials.

LEADERSHIP

Central to a new paradigm for school management must be a clear understanding of the part that leadership plays in creating conditions in which teamwork and cooperation are of a high order. In *Effective Leadership*, John Adair (1983) has suggested that leadership is related to the needs that arise within the organization − in our case, the school. The practice of leadership involves an understanding of three particular sets of needs that are constantly interacting:

1. The needs of the tasks to be undertaken.
2. The needs of the staff team as a whole.
3. The needs of individuals within the staff team.

The role of the leader becomes one of adopting attitudes and behaviours designed to

1. achieve the task;
2. build and maintain the staff team; and
3. develop each individual.

Current models of school leadership place far too much emphasis on the tasks as identified by the head and too little on the second and third sets of needs. Relating this threefold model of leadership to headship in a primary school we have

1. setting up structures to achieve the tasks identified and agreed upon by the staff;
2. creating conditions and setting up structures for effective teamwork; and
3. responding to the needs of individual members of staff in terms of
   (a) their own personal and professional growth; and
   (b) their capacity to work and contribute to the team as a whole.

In this model, leadership needs to be seen more in terms of what leaders do rather than who the leaders are and the positions they occupy in the staffing structure. Leadership, like management, is judged by results rather than intentions. This places the emphasis on behaviour rather than on plans and policies. Leadership needs to be conceived in terms of function of the staff team and not as a responsibility of a named individual. Effective teamwork is successful when there is a capacity in the group to allow the leadership to emerge in response to the need of the moment. When the group regards a single individual as 'the leader' then teamwork can become inhibited, constrained by expectations that relate to status and position rather than need and function.

Certain key qualities in teachers are closely related to successful learning in pupils. These same qualities are likely to contribute most to effective teamwork and group cohesion. Thinking now of leadership these can be defined as

1. the ability to be a good listener and readily understand the world as perceived by colleagues;
2. the capacity to feel a warm, caring respect for each colleague as a unique and individual person; and
3. the ability to engage in a genuine person-to-person relationship with each colleague and to be yourself in those relationships.

This, then, says something about how we need to behave in relation to our colleagues if we are to exercise effective leadership. The relationship of these qualities to the self-concept is considered in detail in Chapter 3. An awareness of the factors that contribute to a strong self-concept is necessary if roles and responsibilities are to be exercised effectively. They are (Elliott-Kemp and Rogers, 1982) as follows:

> **Self-awareness** The extent to which we are conscious of our own attitudes and values and of the effect our behaviour has on others.

Will to achieve The extent to which we seek new challenges in our work and personal lives.
Optimism The extent to which we feel positive about the future and our part in it.
Positive regard The extent to which we respond to others with warmth, caring and respect.
Trust The extent to which we are prepared to place trust in those with whom we work.
Congruence The extent to which we are secure enough to be ourselves with our colleagues.
Empathy The extent to which we are able to understand the circumstances of our colleagues' lives from their point of view.
Courage The extent to which we are prepared to take risks in finding more effective ways of working with colleagues and the extent to which we are prepared to admit to a need for help from them.

(This extract was reproduced by kind permission of PAVIC Publications, Sheffield City Polytechnic.)

When these qualities are well developed in the individual members of a working group then teamwork is likely to be of a high order. Initiatives from any member of staff will be welcomed and status differentials will tend not to get in the way of the team's capacity to solve problems and achieve its tasks.

In moving towards group-focused management there will need to be considerable changes in the ways we conceive and exercise roles and responsibilities. Leadership needs to be seen as a function of the group rather than a role — and more concerned with behaviour than with status. Such a transformation in attitude and practice will not be easy to accomplish. Progress needs to be made, first, by trying to develop accepted patterns and seeking more imaginative uses for existing structures. Let us look now at ways in which a management structure can be created more productively.

The first model, the functional approach, represents an attempt to respond to the question, if there is a school plan, what tasks do we need to undertake? The second model, the developmental approach, has a different question, if there is a school plan, how do we need to be? The first approach responds in terms of tasks and activities. The developmental approach is concerned with the professional skills and qualities the plan demands.

THE FUNCTIONAL APPROACH

In this approach the structuring of responsibilities is related to the management tasks and activities to be engaged on during a school year. These would include

1. curriculum development programmes;
2. organizational changes;
3. financial planning and review;
4. staff development and INSET;
5. policy-making;
6. policy review; and
7. events in the school calendar.

The approach builds on the assumption that responsibility holders are best conceived of as co-managers of the school's affairs. The management tasks considered are those outside the daily classroom work of the teachers and that have implications for the work of the school as a whole.

In traditional management structures the roles of individuals tend to have been created with no end point in mind. A role is occupied until such time as the teacher vacates the post. In the functional approach being proposed here, posts are brought into existence to deal with a discrete and finite set of objectives. On their completion the post is reviewed and redefined. Once in operation a structure such as this becomes a dynamic part of the school's management process, supporting its current needs and planned policies.

Changing from a more traditional structure requires a careful approach and the cooperation of all teachers concerned. The transition is best preceded by some form of school appraisal that focuses on curriculum, organization, staff development, decision-making and staff participation. Such an exercise is often associated with the work of a newly appointed head and involves a comprehensive review of the work of the school (Whitaker, 1983). A less complex approach would resemble the staff-appraisal exercise described in Chapter 4. Its purpose there is related to the process of selection. Here it is concerned with the present management needs of the school.

There are now a variety of review structures available for this type of activity including guidelines for review and internal development of schools (GRIDS) and diagnosing individual and organizational needs for staff development and in-service training (DION – Day, Whitaker and Wren, 1987). This 'management–review exercise' assumes an annual planning exercise towards the end of each academic year, the purpose of which is to define precisely how and when specific policies are to be carried out during the next academic year. Schools are familiar with National Curriculum development plans whereby future requirements are compared with current realities and necessary changes planned.

Figure 2.1 proposes a way of breaking these policies down into discrete activities and events. The left-hand column suggests that policies have three particular dimensions — innovation, maintenance and review. These categories can be further subdivided if required.

The matrix (Figure 2.1) can be drawn on to a large sheet of paper and pinned to the staffroom wall. Brainstorming in small groups of three or four will generate a range of activities that can be transferred to the large sheet. Whole-staff discussion can then follow and agreement be sought on the activities to feature in the allocation of posts.

The next stage is to translate these responses into the discrete tasks to be carried out during the year. Before allocating them to individuals it is important to relate them to a timescale. This is best carried out by

	Curriculum	Organization	Staff development	Finance	Appraisal	Events
Innovation						
Maintenance						
Review						

Figure 2.1 Management-review exercise

locating activities on a year planner. In Figure 2.2, two symbols are used to distinguish between activities that are process-based – occurring over time – and events. The circle indicates the starting point of a process, with the arrow point suggesting the planned completion time. The square indicates events. Coloured stickers are a useful alternative to drawn symbols. By way of example, three particular activities have been entered on the year planner.

Task 1

This is a whole-school project entitled 'Growth', which will occupy the

	Task 1	Task 2	Task 3
Autumn term			
Spring term			
Summer term			

Figure 2.2 Task-planning exercise

spring term. Although the culmination of the project will be an exhibition at the regional science fair, the project is rooted in the school's policy for topic work, a cross-curricular approach incorporating attainment targets from science, English, mathematics and other foundation subjects. Associated with the work are three key events — two whole-day study visits either side of the spring halfterm, and the exhibition in the local town hall.

This project is a major feature of the school's annual plan and will involve all teachers and pupils. The management tasks associated with it will be considerable and it is likely that all members of the teaching team will have some responsibility for it in their job outline.

Task 2

This refers to the innovation of a new approach to drama. A classroom has become available that is to be set up as an expressive-arts studio. The plan, covering most of the academic year, involves a programme of in-service training. The events indicated are those occasions when the adviser will be visiting the school to work with pupils and teachers in the new studio.

This is an important innovatory programme. The planning for it occupied a great deal of staff time during the preceding academic year. A small team of three teachers — one infant, one lower junior and one upper junior — was responsible for the development of the drama curriculum document; the deputy head and another teacher worked with the adviser on the plans for the alterations to the vacant room; and the head working with the three remaining teachers designed the in-service programme. A successful introduction of this new curriculum programme will require considerable teamwork and create a wide variety of tasks and activities. All staff will need to have some element of this programme reflected in their job outline.

Task 3

These are the events associated with decision-making on the allocation of the school's budget. Detailed work will involve the deputy head and two other teachers. These are tasks rotated annually between the staff.

Following the allocation of all the tasks to the year planner comes the process of dividing up responsibilities. A cohesive team will be able to handle this as a whole-staff exercise, making decisions based on an awareness of the needs of individual teachers and those of the school as a whole. It is important to achieve both equity and balance in the composition of responsibilities while, at the same time, achieving optimum conditions for success in the policies defined. Linking the management structure to the school's staff-development policy should ensure that each teacher has the opportunity to

1. utilize specialist skills and abilities;
2. follow particular interests and enthusiasms;
3. acquire and develop new skills and abilities;
4. widen experience; and
5. accept new challenges.

Another set of considerations to apply are those of the various management functions. Each responsibility holder should have some opportunity for

1. planning;
2. creating;
3. communicating;
4. motivating;
5. organizing; and
6. evaluating.

If each of these functions is incorporated into the post then the opportunity to exercise leadership is likely to be a positive feature of the work. While it is important to achieve some spread of functions within each post this should not be gained at the expense of individual expertise. In the examples above, the good planners and motivators should be involved in the overall implementation of policies and programmes and the good organizers in the arrangement of events. In order to provide a satisfactory balance between utilizing existing skills and acquiring new ones it is useful to conceive of each post as having three distinct elements:

1. Involvement in a main project.
2. Responsibility for a key event.
3. A range of supporting activities.

This provides each post-holder with the opportunity to exercise overall leadership for a particular project, to act in support of other projects and to organize a key event. Not only would such a range of responsibilities contribute to the successful management of the school, the work would provide many fruitful professional development opportunities.

When activities have been allocated and each teacher has a clear brief it is vital to ensure that roles and responsibilities are accurately defined and documented. Each member of staff should prepare a job outline containing the following:

1. Job title, e.g. 'Project Leader − Drama'.
2. A statement of objectives.
3. Key dates:
    (a) project deadlines;
    (b) project events; and
    (c) project meetings.
4. List of project groups and committees involved in.
5. Outline of how the post is to be conducted.
6. Requests to colleagues:
    (a) how you would like them to help you; and
    (b) how you would like to help them.

All the job outlines should be prepared to a standard format and distributed to all members of staff, including clerical, welfare and technical colleagues. The success of any management structure depends on everyone knowing in sufficient detail what each other person is planning to do, how they intend to do it and where responsibilities join or overlap. Role conflict can be avoided if this stage is well conducted and if the documentation is clear and comprehensive.

While it is good management and leadership practice for the head and the deputy to take a share of the tasks generated and to undertake project responsibility, it is also vital for them to have a coordinating and evaluating role. These essential functions can be facilitated by bringing into existence two key committees or working groups: the policy group, which deals with the main aspects of project design, and the ways and means group, which is concerned with issues of implementation. In a small school where subdivision is not possible, it is useful to distinguish between these two distinct functions − the form of the policies and the detail of their practical implementation.

A further essential leadership function for the head and the deputy is to facilitate regular, at least halftermly, progress discussions with each responsibility holder. Such a process builds upon and extends the appraisal system currently envisaged for teachers. These discussions should be concerned with

1. assessing progress towards planned objectives;

2. identifying and considering problems;
3. clarifying future plans; and
4. evaluating outcomes.

Reviewing progress should also feature regularly in staff meetings, with time allocated for each member of staff to share current issues and concerns. In addition to this essential face-to-face communicating, it is important to establish an efficient system of information sharing. A specific noticeboard in the school office or staffroom should be set aside for the management programme. It should be subdivided, with headings such as REMINDERS, REQUESTS, NEXT WEEK and URGENT. This latter category should only be used sparingly and items should not be allowed to remain beyond the deadline to which they refer. It is also a good idea to use brightly coloured papers for notices under this heading.

The essential feature of the functional approach to management responsibility is the annual plan. Since posts relate to the implementation of this plan it is important to consider how planning for the next academic year takes place. This can be both an ongoing process, in that future needs are regularly featured in staff meetings, and a particular event in the management calendar. The policy group can be responsible for preparing a discussion document relating to the next annual plan, and the ways and means group can take charge of the process of translating this into practical terms through activities described in this section. It will be essential for both these groups to have regular contact with the governing body of the school and it is a good idea to keep the last half of the summer term clear for these activities.

DEVELOPMENTAL APPROACH

In this approach the emphasis is changed from one of attention to tasks and activities that need to be carried out to one of relating roles and responsibilities to professional growth and development. Like the first approach this one also assumes a clearly formulated programme for school development over a period of time, with its necessary year plans broken down into convenient term plans and more detailed action programmes. The key feature of this developmental approach is the linking of responsibility to the staff-development needs that are created by the nature of the agreed school plan.

Essentially, the developmental approach provides an opportunity for a school to focus on the relationship of the teachers' classroom behaviour to the learning process. Unlike a great deal of curriculum-development work its main concern is not the nature of the learning programmes but how they are carried out in the classroom. Using the six management functions referred to in the previous section, the key areas of focus will be the following:

Planning
1. The content and design of learning programmes.
2. Individual, group and class tasks.
3. The design of the classroom.
4. Working practices and procedures.
5. Monitoring and evaluation procedures.

Creating
1. New approaches to curriculum design.
2. New ideas for classroom organization.
3. Developing teaching styles.
4. Finding ways to involve pupils in classroom management.
5. Trying out new techniques.

Communicating
1. Building personal relationships with pupils.
2. Making time for listening to pupils.
3. Developing groupwork.
4. Developing relationships with colleagues.
5. Contributing to honest and open discussion.

Motivating
1. Understanding pupil behaviour.
2. Building an encouraging classroom climate.
3. Helping pupils to understand the learning process.
4. Relating learning to pupil interests and experience.
5. Helping pupils achieve a sense of belonging.

Organizing
1. Creating and maintaining a stimulating learning environment.
2. Organizing learning activities.
3. Implementing curriculum programmes.
4. Dealing with tasks and activities.
5. Working with colleagues and contributing to school management.

Evaluating
1. Comparing outcomes with plans.
2. Monitoring individual progress.
3. Matching work to ability.
4. Checking continuity and progression.
5. Evaluating policy programmes.

This is a selective list and by no means raises all the issues of classroom teaching. Any subset of this list would make a very useful agenda for a progress interview between head and each member of staff.

In considering the professional development needs of a staff it is important to bear in mind the points made in the earlier section that conceived of leadership as a function of the group as a whole and suggested the following dimensions:

1. The task.
2. The group.
3. The individual.

This provides a useful way of relating roles and responsibilities to professional development. The task represents the desirable future the staff are working to realize. It will exist in the form of clearly defined aims and objectives and the corresponding programmes for achieving them. The programmes will call upon both the collective efforts of the staff working as a team and the individual contributions of each teacher. It is necessary, therefore, that role definitions refer to both group and individual needs. A practical way of raising an agenda for staff development is suggested in Figure 2.3.

Each member of staff should be provided with one form (as shown in Figure 2.3) for each project currently present in the school-development plan. The aim is to invite each teacher to list his or her own particular needs in relation to that programme, categorized under the headings 'knowledge', 'skills' and 'qualities'. They are also invited to suggest what skills and activities will be necessary to achieve the sort of cohesive group process so necessary to effective progress.

When each member of staff has completed a sheet for each of the policy programmes it is necessary to define a role plan. This approach to responsibility focuses very much on the learning process inside the classroom and the teachers' particular skills and abilities. Each role plan is an attempt to provide a clear set of aims for professional development. Part of the headteacher's leadership role is to work with each member of staff

Project	Group needs	Individual needs		
		Knowledge	Skills	Qualities
Teaching				
Planning				
Creating				
Communicating				
Motivating				
Organizing				
Evaluating				
Leading				

Figure 2.3 Identifying professional development needs

to prepare a realistic but challenging role plan. This is best achieved through a series of one-to-one discussions.

The identification of the collective needs of the staff should be a team exercise. Much will depend on the capacities within the working group for frank and honest exchanges about how the group operates and what its strengths and weaknesses are. The staff-appraisal exercise described in Chapter 3 is a very useful activity to help bring out these issues. Developments in humanistic psychology and human-relations training during recent years have provided numerous insights into group processes and practice. Few members of staff are likely to have had the opportunity to be involved in the increasing number of in-service courses that focus on this aspect of management but it is important that part of the whole-staff commitment is towards increasing knowledge about group management and developing the skills it requires.

When individual consultations have been completed and group needs agreed, it is important for each member of staff to commit his or her role plan to paper and to share it with colleagues. Part of the co-managing process is supporting colleagues in their endeavours, and it is essential that each teacher is clearly aware of the development programmes of

Name:	Term ending:
Professional development objectives	
1. Personal – working alone	
Intention	Outcome
1. To attend course on group-focused learning 2. Follow up ideas in the classroom 3. Attend drama workshops 4. Work on Open University pack – *Curriculum in Action* 5. Continue studying Cockcroft Report	
2. Group – working with others	
Intention	Outcome
1. Join drama project team 2. Attend course for staff – 'Developing active listening' 3. Try out peer-group appraisal interview with colleague 4. Contribute to policy-group meetings 5. Run a staff workshop – 'Group-Focused Learning'	

Figure 2.4 Role plan

colleagues. The role plan shown in Figure 2.4 is offered by way of example.

Since the emphasis in this approach is on the teachers' understanding of the learning process and the development of practical skills and abilities it is important that the operating procedures of the scheme provide opportunities for regular review and appraisal. Since appraisal interviews are a time-consuming activity for one person to handle, a system of peer-group appraisal is recommended. This requires each member of staff to work with a colleague to review progress and consider problems. About once a month each pair of teachers agrees to meet for an hour and a half or so. Each partner should complete a form as shown in Figure 2.5 at the beginning of the meeting.

Following the completion of the questionnaires one partner listens while the other talks through the issues raised on the form. The role of the listener is to help the talker to clarify issues, to identify problems and to seek explanations and solutions. The listening role is essentially a helping one, of assisting the talker to be clear about the work under review. It is not an opportunity for giving advice but for enabling the other to deal with the issues under consideration. After half an hour the pair swap roles for the next half hour. The final twenty minutes of the session should be devoted to generating and sharing new objectives that will be reviewed next time. The final task is to fix a date, about a month ahead, when the outcome of this session can be considered. This particular approach to peer-group appraisal benefits if participants have received some training in active listening or basic counselling skills. Opportunities for such training are increasingly available within LEAs, through adult-education centres and from agencies specializing in such training.

IN PRACTICE

Two distinct approaches to the identification of roles and responsibilities have been presented in this chapter. The purpose of offering different

Name:	Date:	
What I had planned to do	What happened	What I still have to do

Figure 2.5 Role-plan analysis

models has been to pinpoint the alternative approaches to the traditional ones. In practice some combination of the two approaches described here is to be desired so that teachers in their co-managing capacities are concerned both with the tasks and activities of development policies and with the extension of their own personal and professional skills. The choice of model is itself an interesting and essential whole-staff exercise. Moving from a long-established pattern to a new one can be a difficult process (see Chapter 5). However, if the exercise is approached as one of the staff team's projects for the year then there is an opportunity for all avenues to be explored, and there is ample time for both group and individual needs to be brought out into the open for discussion and consideration.

Whichever approach is chosen, the structuring of roles and responsibilities is a key management task for the headteacher. The structure is more likely to be successful if it helps to satisfy the motivational needs that were referred to earlier in the chapter. Teacher behaviour will supply plenty of information about how these needs are being met, but in progress interviews with each member of staff the head needs to be listening for clear evidence in each of four key areas (discussed in more detail in Chapter 4):

Affiliation
1. To what extent does each member of staff feel a strong sense of identity with the school, its policies and philosophy?
2. In what ways does this sense of belonging express itself?

Achievement
1. To what extent does each member of staff feel a real sense of achievement about his or her contribution to school life?
2. In what ways does this sense of achievement express itself?

Appreciation
1. To what extent does each member of staff feel valued and appreciated for what he or she brings to the school?
2. In what ways does this sense of appreciation express itself?

Influence
1. To what extent does each member of staff feel he or she is influencing the course of school events and developments?
2. In what ways does this sense of influence express itself?

In practice the aim should be to create roles and responsibilities that are rooted in the daily lives of teachers. In this way they are more likely to make optimum use of the range of skills and capabilities present in the working team. The essential departure from past practice must be in developing the idea that responsibilities are a key feature of an effective management partnership. It is through the exercising of this partnership in corporate planning and decision-making that progress can be achieved. A well-planned and coordinated role structure can facilitate this process of co-managing and help to create the dynamic flexibility necessary to ensure that policies and programmes are responses to the changing needs of society and its young learners. All this presupposes an efficient and effective selection process that will ensure, as far as possible, that roles and responsibilites are perceived clearly by the staff and are of relevance and use to individual and institutional development.

3
THE SELECTION OF STAFF

Having considered the roles and tasks of leadership, and the ways in which the curriculum may be enhanced through shared considerations of priorities and decision-taking, we now move on to the all-important process of recruitment and selection. This chapter offers practical suggestions for systematically appraising the needs of the school; establishing criteria for selection; providing appropriate information for candidates; eliciting relevant information from them about their experience, abilities, interests and expertise; supplying and obtaining reports; and interviewing and induction.

One of the key features of the educational reforms of the 1980s was the shift in a recruitment process largely determined and operated by LEAs to one carried out at the school level by head and governors. It is within this new context that we must consider how selection can best be managed. While governors take the key role in the decision-making process, it is the headteacher who will manage the procedures themselves. Some schools will have a sub-committee of the governing body delegated to take responsibility for recruitment and selection.

A VACANCY BECOMES AVAILABLE

The necessity to make an appointment to the teaching staff is a major management opportunity for the headteacher. The departure of a valued colleague will create a sense of loss, both in the sense that valuable expertise will be lost and also because a significant element of the school's social cohesiveness will be removed. It can be difficult to envisage life in a school without one of its key contributors. Perhaps this is because we tend to be preoccupied more with the task elements of management — the structure of the school, the nature of the curriculum and the professional qualities of teachers — than with the human relationships. There are conceptual models of school organizations and curriculum guidelines in abundance but very little that actually helps to inform about the behavioural dynamics of school life and the way they contribute to the overall effectiveness of the school as a working environment for learning.

In contemplating a replacement for a colleague it is very tempting to allow a dream to temper reality. How nice it would be in one simple appointment to plug all the gaps, satisfy all the needs and accelerate the journey to the promised land. Much of headship is about coping with the gap between the image and the reality, and once the fantasizing is over it is necessary to address the very real question of how the vacancy should be filled.

It is important at this stage to establish who will be involved in the various procedures of the selection process. This has implications for the leadership style of the head and the extent to which individual teachers and the staff as a whole are involved in the overall process of managing the school. In Chapter 1, leadership was described in terms of the providing of an environment. It is very much in this way that we see the context for the process of selection. One of the key themes of this book is the necessity for staff to be involved as active participants in the total managing process of the school. Given such a model of the management process, the needs of the individual are the needs of the organization. Decisions are going to be made about the professional effectiveness of the school and about the nature of the staff as a working team. If the selection process is to be successful in satisfying needs then, clearly, it is vital for staff to be involved. The head has the initiating and coordinating functions and carries responsibility in final decision-making, but he or she needs to work very closely with colleagues throughout the whole process.

ASSESSING THE NEEDS

The assessment of needs is an exercise to determine the current perceptions of the staff about how the school is currently working. Specifically it provides an opportunity to review

1. where we are hoping to go;
2. where we have come from; and
3. where we are at the moment.

This in turn requires consideration of

1. what we are currently engaged on; and
2. what we need to do next.

Before considering what sort of person to appoint it is necessary to be reminded of the work currently in progress and of the plans due for implementation in the future. The idea will be to try to appoint someone who has a positive contribution to make in these specific directions. The head is in an ideal position to summarize the progress made in implementing plans but it is important to gather staff perceptions as well. Raising the five issues listed above can help to provide a clear picture of current work and future tasks. The details provided by schools to potential applicants for posts rarely, if ever, give an indication of the current state of a development programme. This is unfortunate because it robs the candidate of an opportunity to make the written application specifically relevant to current issues and concerns.

In addition to the developmental aspects of the school there are also the general professional requirements that need consideration. Merely holding a generalized image of 'a good teacher' in the mind is unlikely to be very helpful. In giving attention to professional qualities it is necessary to be clear and specific. Figure 3.1 suggests the sort of checklist that can be generated to help in this analysis. The categories listed down the left-hand side allocate spaces for teaching, managing and leadership elements to be identified. It is useful to subdivide these into knowledge, skills and qualities. Such a checksheet should form part of a school's staff-development procedures and can be used by teachers as a self-appraisal instrument. It becomes especially useful in trying to identify the general and specific requirements for a vacant post. (See Chapter 7 for a detailed consideration of staff appraisal.)

Needs identification exercise

A useful strategy for involving the staff in this assessment of needs is the following staff-appraisal exercise. The focus here is the staff as a team rather than its constituent members, and the needs that arise from their corporate activities. The exercise can be handled in various ways. A

Categories	Knowledge	Skills	Qualities
Teaching			
Planning			
Creating			
Communicating			
Motivating			
Organizing			
Evaluating			
Leading			

Figure 3.1 Professional-qualities checklist

reasonably cohesive staff will be able to manage it in an open staff meeting, spending a few minutes brainstorming responses to each category. If the staff is large it is best to subdivide into smaller groups of four or five. The brainstormed responses should be listed and displayed for further consideration and discussion. An alternative approach is to have response sheets printed as illustrated in Figure 3.2. These can be made available to staff to fill in at their convenience. A compilation of responses can be made for circulation or display.

The categories listed are merely suggestions. Staff should be encouraged to create their own categories or delete ones they do not feel are helpful. Choice of categories and avoidance of particular ones can also provide an interesting insight into the current psychological health of the staff.

Having established an idea of the professional qualities required in the vacant post and produced an assessment of the current attitudes and perceptions of the staff as a whole, it is necessary to consider the type of personality likely to match the needs identified.

Personality and behaviour are much more powerful factors in selection than is sometimes realized. Time and again, in our experience, it is personal considerations that prevail in the making of a final choice from candidates shortlisted for interview. Heads and governors are always

As a staff we are:	
Good at	
Bad at	
Short of	
Worried about	
Ready for	
Needful of	
Resistant to	

Figure 3.2 Self-appraisal exercise

anxious to appoint someone who is going to 'fit in'. This implies that there is already an appreciation of how personal factors interact within the school. When heads make this statement about 'fitting in', do they mean someone who fits their ideas of a suitable person, or someone who will blend with the staff and enhance social cohesion? Much will depend upon the way the head relates both to individual members of staff on a person-to-person basis, and to the working team as a whole. No staff is fully cohesive, and interpersonal and intergroup conflict is a feature of all social groups.

In schools where corporate leadership and participatory management are of a high order there is a capacity to deal with conflict in an open and creative way. In these circumstances staff see conflicts as issues to be resolved rather than matters to be settled in terms of winning or losing. Such teamwork is more likely to be achieved where staff members have strong and well-developed self-concepts. Teachers with a high self-concept have been shown to be more effective in facilitating successful learning in pupils than those with a low self-concept (Rogers, 1983). Effective teamwork is more likely in groups where members have well-developed self-concepts. In summarizing the research into personal qualities and teaching, Carl Rogers (*ibid.*) has suggested that in the process of staff selection we should be searching for those teachers who

1. have the ability to be good listeners and can most readily understand the world as perceived by the pupil;

2. tend to feel a warm caring and respect for each pupil as a unique person;
3. are secure enough to be themselves with their pupils, who are not seen as roles but as real persons; and
4. tend to believe that persons are, at core, constructive not evil.

These qualities related to the self-concept are not always the ones we tend to look for in our recruiting. It is not enough to follow hunches about personality (although the intuitive response to people does have distinct value). It is important to try to check out these qualities in those we consider for our vacancies. How we do this will be discussed later in the chapter.

Assessing needs is a crucial part of the selection process. In schools where there is a policy of continuous self-appraisal it need not occupy much time or energy. What is important is that the assessing is looked at from various points of view: the needs of the pupils; the needs of individual teachers; and the needs of the staff as a whole. The intention should be to generate a realistic but comprehensive category of personal and professional attributes necessary for the job in hand. Without this it will not be possible to match the potential skills and qualities of the applicants to the needs of the school.

Before proceeding to the next stage of the selection process it is important to consider whether as a result of the vacancy arising some internal staff adjustments are necessary or desirable. Having identified current needs, consideration should be given to whether the potential to satisfy some of them already lies within the staff. The departure of the school's main musician, for example, could provide an opportunity for another musical member of staff to come forward. Some teachers live in the shadow of more experienced and qualified colleagues and allow their talents to become subdued and under-utilized. When considering specialist needs the first option should always be to give existing members of staff the opportunity to adjust their responsibilities. The departure of a key teacher can be an internal motivator, presenting other members of staff with the opportunity to move into new areas and take on new challenges.

PROVIDING INFORMATION FOR CANDIDATES

The education service has something of a bad reputation in the area of the provision of information for candidates. Potential applicants are expected to consider a major upheaval in their working circumstances on the barest of information about the job being offered, and sometimes when applicants seek an opportunity to visit a school where a vacancy exists they are received only grudgingly. The whole system of appointing staff seems to be built on the wrong assumption. Some schools and local authorities give applicants the impression that they are doing teachers a favour by offering up teaching posts for application. The opposite is true. A teaching vacancy in a school is a staffing problem only those willing to leave their present employment can solve. Those with the power to appoint should be much more grateful than they often appear to the teachers who are prepared to put themselves out to satisfy these staffing needs. While costs are a major consideration they should not be used as an excuse for discourtesy. It is quite appalling that some teachers, having spent considerable time and care in preparing applications in response to advertisements, receive no letters of acknowledgment or even a note regretting that on this occasion they have not been successful.

Cost is the main reason used to explain why advertising for teaching posts is so inadequate. All that an advertisement can be these days is an indication that a teaching post is available at a particular school and that more detailed information can be obtained on request. This part of the appointing exercise — the provision of the further details — is vitally important and should be approached with a determination to provide interested teachers with as clear a picture as possible of the school, and of the teaching vacancy that has arisen within it.

The first purpose these details serve is to limit the number of applicants. There can be no justification for putting anyone to the time and expense of applying for a post for which they are unqualified or for which they do not satisfy the basic criteria. The aim must be to attract positively those candidates who do satisfy the identified requirements and to inhibit those whose applications will not receive serious consideration. From the details the candidate should be able to gain a clear appreciation of the job involved, the type of school, something of the values encouraged in the school and an indication of the experience and professional qualities hoped for in the successful candidate.

It is not easy to summarize these requirements so as to satisfy all the anticipated queries by interested applicants. All schools should have a document that provides a great deal of the information — the school brochure, which is made available to parents. While this has been written with a parent audience in mind it should contain a great deal of the information applicants will need. Clearly, then, this should be one document made available. What the brochure will not contain is any specific information about the post available. It is the nature of this information we must now consider.

A useful exercise, and one that is vastly improved if the whole staff are involved in it, is that of putting yourself in the position of an interested applicant and listing all the queries you are likely to have. This can be conducted in very much the same way as the task described in the previous section of this chapter. Sheets of paper with category headings can be provided and colleagues can be encouraged to brainstorm the sorts of questions they would have if they were in the position of applicant. The following list is offered by way of example:

Type of school
What sort of community does it serve?
How is it organized?
What specialist facilities does it have?
Is it open plan?
Do staff change year groups every year?
How are curriculum decisions made?
Is there a school policy on equal opportunities?

Teaching role
In which age group is the vacancy?
What is the classroom like?
How many pupils?
What range of equipment and resources?
Are there policies about teaching style?
Are there curriculum guidelines?

Special responsibilities
Is there a job description?
To whom would I be accountable?
Are there funds available for development?
Is this a new or a replacement post?

Parents/community
Is there a school policy on community education?
Are parents active in the school?
Is there a PTA or parents' association?
What is the neighbourhood like?

Professional support
Are there regular staff meetings?

Is there a staff-development policy?
Do the staff have the opportunity of regular appraisal interviews?
Is there school-based in-service work?
Are staff involved in policy-making?

This is by no means a complete list but one that provides a useful agenda for preparing documents that supply candidates with information about, and insights into, the life and working of the school.

The next stage is to prepare documentation. How the documentation is presented will convey a great deal about the value system of the school. Shoddy and badly produced papers suggesting that the school prides itself on high standards raises the question about self-awareness. Information prepared in the first person, either singular or plural, always has a more personal quality about it and also serves to initiate a written conversation to which the candidate can respond in the letter of application. One of the best ways to approach the task is for someone to take the list of brainstormed questions and attempt to draft a few paragraphs for each category. Other colleagues can be invited to add information that may have been omitted. There is a lot to be said for this drafting being undertaken by a teacher on the same professional scale as the vacant post. Not only is this good management and healthy delegation but, from the applicant's point of view, it is perhaps more informative to get a colleague's view of the situation rather than the head's. The head will, of course, have other information to supply, particularly in relation to the requirements of the post and an indication of the skills and qualities being sought.

The two key documents that will need to be prepared with meticulous care are as follows:

1. *The job description* This sets out the detailed requirements and responsibilities of the post. It should specify to whom and for whom the post-holder is accountable and list the areas where leadership is required.
2. *The person specification* This sets out the knowledge, skills and experience required for the job. It should specify particularly the professional competencies expected in the specialist area of the job – curriculum coordination or team leadership, for example. Minimum criteria should be established, below which an appointment would be undesirable.

The job description is an essential document for the candidate and should always be sent to potential applicants. The person specification is designed to help selectors in their decision-making and is not sent to candidates. However, it is important to send a summary so that potential applicants can see the sort of skills and abilities expected in the post-holder.

Most LEAs now have well-established procedures for managing selection, firmly setting the process within a framework of equal opportunities. These should be followed in the interests of consistency and fairness to candidates.

Finally in this section, it is important to consider the information provided to candidates about the application itself. Generally the nature, style and composition of the written application is left for candidates to decide. Most teaching posts from main professional grade to headship are applied for in the same generalized way of completed application form and a supporting letter. Written applications could become a much more profound and effective part of the selection procedure if steps were taken to encourage candidates to address themselves to the specific issues of the post under consideration rather than the generalized matters of concern to the profession as a whole. One step towards this end is the preparation for potential candidates of guidelines for completing the application. By specifying the issues for consideration in the application form we are ensuring that what candidates write relates to the post in hand and not to a wider range of general and sometimes not particularly relevant material. The aim should be to get the candidate to prepare an application form that gives the selection panel the maximum amount of relevant information on which to base their judgments. It may be a good idea to issue candidates with a supplementary question sheet designed to elicit particular information not covered by the application form – the question sheet shown in Figure 3.3 is offered as an example. The specimen letter shown in Figure 3.4 is provided as a summary of the main points of this section.

VISITS AND VISITING

It is becoming increasingly common for teachers to want to visit schools before committing themselves to a formal application for a post. This is a very sensible preliminary step for the teacher providing an opportunity for the candidate to gain insights into the school and the way it works. Second, it provides an opportunity for the head and the staff to meet a potential colleague.

Nothing less than a half-day in a school is likely to be adequate to satisfy the candidate's needs. In arranging the visit the head and staff

Please suggest a few strategies for improving staff involvement in curriculum development	
Please comment on your reactions to any of the National Curriculum documents relevant to this post	
How do you suggest topic work can be improved as a central element in the primary curriculum?	
Which particular aspect of in-service training has been of help in preparing you for this post?	
What opportunities for professional development do you see in this post?	
What would you regard as the single most significant contribution you have made to your present school?	

Figure 3.3 Question sheet for candidates

need to be aware of its fundamental purpose — to create conditions in which the match of person to post, and post to person, can be assessed. In the expectation that a number of candidates will accept the invitation to visit it is necessary to have agreed a procedure for managing the visit. The following checklist suggests the different elements of a visit:

1. Seeing the building, inside and out.
2. Visiting classrooms and talking to pupils.
3. Noting specialist facilities: resources, library, etc.
4. Meeting staff informally.
5. Interview with a senior member of staff not involved directly in the selection process.

In organizing such a visit it is important to consider who should do the conducted tour of the school. In the interests of equal opportunities this is best undertaken by a member of staff other than the head. It is good for the visitor to get another teacher's view of the school and it is likely to be easier for the visitor to raise issues that might be difficult if the head were

> Dear Ms Smith
>
> Thank you for your enquiry about the vacant Allowance A post at this school. I enclose the following information which I hope you will find helpful in giving you an idea of the school and how we go about things:
>
> 1. A copy of the school brochure.
> 2. A staff handbook.
> 3. A job description.
> 4. Some information about the school compiled by the staff.
> 5. Some notes about the skills and qualities we are hoping for in the successful candidate.
>
> I also enclose the application papers. If, after having looked at the documents you decide to apply I shall be most grateful if you will submit the application in the following way:
>
> *Application form*
> Please complete pages 1, 2 and 3, leaving the back page blank.
>
> *Question sheet*
> These questions, as you will appreciate, relate specifically to the post you have enquired about. Please write your responses in the spaces provided.
>
> *Supporting letter*
> In a supporting letter about 1500 words I shall be grateful if you would include some reference to your ideas on the following areas:
>
> 1. The role of the allowance-holder in the modern primary school.
> 2. Relationships with pupils.
> 3. Learning from first-hand experience.
>
> We are hoping to hold interviews in the first week after halfterm and invitations will be sent out two weeks before that. In the meantime if you would like to visit the school we shall be very happy to receive you. Please telephone the school and we will try to arrange a mutually convenient time.
>
> Yours sincerely

Figure 3.4 Specimen letter to enquirers

conducting the tour. In order to allow some space and time for the visitor to get a 'feel' of the school it is good to keep the tour reasonably short and then to invite the visitor to wander. This allows the candidate an opportunity just to absorb what is going on, to think out possibilities, to anticipate experiences, to sense the organizational dynamics and to reflect on impressions. Motivation will be a key consideration, and will be based on the answers to such implicit questions as, 'Am I encouraged by what I see here?' and 'Is this school likely to develop me and help me grow, both personally and professionally?'

The discussion with the senior member of staff is really an interview conducted by the candidate. It is his or her opportunity to gain information on a range of issues about the running of the school and the new teacher's part in the scheme of things.

Some controversy surrounds the issue of heads visiting potential candidates in their schools. This is an important issue and in the interests of equal opportunities and good selection there needs to be general agreement in the profession. At present some heads visit before shortlisting; some only visit candidates they have already decided to call for interview; and some heads do not visit at all. This can be confusing for applicants and a code of practice would help to eliminate some of the suspicion that surrounds the issue. Our own view is that in an activity as practical as teaching a complete assessment of a candidate's abilities cannot be achieved without some opportunity to see him or her at work. On the other hand a satisfactory assessment is difficult to achieve from a very short visit, a glance at the classroom display and a brief chat with the teacher about what the pupils are doing.

If the headteacher is considering visiting candidates, the first consideration is when to do it. Should the visits be for the purpose of informing the shortlisting process or of gaining more information about candidates already selected for interview? Only the first of these seems to make any sense. If it is the teacher's practical abilities that are the main consideration then visits should be undertaken to ascertain who have the abilities required. A large number of applicants may present a problem and it may be necessary to draw up a list of the candidates who on paper come closest to satisfying the requirements of the job.

If visits are intended it would be sensible to suggest this in the details sent to candidates. Certainly they should be told of an intended visit and some time should be made available so that the candidate can explain to the visiting head some of the situational factors about the school — catchment area, school building, resources and organization. The circumstances of the visit can provide the basis of very interesting and relevant questions if the candidate is later called for an interview, for example, 'I noticed when I visited your classroom that a number of pupils were undertaking individual assignments. Could you explain to us how that system works?' The answer to such questions should provide a number of opportunities to probe the issue of classroom organization and management in some depth.

When visiting teachers, the head should be very clear about the purposes of the visit. A schedule of factors should be drawn up and applied to each visit. Impressions and supporting evidence should be documented and a summary prepared for presentation at the shortlisting and perhaps again at the final interview. At some stage, perhaps at the end of the visit, the candidate should be asked how far he or she felt that what was seen was a typical representation of the class at work. It is essential that the head should take full account of the context within which the teacher is working and the extent to which the teacher's work is conditioned by school policies and practices.

REFERENCES AND CONFIDENTIAL REPORTS

A reference or confidential report is a formal way of conveying information from someone who knows a candidate to someone who is seeking to fill a vacant post. It is unfortunate that the whole business of seeking and supplying confidential reports is plagued by so much spurious protocol. Far too often reports are merely bland versions of telephone conversations that have already taken place. Heads telephone other heads to gain information in order to shortlist and then seek confirmation of that report in writing if the candidate is shortlisted for interview. When they are actually read out in the final stages of the selection process they usually only confirm views that have already been arrived at. It is rare to find that a confidential report has supplied information that is crucial to the selection process itself.

The fault lies essentially with those who are seeking the report. If specific information is not asked for then it is unlikely to be supplied, and what will be produced is a general appraisal that is characterized by excessive use of superlatives, or couched in the jargon of euphemism. What enquirers often do seek is an indication whether the candidate justifies an unreserved recommendation − a sort of five-year guarantee of good service. Not only is this a naïve request, since it suggests that there is such a thing as all-purpose professional perfection, but it also demeans the whole process of professional appraisal and evaluation. What should be asked for is an assessment of those skills and qualities in the candidate that specifically relate to the job under consideration.

There are a number of ways to obtain this information. Let us first of all be clear about the points the referee needs to be briefed with before he or she can give a useful reference. This briefing involves the following:

1. Providing for the referee a clear written outline of the job in hand.
2. Identifying those particular skills and qualities hoped for in the successful candidate.
3. Suggesting to the referee the criteria for the assessing of those skills and qualities.
4. Enabling the referee to have an opportunity to represent the candidate on issues not specifically referred to.

The specimen letter in Figure 3.5 suggests a possible approach. This letter makes reference to two further documents. The question sheet (Figure 3.6) seeks to gain specific information about the applicant's professional abilities. The assessment sheet (Figure 3.7) invites the referee to make a judgment about specific skills and qualities. Used in combination these two documents can provide a far more detailed and helpful appraisal of the candidate than the four or five paragraphs of general summary usually supplied.

Dear Mr James

Ms J. Smith has applied for an Allowance A post at this school and has given you as a referee. For your information I enclose a copy of all the information which was sent to candidates. I hope this will serve to inform you about the job Ms Smith is being considered for and to give you an idea of the particular qualities we are hoping for in the successful candidate.

I also enclose a question sheet which seeks your comments on specific aspects of Ms Smith's work. Attached to this is an assessment sheet. I shall be most grateful for your responses to the questions and for your evaluation. I shall also be most grateful for any other information you may wish to draw to our attention.

As you may know we are hoping to hold interviews in the first week after halfterm. We shall be shortlisting at the end of this month and would very much like to receive your comments by then.

Many thanks for your help.
Yours sincerely

Figure 3.5 Letter to referee

What are the applicant's particular skills in building a classroom climate conducive to effective learning?	
What are the applicant's particular skills in classroom organization and management?	
What do you consider have been the applicant's most significant contributions in his/her present post?	
Which particular qualities in the applicant would you consider to be especially relevant to the post under consideration?	
What particular contribution has the applicant made to life in the staffroom and to staff discussion?	
Which of the applicant's personal qualities have contributed most to the school?	

Figure 3.6 Referee's question sheet

INTERVIEWING

An interview is a structured interaction between one person and another, or between one person and a panel. Those conducting the interview have the power to control the interaction, deciding how to conduct it, what material to deal with and when to end it. The interviewee acts in a responsive way to initiatives taken by the interviewers. It is important to be aware of this, and to have a capacity to see the experience from the candidate's point of view. Because of its formality and the fact that promotion may depend on it, an interview is usually a nerve-wracking affair. It is not a very common experence for most of us and demands a somewhat unnatural style of behaviour. Also, an elaborate mythology has grown up about the unwritten rules of interviews – the way to dress and how to respond to the panel. Those conducting the interview bear considerable responsibility for helping the interviewee to cope with the situation and to be sufficiently at ease to provide the information the panel will

Please indicate your assessment of the applicant's qualities by drawing a ring round one of the numbers in each category. 1: Excellent 2: Very good 3: Good 4: Adequate 5: Less than adequate					
Creating an effective classroom learning environment	1	2	3	4	5
Planning work	1	2	3	4	5
Building relationships with pupils	1	2	3	4	5
Matching work to the ability of pupils	1	2	3	4	5
Working with colleagues	1	2	3	4	5
Motivating pupils	1	2	3	4	5
Relationships with parents	1	2	3	4	5
Energy and commitment	1	2	3	4	5
Evaluating and monitoring work	1	2	3	4	5
Responding to and developing new ideas	1	2	3	4	5
Flexibility of approach	1	2	3	4	5
Ability to seek help and support	1	2	3	4	5
Awareness of own strengths and weaknesses	1	2	3	4	5

Figure 3.7 Applicant assessment sheet

need if it is to do its work well. It should always be the aim of an interviewing panel to enable candidates to perform at their best.

During the course of the interview (and in the decision-making that follows it) a number of skills are utilized:

1. Questioning.
2. Listening.
3. Observing.
4. Summarizing.
5. Assessing.

Let us look at each of these in turn.

Questioning

This includes all those strategies designed to get the candidate talking. There is always a danger that those interviewing will do far more of the talking than they should, thereby failing to draw from the candidate sufficient data on which to base an informed judgment.

Questions are really invitations for the candidate to talk. Sometimes the best way to facilitate this is not to ask questions at all but to define an area upon which you would like the candidate's comments. For example, on the issue of classroom organization a possible question could be: 'What factors do you need to take account of when setting up a classroom for a class of first-year juniors?'

There are a number of limitations to this question. First, it generalizes the issue, asking the candidate to comment on what teachers in general might regard as significant factors in classroom organization. Second, it invites a somewhat superficial response since situational factors will be of the essence – the size of the classroom, the previous experience of the pupils, the preferred teaching style of the school and the educational philosophy prevailing within it. Third, it limits the candidate to theoretical issues rather than practical ones. Perhaps a better way to get the candidate talking on this issue would be: 'Would you like to tell us about the process you go through at the beginning of each academic year when you prepare the classroom for your new class?'

This 'open' question has a number of advantages. First, since it is not a 'closed' question designed to elicit specific, predetermined information, it does not presuppose a single correct answer. Second, it draws upon the most significant aspect of the candidate's capacity to do the job – his or her practical classroom experience. Third, it provides an opportunity for the interviewer to match the candidate's perception of an issue with information already obtained from other sources – the visit of the head to the candidate's classroom and the specific information about classroom organization received in the confidential report. An important consideration in the interview process is the extent to which the candidate's perceptions of his or her work matches that of others.

In preparing themselves for selection interviews candidates are often preoccupied by the questions they may be asked rather than the areas they may be invited to comment upon. This emphasizes one of the myths about selection – that success depends on getting the answers to the questions right. Such a view misunderstands the nature of the professional examination a selection interview should be. Far more is of interest in the interview than simply the answers. Candidates need to be helped to the view that the interview is concerned more with what they have learnt from their experience and with their particular skills and qualities than with mere knowledge. For this reason it is important that invitations to talk are not merely questions requiring a simple factual answer. Obviously some factual data may need to be established during the interview and some closed questions may be necessary, but the bulk of the interview should be concerned with drawing out from the candidate the more profound aspects of professional ability and potential.

Let us be clear about what we are trying to discover or confirm in the candidate. Basically, it is information about

1. the candidate's knowledge about, and understanding of, the process of education;
2. the candidate's practical skills and qualities; and
3. the candidate's attitudes and values.

There is a relationship between the phrasing of questions and the category of information elicited:

1. 'What' questions usually elicit factual information.
2. 'How' questions usually elicit practical information.
3. 'Why' questions usually elicit attitudes and values.

There is a tendency in candidates to respond to questions with what they are most comfortable with rather than with the information that has been asked for. Interviewers need to be on the watch for this inclination to answer a different question. When probed about attitudes and values, candidates will sometimes try to avoid that issue by offering an example from practical experience. A supplementary question is vital if the panel is to obtain a comprehensive understanding of the candidate's ability — far too often the candidate's answer is accepted and the questioning moved on to another issue or another member of the panel. It is much more profitable to stay on an issue and probe deeper into it, using the candidate's first answer as the cue for a more penetrating enquiry. When, for example, the candidate has offered a 'what' answer to 'why' question, it is important to press the point and seek out the 'why'.

Earlier in the chapter the importance of the self-concept was stressed. Since quality of teaching relates closely to the factors contributing to the self-concept, it is important to cover these factors in the interview. Even without asking specific questions about these factors, the nature of the candidate's self-concept should be revealed during the interview. A checklist of the factors would be a useful addition to the headteacher's interview documents, perhaps arranged as in Figure 3.8, with spaces to record particular instances of each characteristic.

In preparing for the interview the panel need to play around with the phrasing of questions, being very clear about what it is they are hoping to find out. Badly worded questions are unlikely to bring the best out of a candidate, and a complicated preamble to a question is only likely to cause confusion. The best policy is to be very clear about what it is you want to discover, and then put the point to the candidate as simply as possible, following it up with precise supplementaries where necessary.

Listening

The ability to listen effectively in the interview is of fundamental importance. Far from consisting merely of hearing what is said, listening is the active and dynamic process of attempting to gain insights into the perceptual, intellectual and emotional world of the candidate. This involves a capacity to relate the candidate's responses to the questions posed and to pick out the distinguishing features of the candidate's presentation. In terms of the three categories already referred to this means being able to

Self-awareness	
Will to achieve	
Optimism	
Positive regard	
Trust	
Congruence	
Empathy	
Courage	

Figure 3.8 Self-concept factors

distinguish between answers that provide factual information, those that indicate skills and qualities, and those that reveal attitudes and values.

In the interview, listening operates on at least two levels. First, there is listening to make sense out of the current response — the immediate question. Second, there is listening to see how this answer relates to others that have come before or that will follow later. This is listening for consistency — the extent to which the candidate reveals a cohesive and compatible pattern of theory and practice. This second level of listening requires a capacity to pick out the underlying themes in the candidate's package of responses, in particular prejudices, ambiguities and inconsistencies.

Note-taking is a vital aid to effective listening in the selection interview. Since the process of interviewing itself requires considerable concentration it is important that data is recorded so that it can be recalled during the decision-making process. Figure 3.9 suggests a form that can be used by panel members to jot down significant points arising from each candidate's interview. A standard format makes for clarity and consistency between the panel members.

Observing

This is the skill of drawing inferences from the candidate's behaviour during the interview. Most interviewers can detect signs of nervousness in a candidate — a somewhat stiff posture, fidgety hands, a shaky voice — but may not be so aware of other aspects of non-verbal behaviour. Since the candidate's behaviour is likely to make an impression on each member of the interviewing panel it is important to make it an explicit feature of the selection process. During the summing-up and decision-making process it is essential that these aspects of the candidate are dealt with openly, rather than left only as private impressions. The purpose of observing how people behave is to gain an understanding of why they behave as they do. The categories of non-verbal behaviour of significance in the interview will be

1. facial expression;
2. eye contact;
3. voice; and
4. gestures.

In combination these represent the candidate's 'presenting image'. There

Name:				
Appearance	Facial expression	Eye contact	Voice	Gestures

Knowledge

Skills and qualities

Attitudes and values

Specific points	General comments

Figure 3.9 Interview recording sheet

is a considerable literature on non-verbal communication and it is important that someone on the interviewing panel has some knowledge and skill in this area. (Chapter 4 goes into this subject in some detail.) There is always a danger that incorrect interpretations will be drawn and this is another reason why some discussion of this dimension is important.

Perhaps the most significant aspect of the 'presenting image' is that of dress. There is much talk of 'the interview suit' and whether women candidates should wear trousers to an interview. There are many prejudices relating to this aspect, which is why the issue of appearance should feature in the discussion. In these times of changing fashions and social codes it would be good to see an initiative being taken by selectors, suggesting that candidates should attend interview in the style of clothing they would normally adopt in the classroom.

Summarizing

From time to time during the interview it is helpful to summarize progress. This provides an opportunity to check out with the candidate ground that has been covered and also that the candidate's view has been correctly received. In addition it provides an opportunity for the interviewing panel to assess its own progress. It is during the final decision-making discussion that the skill of summarizing is most important. It is important, when reviewing the interviews of each candidate, to be able to bring in front of the panel a complete appraisal of the candidate's strengths and weaknesses as revealed by the interview. This view will need to be supplemented later with information and assessments from visits and confidential reports.

To present such a summary requires some sort of framework. A summary could be built on the interview recording sheet illustrated in Figure 3.9. Alternatively the summary could be arranged under a set of categories decided upon before the interview:

1. Ability to deal with the interview.
2. Interview behaviour and 'presenting image'.
3. Professional knowledge and understanding.
4. Skills and qualities.
5. Attitudes and values.
6. Relationship of abilities to job requirements.
7. Estimation of potential to do the job.

Wherever possible the panel should be encouraged to adopt a standard procedure for summarizing and assessing each candidate. Far too often the final selection procedure rests on the exchange of personal impressions unrelated to the requirements of the job under consideration. Such an approach can be achieved if the panel includes a representative of the LEA's central administration, either an adviser or an officer.

Assessing

This is the skill of drawing conclusions from the evidence obtained about each candidate. This part of the procedure is facilitated considerably if the summarizing described above has been of a high order. In working towards the final choice of candidate it is important to proceed by elimination — no candidate should be eliminated without some discussion. If the procedures before the interview were carried out effectively all the candidates called should have the potential to do the job well. Some may not interview as well as others and the skill of assessment is about distinguishing between interview expertise and wider professional ability. It is at this stage that it is necessary to remind the panel of those particular abilities and aptitudes hoped for in the successful candidate and also the important personal qualities that need to accompany them. The following checklist suggests the factors that need to be included in the assessment that precedes the final choice of candidate:

1. A restatement of the current and future needs of the school.
2. A restatement of the job requirements.
3. A restatement of the skills and qualities hoped for.
4. Summaries of the interviews of each candidate.
5. Discussion of each candidate's interview.
6. Presentation of information previously received from
    (a) visits of candidates to the school;
    (b) visits to the candidates in their schools; and
    (c) confidential reports and references.

If the last item has been dealt with by a presentation before the interviews then it will be necessary to go over some of the main points concerning each candidate. Part of the assessment is the process of comparing the first-hand evidence of each candidate in the interview with reports received from other sources. It is not enough to make a choice purely on the basis of the interview itself. The interview stands as a part of a comprehensive selection process and needs to be seen in the context of that wider perspective.

Most interviews for teaching seem to last between twenty and forty minutes. If the interview, as perceived in this chapter, is to succeed in becoming a more effective instrument in the process of staff selection it is necessary to plan for interviews that are somewhat longer. This will provide an opportunity for more supplementary questioning, a chance to go into some issues in greater depth, and more scope for exploring the range of a candidate's qualities and abilities.

INDUCTION

Once an appointment has been made there is a tendency to regard the selection process as complete. In a sense the interview itself could be regarded as the beginning of that often neglected process — the induction programme. This officially comes into operation the moment a post has been offered and accepted. Although the successful candidate will have to serve out time in an existing post there is much that can be done to prepare for the new job ahead.

Before leaving the school after the successful interview the candidate may well have the opportunity to meet future colleagues and to make some arrangements to visit before officially taking up the post. This would also be a good time to pass to the candidate such documents as curriculum guidelines, pupil profiles, minutes of staff meetings and recent newsletters to parents.

A comprehensive induction programme should be an essential ingredient in a school's staff-development policy. Some care should be taken to anticipate the needs of a colleague joining the staff, and key members of staff should be briefed to undertake important introductory activities. Far too often new members of staff are left to tease out for themselves those all-important behavioural rituals and customs such as terminology, use of first names, and procedures for administrating the school's bureaucracy. Certainly, the induction of a new colleague should be the subject of at least one staff meeting.

The relationship between staff development and staff selection is fundamental. As has already been stated, those schools that have well-established staff-development practices will see selection as a natural part of that process. The need to appoint a new member of staff also provides a creative opportunity to exercise staff development by involving the whole of the professional team in the process of selection. Such an involvement has the potential to build effective teamwork and strengthen the social cohesiveness at the heart of all effective management. Indeed, both the newest and the longest-serving members of staff have a right to continuing opportunities for developing their awareness and expertise as individuals and as members of a team.

4
DEVELOPING PROFESSIONAL AWARENESS AND EXPERTISE

It is not enough to have a stable staff. Without help and encouragement in tackling not only new issues caused by external interventions but also the day-to-day challenges and problems caused by virtue of being a member of a teaching and learning community, many teachers will 'die on the vine', become disenchanted or settle into a routine that may ultimately become dysfunctional. It is therefore important that the head ensures that opportunities for updating skills and knowledge are provided on an individual and collective level, and that the psychological health of the school is maintained. This chapter provides both useful ideas for further thought and practical suggestions for action by the head in, for example, staff meetings and staff appraisal.

The term 'staff development' is used a great deal these days and sometimes it seems to be interpreted as an activity that happens at specific times during each school year or a teacher's career. What it ought to be is an ongoing process taking place every day in the school, and one whereby the head, through leading the teachers in a professional manner, ensures that they are well informed and fully aware of their roles and the responsibilities they have to the head, their colleagues and the children they teach. One of the most satisfying aspects of the head's job is the growth of personnel under his or her supervision. It is important, therefore, that the head has given very careful consideration to the management of a personal leadership style in order to get the best out of the staff and develop their potential. Consequently, the head will need to reflect on how to communicate with staff, establish responsibility and motivate the staff. Without frequent thought on these issues he or she is unlikely to develop the teacher's professional awareness and expertise, and the teachers are, after all, the most important resource available within the school.

KEEPING EVERYONE INFORMED

How can ideas be communicated to others effectively? This is a question every head should ask when preparing for staff meetings or parents' evenings, or talking to individual members of staff. Just because the head is familiar with the topic to be talked about does not mean that the teachers or the children's parents are. As schools grow in size and complexity there is a temptation for the head to rely heavily on formal written statements to spell out policy and philosophy, although experience suggests that written statements may not be the most effective method of getting ideas across. There are other ways of communicating within schools that are more likely to unify the school and project a positive image and outlook.

The head must become the catalyst for keeping information flowing throughout the school. Everyone involved in the life of the school — pupils, teachers, other staff, parents and governors — must be informed about those policies and practices that affect their lives. Teachers are unlikely to be highly motivated when they read about new approaches to the organization or curriculum of the school in a letter to parents. Parents want to be informed about changes in organization before they take place, while governors will be more than frustrated if the head acts on all matters without consultation. It is the head's role to make certain that every school group has some input in making decisions and carrying out mutually agreed goals and objectives.

Timing is a key factor in keeping everyone informed and, when change is planned, it can be worth while to list all the people who may initially be affected by it. Everyone should be informed *before* the change becomes effective and it is essential that they have had the opportunity to air questions and comments at an early stage and in an informal atmosphere where communication can move freely. Statements of school policy seldom run foul when there is free access of staff members to the head. Ideally, all the staff members will be part of the policy-making team. People who feel that they have been an integral part of a policy decision then have a vested interest in seeing that it succeeds. The teacher who is merely told of a change via a written memo is likely to become disgruntled and feel left out. (See Chapter 5 for a full consideration of possible effects of innovation and change on teachers.)

Keeping people informed is more than telling them in a pleasant manner. They must understand the reasons for the change. Alternatives should be presented. Suggestions must be considered and objectives should be studied. The final decisions should take into account the feelings of every group. Gone are the days when the head maintained an 'I know best' attitude and imposed his or her will on docile teachers, obedient pupils and awestruck parents.

SYSTEMS OF COMMUNICATION

Every head wants good staff morale and this is largely dependent on the effectiveness of the systems of communication. In most cases the two main means of communication used will be written communications and face-to-face meetings. The latter must always predominate and the most obvious way is to get around the school during the day. Visiting every classroom every day should be the first priority so that staff have access to the head of the teaching team who in turn can use such opportunities to communicate philosophy and influence classroom practice. In some rooms it may be a cursory visit, while in others it may be long enough to participate in a discussion or assist with children's activities. Teachers and pupils must know that the head takes an interest in them in their place of work. They should not see the head solely behind a desk in an office. It is important that the staff see the head when they arrive in the morning and, however the head may be feeling, a cheerful word of welcome will usually not go amiss. Seeing the teachers at the end of the day is probably more important because it is a good time for a head to compliment a teacher for something outstanding observed when making the rounds of classrooms. Offering praise to a teacher when other staff members are within earshot can be an effective motivator, but if there is a desire to make suggestions for improvements then this should always be done in private.

STAFF MEETINGS

These are an essential ingredient in the development of effective communications as they offer an opportunity for everyone to share ideas. It is important to remember that the staff have not come to a meeting just to listen to the head's magnetic voice, and any announcements the head needs to make should be kept brief, as people cannot sustain interest for long periods of time. Staff meetings must be planned well in advance — generally at least a term ahead — so that staff know what their commitment is likely to be. This is particularly important if the meetings are taking place after school, in which case a specific time should be fixed for the meetings to start and finish. All the staff must fully understand the purpose of such meetings and an agenda should be drawn up that includes all topics of interest suggested by individual teachers. A written agenda should either be given to each staff member or placed on the staff noticeboard at least 24 hours before the meeting is due to take place so that everyone has time to think about their own contribution on the topics raised for discussion.

An opportunity should be offered at the start of the meeting for staff to add items, and an effort should be made to establish the initial priorities and order of business. The agenda should not be sacrosanct, however, and if more important issues emerge during the meeting, which members are keen to pursue, then agreement should be sought to postpone the rest. The purpose of the meeting should always be clear, whether it be decision- or policy-making, exchanging information or keeping in touch. The chair's role is to help the group to achieve its task of completing the agenda whilst helping the members to work with each other effectively. It is good practice to allow the deputy head and those with incentive-allowance posts to chair specific meetings, especially when a curriculum area that relates to a teacher's specific responsibility is under discussion. Keeping a record of decisions reached is also an important aspect of staff meetings sometimes overlooked and this task can be delegated to staff members in turn with the notes of each meeting subsequently displayed on the staffroom noticeboard for perusal at leisure.

In order to make meetings work effectively, the leader (in many cases the head) needs to give careful consideration to working with the participants before, during and after the meeting. The following reminders are a guide to the strategies that need to be employed:

Before the meeting
1. Consider the individuals involved and the interests they will bring to the meeting.
2. Consult with staff regarding the agenda and time of the meeting.
3. Provide any necessary information prior to the meeting.

4. Organize tea or coffee and ensure the room will be comfortable and appropriately laid out. Staff should be able to look at and talk to each other.

During the meeting
1. Ensure that it starts on time.
2. Establish contract related to the content, style and purpose of the meeting.
3. Check out the feelings and understanding of staff members as the agenda progresses.
4. Use humour appropriately.
5. Bring any latecomers up to date.
6. Convey in behaviour that members are respected and contributions to the meeting are valued.
7. Listen, encourage, respond, link, bring in, ask clarifying questions, support, offer feedback to members.
8. Check any domination and work for a balanced contribution amongst staff members.
9. Encourage the talking out of differences.
10. Thank those attending and observe the agreed time limits.

After the meeting
1. Follow up contact with individual teachers who may need a further chance to talk on matters arising from the meeting.
2. Check out the staff feelings about the meeting and whether there are any suggestions for making the next meeting even more efficient.
3. Support any agreed follow-up action undertaken by the staff.

The staff meeting is perhaps the most used and least effective medium in most schools. If it goes well, the gains, in improving communication, participation, commitment and a sense of teamwork, are appreciable. If it does not, if issues are not clearly presented, if agendas are mismanaged or people left feeling confused, manipulated or frustrated, the individual and organizational costs can be appreciable.

ENCOURAGING PARTICIPATION

There are a number of effective strategies that can be employed to increase staff participation in meetings. For example, when developing school-based in-service curriculum meetings, the following strategies could be used:

1. The leaders of the development (which should include either the head or deputy head and, where appropriate, one other member of staff) must define their roles: they must see themselves as learners, refrain from 'selling' ideas, and allow staff to elaborate those ideas they see as relevant to the needs of the school.
2. Two team leaders are of great help in the planning stage to ensure the application of a breadth of experience to the development of the programme. Their role is also to stimulate discussion of the work undertaken when each session is concluded.
3. Before the 'course' begins there must be a slow build-up to the first session, during which time staff are given the opportunity to become acquainted with the philosophy involved.
4. The involvement of teachers from other schools within a local area can broaden the discussion and prevent staff from becoming too inward-looking.
5. Group sizes for discussion should be kept to a minimum of three and a maximum of six – this results in greater teacher participation, especially when careful consideration is given to the membership of each group.
6. In order to ensure full involvement by each staff member, it is desirable to appoint individuals on a rota basis to act as rapporteur to any plenary sessions.

Noticeboards in the staffroom are another effective way to communicate ideas and administrative details. Far too often such boards become cluttered with papers pinned at random in any available space and as a result lose the impact they were designed to have on the reader. Such a staff noticeboard should be clearly subdivided in sections so that staff know where to seek information. There should be sections on in-service courses, duty schedules, teacher union announcements, etc., and a 'special' section should be reserved for items of immediate concern. All items should be neatly displayed, and stale, out-of-date notices should be removed promptly.

However, the more formal systems of communication are not the only ones operating in the school. A great deal of information is likely to be transmitted through both the informal system and the inferential system. The informal system, the 'grapevine', is certainly at work in any school and there is little that can be done to prevent it functioning. It clearly differs from the formal systems in that it tends to be quicker and less accurate, and to thrive on 'news' that threatens and alarms. The head needs to recognize that rumour and gossip are essential elements in the social psychology of any institution. To ignore such elements would be foolish, and the head at least needs to take them into account. The grapevine can have considerable impact if left to grow wildly.

NON-VERBAL COMMUNICATION

The inferential system consists largely of non-verbal communication that, by its very nature, will always be present yet is often not given careful consideration. Non-verbal communication can be split into two categories, visual and non-visual, both of which are important in their own right. The different areas of visual non-verbal communication are as follows.

Proximity

How close (physically) you get to an individual will be taken as an indication of how close a relationship you have with him or her.

Orientation

The way you sit or stand in relation to someone is an indicator of the type of relationship you have with him or her. People will always try to face those with whom they are in conflict, or whom they are trying to prove superiority to, whereas people who are cooperative and friendly will either be side-by-side or at 90 degrees to each other.

Bodily Posture

This will indicate your attitude towards someone as well as your self-image. It is easier for a leader to attain a relaxed position in a group if he or she sits or stands in the group-norm position.

Gestures

There are two types of gestures – head nods and other body movements such as hand or arm movements. A single nod is a method of showing attention when talking to someone, and a rapid series of nods usually shows that you wish to interrupt the speaker and get your own point of view across. The other type of gestures (other body movements) can be a great source of information, especially when spontaneous – they can show specific as well as general emotions.

Facial Expression

People's expressions indicate their attitudes and emotions toward each other and situations. A smile may sometimes indicate happiness, interest or greeting: a frown can mean distaste or concentration. One of the problems with the interpretation of facial expressions is that they can be manipulated to give a false impression.

Eye Movement

These can indicate attention as well as moving in synchrony with speech. The amount of eye contact with speakers can also indicate the degree of interest being shown in what people are saying.

Appearance

People's hair, clothes, make-up, etc., can indicate self-image, personality, mood, occupation. You decide how you wish to look and what others see may well determine their reaction to you.

When considering non-visual, non-verbal communication there tends to be a problem of perception. As so much information is taken in visually, it becomes difficult for people to perceive other types of non-visual information, especially if it contradicts the visual sense. There are four types of non-visual, non-verbal communication that can give information about people's feelings and attitudes.

Touch

It is remarkable how even such a formalized gesture as a handshake can convey an impression of someone's personality.

Aura

This is difficult to define but one's perception of it could be termed 'intuition'. People who are experiencing very strong emotions generate a strong aura that can be detected fairly easily by other people.

Voice

One of the best indicators of a person's feelings is the voice. The speed of speech, the tone of voice, the choice of words and the loudness as well as hardness of the speech, can all indicate general and specific emotions.

Olfactory

A person's choice of perfume, aftershave, etc., can give an impression of self-image, personality and mood.

Non-verbal communication is a powerful means of indicating attitudes and emotions and probably has two other main uses: first, re-enforcing, contradicting or complementing verbal communication; and, second, replacing speech.

KEEPING IDEAS FLOWING

Not every good idea originates in the head's office. Seeds of ideas are more often developed in the classroom, where the good head is constantly on the look-out for such ideas and innovations. It becomes the head's job to help these seeds germinate and to nurture their growth. He or she must also provide the atmosphere and structures in which teachers are willing to share ideas and pass on successful practices. The head should therefore encourage informal meetings between groups of teachers in order that an interactive flow of information and attitudes is stimulated. The technique requires little more than an openness that allows ideas to rise from the grass roots rather than percolate down from the head's office.

Heads have developed many ways of finding out what their teachers are thinking. They can range from interview techniques to simply leaving the office door open. Each listening device has its virtues and its limitations. While some are clearly better than others there is no single method that can give you all the information you need about teacher ideas and attitudes. The daily face-to-face communication with the staff is unquestionably a fruitful source of information about what is really going on in the school. Without these contacts no other method of listening is likely to be very meaningful.

Yet, no matter how free and open heads may try to be, staffs will always have a strong tendency to tell them what they think they want to hear. Communication is most likely to be 'taken on board' if it is personal and fulfils a need or meets an interest in the receiver. When the head spends time listening to individual teachers he or she will often be drawn into impromptu conversations. This is an ideal opportunity to develop a good working relationship with staff, and will not only give a close personal insight into their ideas about the school but also provide an opportunity for the head to share thinking about the way the school and their work is developing. By responding to teachers' needs the head will be creating an atmosphere of trust and understanding. Every effort should be made to be clear and consistent in any replies, otherwise all the head may do is confuse the situation, and this may well lead to rumour and misunderstanding. There will be occasions when people will misunderstand him or her and on analysis it will probably be the case that it was the head who did not achieve the necessary degree of precision and lucidity in the first instance.

ACTIVE LISTENING

A developed skill of active listening will be of great help in communicating effectively with other people. By active listening we mean the ability to see the expressed idea and attitude from the other person's point of view, to sense how it feels to him or her and to achieve his or her frame of reference in regard to the topic being talked about. Active listening is the skill of feeding back to the sender the feelings perceived from his or her verbal and non-verbal communication. The goal of active listening is really to 'hear' what senders are communicating about their feelings through their verbal and non-verbal language; in other words, hearing what is said accurately and interpreting what is not said. The skills of active listening will usually be a help to someone who is bothered by a professional or personal problem. In order to develop the skill there is a need to

1. concentrate – aurally and visually;
2. clarify and help the discussion by

    (a) paraphrasing what has been said, and
    (b) summarizing at appropriate stages;

3. hear the speaker out;
4. respond to feelings and emotions – don't sweep them aside; and
5. respond to non-verbal cues.

ESTABLISHING PRIORITIES AND PROCEDURES

Think carefully about your school – what are your goals or objectives for improving it? What steps have you taken this year to implement your plans? Have you only managed to maintain existing practices or are developments clearly recognizable? Some heads seem to have difficulty planning because they regard it as limited to 'thinking', whereas in fact it ought to be thought of as a writing exercise. In one way or another, whether you have been aware of it or not, you will have been thinking about the goals for your school. But thinking about your goals is different from writing them down. Unwritten goals often remain vague dreams. Writing goals down tends to make them more concrete and specific and helps you probe below the surface of the same old clichés you have been telling yourself for years.

By reading your thoughts committed to paper you will gain a valuable new perspective because you can then examine them more closely. Once they have an independent existence you can scrutinize them better – they can be analysed, refined, updated, pondered and changed. At the same time, write down the names of the people who could help you achieve some of the goals and in this way you will begin to realize specific ways the skills and efforts of such people can be utilized.

Before the start of a new school year set yourself the task of writing three or four goals you would like to accomplish during each year. Early in the autumn term meet with each of your staff members and talk with them about the year ahead. Ask them what some of their plans are and discuss them in detail. At the first convenient staff meeting, after seeing each of your teachers, the goals for the school year should be discussed. However, long-term planning must be complemented by short-term planning. This kind of planning requires specifying the activities teachers should perform. Most, if not all, of the activities specified in short-term plans should contribute to the realization of the goal specified in long-term plans, and should be planned in such a way that they are recognized as achievable by your staff. To set them tasks they feel are completely beyond them is pointless. As head it is vital that you examine the precise job to be performed by each of your staff involved. Each teacher will have a different set of experiences, attitudes and ideas and your role is to develop each of your staff to a level that utilizes their existing expertise yet takes them one step further in the development of classroom practice. In writing specific objectives for your staff the following suggestions will help in your planning. An objective should

1. be mutually agreed;
2. be recorded in writing;
3. specify a single result to be accomplished;
4. set a target date for its accomplishment;
5. be measurable and verifiable; and
6. be realistic and attainable but still represent a challenge.

Establishing priorities with your staff and listing them is only part of the planning process. All the items on the list will not be of equal value so it is important to agree with your staff the ones that are of the highest priority. Having done this you will end up with a first priority that should be of very high value and that you need to build into your daily schedule. Teachers may need help in ordering their priorities for the year and it is your job to review their progress.

THE EFFECTIVE MANAGEMENT OF TIME

Some teachers and heads can get vast amounts done during a working day while others continually complain that they do not have enough time. It seems that some people are able to use their time better than others, and heads who recognize planning as an important function of their role usually find themselves in the former category. Planning separates the effective head from the neurotic one, and in today's primary schools it is as important for the head to have knowledge and skill in implementing the management process − planning, organizing, directing and controlling time − as a knowledge of the curriculum. Planning is determining what needs to be done, who will do it, and when it has to be done.

The first step you need to take in effectively managing your own time is to find out how you spend it at present. A precise study is not necessary, but a time-analysis chart (Figure 4.1) using a check mark for each ten minutes of each day, can give a fairly accurate picture of how most of your time is spent. The same sheet can be used for an entire week as this will have greater impact and be easier to check. The total check marks for the week in each column multiplied by ten provide a fairly accurate picture of how many minutes are spent in a week on each activity. (You will have to determine the column headings for yourself in order to choose those that best cover your own activities.) Once you have discovered how your time is spent you may well realize that it does not allow for any of your set priorities and this is where a personal planning sheet (Figure 4.2) can help you to organize your time for the coming week. It will force you to evaluate activities, set priorities and schedule each activity when it will not be crowded out by a dozen others. During the week some tasks will not be completed, and so will need re-scheduling. Nevertheless, this kind of planning, where an explanation in writing is given to oneself for non-completion of tasks, will give you a better understanding of, and more control over, how your time is used.

Managing personal time in this way is obviously good in theory but many heads back away when they look at the countless activities they must engage in every day. Feeling that it is hopeless, they never start, and so put personal time planning far down on the mental list of things they will do as soon as they get more time. None of us is perfect. None of us should be disappointed if we are not planning our work − and working our plan − every minute of the day, but you will be taking several steps in the right direction if you get into the habit of doing the following:

1. Keep long-term goals in your mind even while doing the smallest task.
2. Plan first thing in the morning and set priorities for the day.
3. Keep a list of specific items to be done each day, arrange them in priority order and then do your best to get the important ones done as soon as possible.

TIME	Teaching	Visiting classrooms	Paperwork	Telephoning	Informal meetings with individual teachers	Staff meetings	Parent consultations	Visitors – governors, Advisers, etc	Duties – dinner, playground	Visits to other establishments
08.00										
08.30										
09.00										
09.30										
10.00										
10.30										
11.00										
11.30										
12.00										
12.30										
13.00										
13.30										
14.00										
14.30										
15.00										
15.30										
16.00										
16.30										
17.00										
17.30										

Figure 4.1 Personal time analysis

Week commencing:										
Activity	Monday		Tuesday		Wednesday		Thursday		Friday		Comments
	a.m.	p.m.	a.m.	p.m.	a.m.	p.m.	a.m.	p.m.	a.m.	p.m.	

Figure 4.2 Personal planning sheet

4. When under pressure, ask yourself, 'Would anything disastrous happen if I didn't do this now?' If the answer is no, then don't do it.
5. Do your thinking on paper.
6. Set deadlines for yourself and your staff.
7. Delegate all routine items.
8. Generate as little paperwork as possible.
9. Recognize that some of your time will be spent on activities outside your control and don't worry about it.
10. Ask yourself hourly, 'Am I making the best use of my time right now?'

There are other techniques that can be developed for getting maximum benefit from minimum investments of time. Some of the most helpful we have found are as follows:

1. *Concentrate* Of all the principles of time management, none is more basic than concentration. People who have serious problems managing their time are invariably trying to do too many things at once. The amount of time spent on a project is not what counts; it's the amount of uninterrupted time. Few problems can resist an all-out attack. Equally, few can be solved by erratic attention.

2. *Take breaks*   To work for long periods without taking a break is not an effective use of time. Energy decreases, boredom sets in and physical stress and tension accumulate. Switching for a few minutes from a mental task to something physical − walking around the school, even changing from sitting to standing for a while − can often provide relief. Merely resting, however, is often the best course and you should not think of a 'rest' break as poor use of time. Not only will being refreshed increase you efficiency but relieving tension will also benefit your health. Anything that contributes to health is good time management.

3. *Avoid clutter*   Some people have a constant swirl of papers on their desks and assume that somehow the most important matters will float to the top. In most cases, however, clutter hinders concentration and can create tension and frustration − a feeling of being 'snowed under'. Whenever you find your desk becoming chaotic, put some time aside to re-organize. Go through all your papers (making generous use of the rubbish bin) and divide them into categories: immediate action, low priority, pending, reading material. Put the highest-priority item from your first pile in the centre of your desk, then put everything else out of sight. Remember, you can only think of one thing at a time, and you can work on only one task at a time, so focus all your attention on the most important one. A final point: clearing the desk completely each evening should be standard practice. It gets the next day off to a good start.

4. *Don't be a perfectionist*   There is a difference between striving for excellence and striving for perfection. The first is attainable, gratifying and healthy. The second is often unattainable, frustrating and neurotic. It's also a waste of time.

5. *Don't be afraid to say 'no'*   Of all the time-saving techniques ever developed, perhaps the most effective is the frequent use of the word 'no'. Learn to decline, tactfully but firmly, every request that does not contribute to your goals. If you point out that you are not just being lazy but saving your time to do a better job on the really important things, you'll have a good chance of avoiding unproductive tasks. Remember, many people who spend time worrying about offending others wind up living according to other people's priorities.

6. *Don't procrastinate*   Procrastination is usually a deep-rooted habit. But habits can be changed, provided the right system is used. It works as follows:

- Decide to start changing as soon as you finish reading this chapter, while you are still feeling enthusiastic. Taking that first step promptly is important.
- Don't try to do too much too quickly – just force yourself right now to do one thing you have been putting off. Then, beginning tomorrow morning, start each day by doing the most unpleasant thing on your schedule first. Often it will be a small matter: an overdue apology, an annoying chore you know you should tackle. Whatever it is, do it before you begin you usual morning routine. This simple procedure can set the tone for the day. You will get a feeling of exhilaration from knowing that although the working day is only fifteen minutes old, you have already accomplished the most unpleasant thing you have to do all day.
- Do not permit any exceptions. Be tough with yourself for the first few minutes of each day, for the next two weeks, and a new habit of priceless value will have been acquired.

7. *Apply radical surgery* Time-wasting activities are like cancers. They drain off vitality and have a tendency to grow. The only cure is radical surgery. If you are wasting your time on activities that bore you, divert you from your real goals and sap your energy, cut them out, once and for all. The principle applies to personal habits, routines and activities as much as to ones associated with your work. Check your calendar, your social life, your reading list, your television viewing habits and axe everything that doesn't give you a feeling of achievement or satisfaction.

8. *Delegate* Learn to delegate the challenging and rewarding tasks, along with sufficient authority to make necessary decisions. It can help to free your time for other things. One caution: giving teachers jobs that neither you nor anyone else want to do isn't delegating, it's assigning.

9. *Don't be a 'workaholic'* Most successful people work long hours but they don't let work interfere with the really important things in life, such as friends and family. This differentiates them from the workaholic, who becomes addicted to work just as people become addicted to alcohol. Symptoms of work addiction include refusal to take a holiday, inability to put the school out of your mind at weekends, a bulging brief-case and a husband, wife, partner, son or daughter who is practically a stranger. Ask yourself whether the midnight oil you

are burning is affecting your health. Ask where your family comes in your list of priorities, and whether you are deceiving yourself by pretending that the sacrifices you are making are really for them. Above all else, remember – good time management involves an awareness that today is all you ever have to work with. The past is irretrievably gone; the future is only a concept.

MANAGING TEACHERS EFFECTIVELY

Communication is a two-way process and it is important from the head's point of view to be specific. Decisions, as well as the reasons for them, have to pass both ways before coordination and cooperation can be achieved.

Heads of schools should not hesitate to go into classrooms to find out what is going on. They should not have to pause to think twice before entering the classroom of one of their teachers. Only by frequent visiting will they be aware of the teachers' techniques, strengths and limitations. Only then will they be able to guide and provide true supervision by improving the level of instruction.

To manage teachers effectively, therefore, heads must resist any temptation to go into isolation. Teachers must see them in their classrooms and around the school – their 'aura' must pervade the entire school. By making their presence felt through communicating face to face they will begin to be truly effective in keeping their staff informed. But they must not assume that teachers know everything they know, or even that the teachers care about the same things as they do.

Teachers can be trained to improve their daily performance if they are approached in the right way. The best in-service programmes in the world may look good on paper but will be worth little if the wrong person is put in charge of implementing them. As leaders of the school, heads must set an example of concern for self-improvement. They must show their teachers that they care about their feelings before they will be able to get the teachers to care about refining their techniques. The following suggestions are intended to help in the planning of a programme of school-based in-service training:

1. Make sure all your instructions are detailed and that you have anticipated any questions your staff may have.
2. Tell your staff the 'why' and 'what for' of any development.

3. Carefully describe the standards you expect.
4. Allow sufficient time for the completion of any task.
5. Plan for staff to visit each other's classrooms and other schools.
6. Demonstrate how you would like something taught.
7. Supervise closely.
8. Help the staff to set goals and objectives.
9. Be patient. Encourage with praise when earned.
10. Use staff expertise to encourage others.
11. Set the tone for self-improvement by being honest about your strengths and weaknesses.

In all his or her dealings with teachers and others in the school, the head needs to be ever protective of their egos and feelings of self-worth. This is perhaps the most important element in any programme of staff development. The head may be right about something, but if he or she presents correction in a manner that demeans the recipient, the latter will pay little or no attention to it. There will be times when the head must criticize, but it should always be done in a way that is constructive and not destructive. In addition, management of teachers will improve if the head remembers that positive feedback on the performance of teachers is also possible.

HANDLING STAFF COMPLAINTS

The handling of staff complaints about the decisions made by a head demands the sharpest human-relations skills from beginning to end. This skill can frequently make the difference between a satisfied, cooperative staff member and a staff member who is a constant source of irritation. It only takes one or two disgruntled staff to lower the morale of an entire school. The justification for a complaint may be either real or imaginary, but it is vital to understand that, from the staff member's point of view, it is real. Downgrading the importance of a complaint or ridiculing an individual only adds fuel to a fire that is just starting.

Even in the best-run school there will be complaints. In fact, a complete absence of complaints, say many experts, is an indication that people are afraid to voice their feelings and concerns. When handling complaints, a number of particular points have been gleaned from successful and management-minded heads. They are as follows:

1. *Listen with interest* Listening is perhaps the best way of sizing up another person in a disagreement. Listening is a way of showing

respect. It helps the head understand the depth of feeling the staff member has about the issue, and is the first chance to start developing an understanding of what is really bothering the individual.
2. *Dignify the complaint* Many complaints are without foundation and are a result of poor communication – or an overactive imagination! To the staff member, however, the complaint is real. It may have taken much courage for that person to express it to the headteacher. The least the head can do is demonstrate that the complaint is considered important and that it will receive full and sympathetic attention.
3. *Remain poised* Proper handling of complaints requires clear thinking. Most complaints challenge methods of management and organization. The temptation to become angry is great, but the head's main objective should be to stay in control. Loss of temper tends to lead to loss of control and also a loss of dignity as a member of the management team.
4. *Assemble the facts* The pressure is often on the head to make a decision as quickly as possible, yet this should not be done without the benefit of factual information. There is always the possibility that a complaint might develop into a full-blown grievance. The head needs the whole story and may need to ask questions of a number of people, check records or review conditions of service, and investigate anything that will help make an informed ruling or decision.
5. *Be direct* Hedging and stalling are annoying and can be inflammatory. It is safe to assume that anyone coming to a headteacher with a complaint would like a direct answer. If it is within the scope of the head's authority to give an answer, then it should be given in clear, definite, understandable terms. A decision beyond the head's authority should be sought and communicated to the individual concerned as soon as possible. If the answer is slow in coming then the employee should know the reasons for any delay. Since the complaint is serious to the employee, the longer the wait for an answer, the deeper the concern and convictions are likely to become.
6. *Stick with the decision* Telling the staff member that he or she is right and that the request will be granted is the easiest thing in the world. The test of the head's skills is in saying 'no' and in helping the member of staff accept the decision. Reasons that are clear and understandable from the staff member's point of view should always be a part of rendering a negative decision. A hard, cold 'no' does nothing to strengthen future relations. This is the critical point in

preventing a complaint from becoming a grievance, and a grievance from going to a higher level.

DEALING WITH CLIQUES

In almost every school there are informal groups of teachers who have banded together because, for one reason or another, they find themselves congenial. These groups can have considerable influence over the behaviour and job attitudes of other individuals, especially new teachers. Whether a clique is disruptive or cooperative depends a great deal on how the head decides to meet the challenge. In every group there is someone who is the most popular and someone who is the acknowledged leader. There is a strange psychological factor in this leadership because it hinges on the group member's desire for authority that is not imposed by anyone − they decide for themselves that one of their member deserves their loyalty. In most cases the problem of dealing with cliques becomes a question of recognizing the popular leader and finding a way to ensure that person's cooperation. Most of the time a head will find no cause for alarm that various groups of teachers have emerged within the school as long as they continue to perform up to expected standards and cooperate when a special effort is needed. Yet there is no denying that many such groups are anything but productive. If the following characteristics are true for some of your staff, then it is time for the head to intensify efforts to gain their cooperation:

1. They keep their performance to a level that is far below their capacity, but equal to their past performance.
2. Newcomers to the staff, no matter how well they are inducted, quickly adjust their performance to the group's normal low level.
3. If a teacher does do something 'extra' it is made quite clear by that person that this is a 'favour' for the school and should not be expected to last.

A headteacher is most likely to gain the cooperation of any clique of workers that exists in the school if

1. recognition is given to the group's leader as well as all the members, and their cooperation is encouraged instead of fighting the clique's existence;
2. interest is shown in the goals of the group and they are supported when their requests are reasonable;

3. the group's interests can be developed in the school and that their ideas are understood and each group member treated in a considerate manner; and
4. the successful head learns to work with the informal leaders among the staff to develop a mutual understanding of the school's aims and objectives.

FEEDBACK

Feedback is to help the receiver achieve the desired learning goals and objectives. It increases a person's awareness of how he or she affects others. Feedback is a mirror for observing the consequences of one's behaviour. Before giving feedback a good relationship with the receiver needs to be established so that both parties can be open and honest with each other. A good relationship will increase the chances of the feedback being accepted, not rejected, by the receiver. When giving feedback it is necessary to concentrate on the following:

1. What is done or said — not who said it or why (i.e. do not make assumptions about motives or intent).
2. Observations — not inferences (they may be wrong).
3. Description — not judgments or evaluations (which will be based on your own values).
4. 'Here and now' behaviour — not 'there and then' (which tends to become distorted or fantasy).
5. Sharing ideas and information, and explaining alternatives (rather than giving clear-cut standard solutions).
6. Behaviour that can be reasonably changed (in order to avoid frustration or the rejection of the feedback).

Other factors you should consider are as follows:

1. The value of feedback to the receiver — not your own self-satisfaction.
2. The desirability of limiting yourself to a few major observations to avoid overloading the receiver.
3. The appropriate time and place to avoid emotionally harmful effects.

It may be helpful to check with other observers, before giving feedback, whether they have the same impression as yourself. It is also very important to check whether the receiver has understood and accepted the feedback by asking him or her to recap on what you have said. There is little point in giving feedback unless you are aware of any obstacles to the receiver accepting feedback. Some people find it hard to admit their weaknesses and difficulties, often because they are so concerned about what others think of them. They may fear being dependent on others or being without anyone upon whom they can depend for support and sympathy. Also they may feel that their problem is so unique that no one will understand or, equally, that the problem is too trivial to bother someone else with.

REVIEWING TEACHER PROGRESS

Providing feedback is an activity that can happen at any appropriate time during the school year but, in addition to this, there is probably a need for a more structured session when the head can review the progress and future objectives of each teacher. Work review is an important part of motivating staff, improving performance and determining future developments. Some heads feel that because they are in daily contact with their staff there is no need for formal work reviews. However, daily contact is often superficial and does not allow people time to discuss their ideas in depth. The work review can allow staff the time to consider their influence over the development of their skills and attitudes and, where appropriate, future promotional opportunities. The need for this type of review has probably never been greater than in the present climate, where there is now more staff stability in primary schools. Every effort needs to be made to help teachers develop their expertise over a longer period within each school. The work review can assist both teacher and head in their personal and professional growth. A number of stages can be identified that lay a good foundation towards understanding and accepting the review:

Stage 1: preparation Prepare yourself, as well as asking the teacher to prepare him or herself, for a prearranged meeting at a mutually agreed time when there will be at least forty-five minutes available for an uninterrupted conversation. Come to the meeting expecting to compare notes, as this will allow for a review of the facts that have influenced the teacher's performance during the previous year.

Stage 2: review Compare the teacher's accomplishments with specific targets. Do not be vague or resort to generalizations. Be specific about what was expected and how close the teacher has come to meeting those expectations.

Stage 3: giving praise Be sure to give adequate credit for what has been accomplished. It is a temptation to concentrate on the mistakes and take for granted those things that have been done well.

Stage 4: noting areas for improvement Review those things that have not been accomplished and emphasize where improvement is needed. Explore together with the teacher why improvements are necessary and how they can be tackled.

Stage 5: protecting the other's ego Avoid the feeling of being judgmental. Never compare the teacher with a third person. Stick to a mutual examination of the facts and what they imply to both of you.

Stage 6: future targets Agree on targets to be met during the year ahead. Be specific about them. Relate them to what has been accomplished during the previous year.

Stage 7: offering help Review what you can do to be of greater help. Improvement is almost always a mutually dependent activity. It is likely that the teacher will approach the task with greater confidence and enthusiasm if you and he or she have jointly accepted responsibility for improvement.

You should be the best judge of how one of your teachers will take what you have to say. Try to anticipate people's reactions so that you are not taken by surprise. A work review is unlikely to be helpful if the head is shocked by a teacher's unexpected antagonistic or hostile attitude. By expecting specific reactions you can try to plan your responses well ahead. It may be that you will learn much about your own interpersonal skills in such situations. (In an honest interchange your own ego may well take a knock!) Careful forward planning in terms of the type of open-ended questions you could ask will help you to feel confident and relaxed. The following questions will provide useful starting points for much discussion:

- What aspects of your teaching have interested you most?
- What aspects interest you least?
- How do you feel you have carried out the main tasks you are responsible for?
- What tasks do you feel you have performed particularly well and why?
- What areas, if any, are unclear to you about any aspect of school life?
- What extra help or guidance do you feel you need?
- What can I do to assist in your professional development?
- Where do you see your future in, say, three years time?

The work review can be seen as part of the school-based in-service training programme for teachers. Such a programme will have other necessary components, including the following:

1. A good staff library where, occasionally, certain books relevant to the school's curriculum or organizational developments are specially featured. Staff should be encouraged to read in order to inform others.
2. The facility for discussion on relevant issues. There are a number of types of discussion groupings, all of which may have a place, according to the school's general development policy. Some discussions may take the form of workshops, run by staff or visitors, whilst others could include a review of published materials, talks by colleagues, or general staff meetings.
3. A series of purposeful visits to other schools when specific ideas are being considered.
4. Opportunities for the production of written material by staff to act as guidelines for the development of all curriculum areas.

DELEGATING RESPONSIBILITY

Some heads are afraid to delegate responsibility even though members of their staff are paid an additional allowance to be specifically responsible for an area of the curriculum or school organization. There are heads who look upon delegation of authority and responsibility as a loss of control. It should not be like that and, in fact, the good head will delegate responsibility for work along with the necessary authority to carry it out, establishing the proper control measures that will allow for immediate corrective action to be taken if things go wrong. A checklist on control measures might be as follows:

1. Is the teacher thoroughly trained, ready and willing to do the job?
2. Have you mutually agreed the nature of the job?
3. Have you delegated the responsibilities gradually or all at once?
4. Have you corrected mistakes and praised progress?
5. Can you intervene at any time without causing great upset?

The head can build the confidence of staff members by delegating the responsibility and the authority to carry it out. This gives them the concrete evidence that the head has faith in them and their abilities and will give the staff the chance to grow and to develop more confidence.

Once responsibility has been delegated there is a need to develop the initiative of each member of staff, which can be accomplished by giving open-ended instructions to each teacher. Such an instruction tells a person what you want done, but it does not tell him or her how to do it. Open-ended instructions will give each teacher the opportunity to carry out the same task differently, according to his or her experiences and training.

An open-ended instruction is composed of three basic parts. First, state the problem to be solved clearly and concisely, and make sure it is understood completely. Second, the limitations imposed must be carefully outlined in order that members of staff know just how far they are free to try out their own methods. Third, spell out the resources available so that the teacher knows exactly what can be used to accomplish the job. In a good instruction of this type the head acts as the catalyst, leaving the main task for the staff to execute – this is the key to effective leadership.

If the head is going to hold one of the staff responsible for a particular task, then the head should also give the teacher the authority to carry out that responsibility. It is not possible to be responsible for arriving at a solution to a problem if you must go to someone else to get the authority to carry out your responsibility. In addition, the staff should realize not only what their responsibilities, and what authority they have, but also that they are accountable to the head. Unless this last concept is understood, the head will not be able to achieve the desired results. All members of the staff must have a clear understanding of what is expected of them individually. They should know what their responsibilities are and just how much authority they have. Then, if mistakes are made, they can be corrected without hesitation. If a head is afraid to hold one of the staff accountable for results, then the consequences for their failures must be accepted by the head who, in turn, must be held responsible. A good head is one who knows when to take corrective action and when to offer praise for a job well done.

How you delegate responsibility is an expression of how you see yourself. If you have a good self-image you will not be threatened by the delegation of authority. Nevertheless, the delegation of authority requires very careful thought and planning – it is not an art that is necessarily easily acquired. To build a truly decentralized organization that succeeds in inspiring initiative, imagination, self-discipline and loyalty among the staff, the head must demonstrate four important personal attributes. He or she must

1. be receptive to other people's ideas;
2. realize that people will make mistakes;

3. be tolerant when let down by those to whom authority has been delegated; and
4. be able to exercise powers of self-restraint.

Once the head has mastered the art of delegation, there are four specific aspects to which attention must be paid if authority is to be effectively delegated at all levels within the organization of the school:

1. Jobs must be clearly defined and mutually agreed. Every staff member to whom authority is delegated deserves a clear written statement of their responsibilities. Within such job descriptions there needs to be a recognition that an incentive allowance post-holder has to accept responsibility for a general quality of teaching and a leadership role throughout the school. There will be occasions when this will require involvement in other tasks outside those that have been specifically defined.
2. Goals must be set and clearly understood so that everyone knows which specific goals relate to every delegated task.
3. Ideas must be communicated to everyone at every level in the school to help them make the 'right' decisions.
4. Controls must be established. A good head can delegate authority to do a task, but cannot be rid of the responsibility for getting the task done. Therefore, there must be ways of knowing what is done and of knowing when to step in and take action. You cannot have delegation without control.

NEEDS AND MOTIVATION OF STAFF

It hardly needs underlying that whatever his or her enthusiasm, expertise and competence, no head can be effective without well-motivated staff. It is the willingness of teachers and other staff to work hard, to throw themselves with enthusiasm into work, that makes organizational change possible.

From the work of Herzberg (1966) it seems clear that if you undertake to 'motivate' people so that the work will then be done better, you are on the wrong track. What is needed is the structuring of the work in such a way that the work will have the motivators in it. The work itself, then, will motivate people and the enterprise will have expanded its capability of achieving its objectives. That is the way to ensure the full utilization of teacher talents. The planning and organization of the work environment, therefore, is a key to successful school management, as it is to successful classroom teaching. An understanding of human motivation is important if you are to understand why people behave as they do, and it helps to understand your own behaviour.

There is a very extensive literature on the theory of motivation as part of the theory of learning. Maslow's pioneering work helps us to understand the pattern of human motivation. Motivation is not administered externally: it is the result of needs within us that cause us to act as we do. The general view starts with the belief that people tend to be most strongly motivated when certain needs are met. According to Maslow, we are first motivated by our physiological needs – for food, shelter and survival. Once these needs are satisfied, safety and security become the major motivators, then participation and roles in social groups and society, then status and ego satisfaction, and finally self-actualization. Clearly, it is not assumed that everyone has each of the needs in equal strength. Some people may have one or more of the needs very strongly in evidence, while others have a different patterning of needs. Because people have different needs at different times they will respond differently to the same conditions. The theory is that while each person may have a unique profile of needs we each share the same set that go to make up that profile:

1. *Affiliation* The need for a sense of belonging. Do all staff really feel that they belong in the school and are regarded as part of the team? The head's skills as a communicator are of great importance in meeting this need.
2. *Achievement* The need for a sense of 'getting somewhere' in what is done. Do the staff feel that they are achieving things in the tasks they undertake? The head's ability to ensure that roles and responsibilities are clearly defined and understood will help people meet this need.
3. *Appreciation* The need for a sense of being appreciated for the efforts one makes. This relates very closely to achievement – does the head show appreciation to the staff for both effort and achievement? People thrive on praise and it is probably one of the highest motivational factors – when did the head last offer praise to someone on the staff? Has the head praised all the teachers during the last term?
4. *Influence* The need for a sense of having some influence over what happens within the work setting. The ability of the head to delegate effectively has considerable bearing on this issue. Staff do not wish or

expect to have complete control over everything that happens in school but there are specific areas where they are able to lead their expertise and have some influence. Teachers are most highly motivated when they feel that they can contribute significantly to the shape of the curriculum.

In addition to these four basic areas of need, there is another closely related factor that influences teachers' motivation. This is self-concept. Each of us has a view of ourselves, of our abilities and potential, and of the sort of person we are, and of what we are capable of. This self-concept is developed over many years and is related very closely to the view of ourselves we see 'reflected back' to us by others. None of us is very keen to attempt that which we believe to be impossible – to expand effort, time and other personal resources – unless we believe we are reasonably capable of achieving worthwhile goals. Where you believe you are not able to achieve goals set, or do specific things that may be required of you, then you are unlikely to try very hard – you will not be well motivated. The system may require you to try but it cannot force you to try hard. You tend not to be well motivated when asked to do that which is not consistent with your view of yourself and your capabilities – your self-concept. This is certainly an important factor to consider when attempting to change the curriculum responsibilities of a teacher on your staff. When groups of teachers have been asked to discuss strong and weak motivational factors within schools they have arrived at lists that strongly reflect the patterning of needs already discussed. The lists below, which have been compiled over recent years on in-service courses considering aspects of primary-school management, represent a sample of teachers' views.

First, teachers are *most* likely to be well motivated in regard to changes when the following apply:

1. They are involved in the formulation of the new approaches.
2. There is a feeling of 'solidarity'/community among the staff.
3. There is a demonstrable need for change.
4. Staff are confident of their own abilities to deal with an activity.
5. Skills for dealing with an activity have been fostered within teachers, or will clearly be developed in the future.
6. The head recognizes the extra time/effort put in by staff.
7. The head provides positive support and involvement.
8. The teacher feels generally secure within the school.

9. There is a sense that what is being done is also laying a foundation for future success.
10. As a venture, it is easy to join in at any time.
11. Clear educational and social goals are obvious.
12. There are regular discussions for the interchange of ideas, information and experience.
13. The previous experience of staff in comparable situations is utilized.
14. There is an open and friendly atmosphere generally within the school.
15. Teachers are sure of support in the case of difficulty being experienced.
16. The staff have confidence in the head, based upon his or her credibility and reputation for success.
17. The staff concerned have specific and clearly defined responsibilities.
18. A provision of time in 'working hours' is made.
19. The senior staff are actively involved in the work.

Teacher are *least* likely to be well motivated when the following apply:

1. They are simply told that they *must*...
2. They are put into a threatened position.
3. The activity is not well planned.
4. It is felt by teachers that the plan is a 'gimmick' promoted by a senior member of staff to further his or her own ends.
5. The teachers feel that the plan is mounted merely to satisfy higher authority.
6. A lot of hard work is involved without any apparent or obvious results.
7. Initial moves are badly organized, with consequent initial negative feedback.
8. The teachers feel alienated from the school or from whoever is responsible for the plan.
9. The head assumes the role of the 'expert', and there is a lack of opportunity for teachers to develop, or to exercise, responsibility.
10. There is group pressure from colleagues to 'opt out'.

The practical steps a headteacher might take to increase the likelihood of the staff being well motivated include the following:

1. Facilitating early initial discussion within the staff.
2. Keeping an overview of the programme.
3. Developing staff, especially their skills, understanding and self-confidence.

4. Making available as much time as possible (and letting it be seen that he or she is doing so).
5. Leading by example.
6. Involving *all* staff, and not just teachers.
7. Providing aid, back-up and support, especially when there are particular difficulties.
8. Utilize the skills and expertise of particular staff.
9. Making a very careful appraisal of the status quo, prior to committing the school to change.
10. Encouraging staff to suggest developments and modifications once the change process is under way.
11. Building up a system of steady, reliable support for teachers who are attempting to innovate in their own work.
12. Building upon success and not failure.
13. Delegating carefully; and delegating authority as well as responsibility.
14. Appreciating work already done, however trivial – not alienating those who are committed to the system you may wish to change.
15. Not personalizing opposition – keeping it on a professional level.

Stripped of its essentials, good school management is appealing to the basic emotions of the staff. Teachers will want to do what the head wants them to do if they get what they want and need while they are doing it. The head holds the key to motivating staff, and only when staff respect and acknowledge the needs of their own position, and the needs of the school, will the head ensure loyal cooperation and full staff support. It is important that the head learns about the staff and their families, their hobbies and interests. As a head, demonstrate that you care for teachers as individuals: look them in the eye when talking to them and listen to what they have to say to you. Find at least one positive item to mention when you know that someone is discouraged or depressed. Always try to help your staff to achieve success in some small way so that they feel important and, above all, needed, whilst accepting that not everyone in your team is going to be a brilliant teacher.

There is little purpose in heads formulating a programme to develop the awareness and expertise of a staff of teachers until they have carefully considered their own interpersonal skills. According to Maslow (1968), in order to grow you must satisfy a variety of human needs. Interpersonal skills can be seen, from one point of view, as instruments enabling you to satisfy a number of your human needs. The skills of expressing yourself, responding to others, placing legitimate demands on others and opening yourself up to being influenced by others, help you to satisfy safety needs (the need for a secure, orderly life) and esteem needs (the need for both self-respect and for respect from others). Successful interaction with other people requires the development of effective interpersonal skills. Therefore interpersonal skills are important not only to help you gratify legitimate personal needs but also to enable you to gratify the legitimate needs of others, work through interpersonal conflict and establish effective working relationships. You will need not only to know how to disclose yourself appropriately to others, but also to be aware of your characteristic ways of thinking and feeling about, and interacting with, other people. You will also need to recognize that your staff, too, will have different motivations, needs and aspirations. Not all will wish to involve themselves in development and its companion, change.

5
INNOVATION AND CHANGE: THE HUMAN FACTOR

At the heart of the headteacher's role is a responsibility for ensuring that every child and teacher in the school receives the best possible education. In order to achieve this, he or she needs not only to keep up to date with developments in both curriculum and in the understanding of effective teaching and learning but also to have the skill to enable his or her staff to do the same. Such information and new understandings will, from time to time, challenge the existing theory and practice of one or more members of staff, and it will be for the head to ensure that his or her particular leadership style provides the best possible spur and support for change. This is particularly true in the 1990s when teachers will still be having to deal with the practical implications of the Education Reform Acts of the 1980s. They will be engaged in changed approaches to teaching and assessment, teacher appraisal and more active involvement of governors and the local community. There are no known 'recipes' for successful change, but there are a number of different practices that seem to have achieved success in a variety of schools and other institutions – and these are all based on similar principles of leadership, intervention and professional learning. It is the purpose of this chapter to discuss such principles in relation to innovation and change. The focus will be on what we have called the 'human factor' for two reasons: first, because change involves people in a re-examination of values, attitudes and feelings that, arguably, are not governed by rationality nor are amenable to prescription; and, second, because attempts to promote change are unlikely to meet with success unless there is an active consideration by the headteacher of the psychological and social dynamic in its planning, process and evaluation.

> There is nothing more difficult to carry out, nor more doubtful of success, nor more dangerous to handle, than to initiate a new order of things. For the reformer has enemies in all who profit by the old order, and only lukewarm defenders in all those who would profit by the new order. The lukewarmness arises partly from fear of their adversaries who have law in their favour, and partly from the incredulity of mankind who do not truly believe in anything new until they have had actual experience of it.
>
> (Machiavelli, 1513)

'Innovation' as used in this chapter refers to ideas or practices that are new or different from those that exist in the school and classroom. The introduction and use of anything that is new also implies change. So the focus for this chapter is school-centred change planned as a deliberate and collaborative process involving a change agent (who may be any member of the school staff) and client, or group of clients, in solving a problem in order to increase the effectiveness of children's education. Change itself, whether major or minor, requires time, energy, skill and, most importantly, the commitment of the person who is being expected or encouraged to make the change. Problems of commitment especially arise where the need for change has been identified by someone other than the person expected to change.

The problem for the head, deputy head or any other member of staff who may take a leadership role is how to achieve and support a commitment to change that will be more than 'token'. Rather than beginning, in this chapter, by describing various approaches or models that might be adopted or, indeed, the well-documented innovation overload of the late 1980s, it is necessary first to investigate the likely psychological and social contexts that influence the attitudes of the teachers involved.

PROFESSIONAL LEARNING

If we assume that professional development is a normal rather than an exceptional process, and that most teachers are capable of reflecting on their performances and improving them in the light of such reflection (Elliott, 1976), then it follows that they are no strangers to innovation. Indeed, they are constantly having to take decisions about teaching that involve change. Many are immediate 'on-the-spot' decisions taken in the classroom when there is no time for reflection; others are the result of a conscious thought process that occurs outside the classroom. These are 'reflective' decisions (Sutcliffe and Whitfield, 1976).

It may be argued, however, that while these decisions are based on the teachers' identification of need, and while development of this kind occurs naturally and without intervention, such development is limited by the physical and social environment or context in which the teachers work and by their perceptions. For example, the classroom in which they work contains much more 'information' than they can handle, and their decisions about practice are concerned with finding ways in which they can survive, cope and teach effectively in a world that is stable. Thus practices are in a sense rules of action that allow them both to maintain a stable view of, for example, the classroom or the school, and to give priority to certain kinds of information while ignoring other kinds. They are theories of control. A new teacher very quickly develops assumptions about practices that allow him or her to cope with the complexities of teaching and being a member of staff. However, since it is rare for these to be made explicit or tested, the possibilities for evaluating these assumptions — which underpin his or her teaching — are minimal. As we have seen in Chapters 1 and 4, the need for reflection and self-confrontation is part of a process of professional development.

To survive in a school it will be necessary for a teacher to accept into his or her system of behaviour the often unstated norms and expectations of the community and his or her colleagues in school. In the staffroom setting, for example, talk about teaching is governed by assumptions about the nature of talk about teaching. Thus, what happens in the classroom and what is said to happen in the classroom may be quite different, and it may not be surprising if the 'doctrine' of teacher as educationist is contradicted by the 'commitments' that arise in the classroom situation of teacher as practitioner (Keddie, 1971). The imperatives of the National Curriculum may provide help in minimizing these contradictions but they will not remove them.

So there are both perceptual and contextual constraints that may militate against teachers exercising their capacities to be self-critical. Indeed, all but the newest teachers are likely to have found their own personal solutions to problems shortly after entering the school. These enable them to strike a balance between opposing forces of teacher-personality factors, ideological factors, presentation and nature of material, external requirements and the characteristics of pupils (Lacey, 1977). It is only when the teacher perceives that this personal solution is itself inadequate in, for example, reaching an agreed target or implementing, in the best possible way, aspects of the National Curriculum or agreed school policy that he or she will be moved to search for means by which he or she can change. The responsibility of the headteacher is crucial both in creating a climate for examination of thinking and practice by ensuring regular opportunities for teachers to review their personal solutions and by providing appropriate support.

PROMOTING CHANGE

'Finally, the importance of the teacher as the implementer cannot be over-emphasised. How (s)he perceives the innovation, its effectiveness, its fit, and the importance that gets attached to implementation, and continued use, determines whether or not something new gets used' (Lewis, 1987). Genuine innovation is unlikely to occur unless the teacher him or herself feels a great sense of ownership of the innovation, is committed to its value for the pupils in his or her classroom and can call upon support for its implementation, particularly in terms of training and resources. Clearly, in an ideal world it is changes that teachers have initiated that are most likely to work, 'since it is they who experience directly the pressure of the classroom and staffroom and can thus weigh the advantages and disadvantages' (Barnes, 1982).

In the world of the 1990s, teachers are expected to implement a curriculum designed by others and, at first sight, this may appear to be a repeat of centre-periphery innovation models of the 1960s that failed to permeate the majority of schools. However, innovation of the late 1980s and 1990s is legislated and monitored so that the issue of choice of implementation is no longer appropriate. Nevertheless, those who promote legislated change at grass-roots level will still have to be convinced of its value in order to assimilate, accommodate and, where necessary, transform practices. Knowing how to manage the individual and group involved in innovation is the key to successful change.

In a sense, changes in conditions of service imposed in the 1980s have, at least in theory, assisted the headteacher in promoting change. The practice of 'directed time' within teachers' designated 1265 hours, the five 'professional development' days each year and teacher appraisal provide potentially rich opportunities for institutional and personal review and target-setting. The LEA Training Grants Scheme (LEATGS) has ensured that each school has an annually reviewed school-development plan. This and local management of schools (LMS) have, for most schools, provided finance that may be used to release teachers from classroom duties. All provide potentially rich opportunities for teachers to engage in reflective curriculum and professional development. Most heads, however, have received little or no training in the management of these opportunities (DES, 1989b). Indeed, few training opportunities exist that focus upon the knowledge that educational change agents need to exercise in managing change (Figure 5.1).

American research (Miles, Saxl and Lieberman, 1988) has revealed 18 skills needed by educational change agents. Whilst the relative importance of each of these skills will vary according to time and social contexts, the list provides an interesting repertoire upon which to reflect. Of the 18 skills, 6 were classified as general skills. These were interpersonal ease, group functioning, training/doing workshops, master teacher, educational content and administrative/organizational ability (see Figure 5.2). Regardless, however, of a change agent's knowledge, skills and organizational abilities, there will still be those in the school who, for a variety of reasons, will be resistant.

RESISTANCE TO CHANGE

There is no assumption here that all innovation or change is for the better, nor that what is right for one teacher is necessarily right for another. As we saw in Chapters 1 and 4, teachers, like children, will be at different stages of development and have different needs; and these needs may be expressed through an apparent or real aversion to new ideas that involve them in change. Doyle and Ponder (1976) identify three types of response by teachers who are 'invited' to change:

1. The rational adopter − someone who might be said to adopt a step-by-step approach to solving problems. This person will
   (a) clarify goals and problems;
   (b) collect information about how the problems arise;
   (c) consider ways to resolve the problems;
   (d) implement these; and
   (e) evaluate the success of the strategies implemented.
2. The Stone Age obstructionist − who neither accepts the need for change, nor responds to 'invitations' to be involved.
3. The pragmatic sceptic − who expresses 'a concern for immediate contingencies and consequences'. This person will evaluate change proposals in terms of their validity for him or her in his or her classroom. The pragmatic sceptic will ask three questions:

1. Assess the situation (people, resources, constraints). For example, you may approach or be approached informally by individuals, or formally through your appraisal system, or 'hear' a need voiced during a staff meeting, or initiate a staff meeting yourself.
2. Identify an area of concern (general or specific). The realization that there is a need for change may come through listening to staff and being aware of their thoughts, needs and relationships. If not, the ground has to be prepared for change. This will include planning how and when to implement change.
3. Communicate the concern formally to:
    (a) headteacher/deputy headteacher
    (b) staff colleagues
    (c) other involved people, e.g. parents/ancillaries.
4. Meet formally with colleagues to:
    (a) identify the specifics of the problem(s)
    (b) clarify issues
    (c) generate discussion of new ideas
    (d) decide on group aims and specific strategies: consensus seeking; joint formulation of valid alternative strategies, leading to establishment of priorities and agreed deadlines
    (e) decide on ways of monitoring the implementation of the plan.

    } Negotiation of meanings and contracting

5. Implementation of the plan (with back-up provided, e.g. time and resources).
6. Revision of plan in the light of experience (a recognition that the logic of planning and the logic of action may not match).
7. Reflective monitoring and appraisal of the effectiveness and new planning if appropriate.
8. Consolidation of new pattern/plan.

    } Flexibility as a criterion of action

9. Long-term 'after-care' support and evaluation.

Figure 5.1 Procedures in the management of change

(a) What do I/my pupils get out of it?
(b) Can I relate it to what I do/how I teach?
(c) What is its cost (in time, energy and finance)?

The pragmatic sceptic wants to see a return for his or her investment.

There may be connections between these responses and those of teachers influenced by their own career expectations and the broader political context of education. For example, schools may be faced with changing pupil populations and diminishing financial resources. Staff find increasing difficulties in achieving promotion. Some may be unhappy with systems of short-term 'merit' allowances established under LMS. There is more 'intervention' in school life by parents, LEAs and central government through the National Curriculum, governing bodies, calls for curriculum monitoring and institutional appraisal and greater central control of the curriculum. The increase in internal and external pressures may lead to perceptions by teachers that there is less trust in their 'professionality'. The head may therefore have to help motivate some teachers who are frustrated, apathetic and resentful. Hand (1981) divided the teaching force of the 1980s into three categories:

1. Those who are frustrated in their ambitions.
2. Those who are happy to be in their final school posts.
3. Those likely to gain (further) promotion.

A fourth category may be added to the teaching force of the 1990s:

4. Those who are happy to be in their present posts but who find it difficult to cope with the stresses caused by externally imposed innovation.

Not all schools will contain all of these clear-cut categories of teacher and, indeed, these categories are not in reality mutually exclusive — people and contexts can and do change. However, they do serve to draw the attention of headteachers and others concerned with innovation to the complex web of role expectations, institutional constraints, professional experiences, teaching attitudes and approaches and personality factors that may influence the responses of teachers to any form of new idea or practice the head may wish to introduce into the school. After all, it is the head's responsibility, with the teachers, to try to match individual and institutional needs, and there may often be conflict created by the tensions between the two.

A group of headteachers attending a management training programme identified the strategies in Figure 5.3 for managing difficult people. It is

Skill and description	Examples
Interpersonal ease Relating simply and directly to others	Very open person...can deal with people...nice manner...has always been able to deal with staff...you have to be able to work with people, know when to stroke, when to hold back, when to assert, know 'which buttons to push'.... gives individuals time to vent feelings, lets them know her interest in them...She can talk to anyone ...
Group functioning Understanding group dynamics, able to facilitate team work	Has ability to get a group moving ...He started with nothing and then made us come together as a united body...good group facilitator...lets the discussion flow
Training/doing workshops Direct instruction, teaching adults in systematic way	Gave workshops on how to develop plans...taught us consensus method with 5-finger game...He prepares a great deal and enjoys it. He has the right chemistry and can impart knowledge at the peer level...
Educational general (master teacher) Wide educational experience, able to impart skills to others	Excellent teaching skills...taught all the grades, grade leader work, resource teacher have done staff development with teachers... Title I programs where I was always assisting, supporting, being resource person to teachers ...a real master teacher, much teacher training work
Educational content Knowledge of school subject matter	Demonstrating expertise in a subject area...Parents thought kindergarten would be all academic. She showed them the value of play, of trips...knows a great deal about teaching, especially reading. What she doesn't know she finds out...
Administrative/organizational Defining and structuring work, activities, time	Highly organized, has everything prepared in advance...I could take an idea and turn it into a program ...Well organized, good at prioritizing, scheduling, knows how to set things up...

Skill and description	Examples
Initiative-taking Starting or pushing activities, moving directly toward action	Assertive, clear sense of what he wanted to do...ability to poke and prod where needed to get things done...I had to assert myself so he didn't step on me
Trust/rapport-building Developing a sense of safety, openness, reduced threat on part of clients; good relationship-building	A breath of fresh air. In two weeks he had gained confidence of staff...She had to become one of the gang, eat lunch with them. A skilled seducer (knows how to get people to ask for help)...I have not repeated what they said so trust was built...Even those who knew everything before, now let her help because they are not threatened...She was so open and understanding that I stopped feeling funny
Support Providing nurturant relationship, positive affective relationship	Able to accept harsh things teachers say. 'It's OK, everyone has these feelings.'...A certain compassion for others. Always patient, never critical, very enthusiastic
Confrontation Direct expression of negative information, without generating negative affect	Can challenge in a positive way...She will lay it on the line about what works and what won't...He is talkative and factual. His strength is being outspoken...He can point out things and get away with being blunt ...Able to tell people they were wrong, and they accept it
Conflict mediation Resolving or improving situations where multiple incompatible interests are in play	Effected a compromise between upper and lower grade teachers on use of a checklist...Teachers resented the chair's autocratic behavior. So she spoke openly to him about it. Things have been considerably better...The principal is very vindictive. He was constantly mediating, getting her to soften her attitude...Can handle people who are terribly angry, unreasonable, keeps cool

Figure 5.2 Skills needed by change agents (Source: Miles, Saxl and Lieberman, 1988)

Skill and description	Examples
Collaboration Creating relationships where influence is mutually shared	Deals on same level we do, puts in his ideas...I've never seen a time where teachers felt they were told to do something...Leads and directs us, but not in a way like professors and students, but as peers. Doesn't judge us or put us down...Has ideas of her own, like in math, but flexible enough to maintain the teachers' way of doing things too
Confidence-building Strengthening client's sense of efficacy, belief in self	She makes all feel confident and competent. Doesn't patronize... 'You can do it.' She'll help...He has a way of drawing out teachers' ideas. He injects a great deal, but you feel powerful...She makes people feel like a million in themselves. Like a shot of adrenaline boosting your mind, ego, talents and professional expertise...Her attitude: 'try it, you'll like it.'
Diagnosing individuals Forming a valid picture of the needs/problems of an individual teacher or administrator as a basis for action	You need to realize that when a teacher says she has the worst class, that means 'I need help'....He has an ability to focus in on problems and get rid of the verbiage...picking up the real message...sensitive, looks at teacher priorities first...knows when an off-hand joke is a signal for help
Diagnosing organizations Forming a valid picture of the needs/problems of a school as an organization (including its culture) as a basis for action	Analyzing situation, recognizing problems, jumping ahead of where you are to where you want to go...when I analyzed beyond the surface, I saw the principal was using meetings for administrative purposes ...Anticipates problems schools face when they enter the program ...brought in report on reading/ math and attendance, helped us know where we should be going ...helped team look at the data in the assessment package

Skill and description	Examples
Managing/controling Orchestrating the improvement process; coordinating activities, time and people; direct influence on others	She filled all the gaps in terms of legwork, preparing materials and coordination of our contact with admin. and district...a task master and keeps the process going...makes people do things rather than doing them himself ...He sets a pace, like the bouncing ball on songs...
Resource-bringing Locating and providing information, materials, practices, equipment useful to clients	If it's broken he fixes it. He uses his network to get us supplies... Brings ideas that she has seen work elsewhere...Had the newest research, methods, articles, ideas, waters it down for our needs...Brought manipulative materials for help with multiplication...
Demonstration Modeling new behavior in classrooms or meetings	He's a great story teller – gets the kids very interested...willing to go into classrooms and take risks... modeling...was real, did demos with their classes... Watching someone else teach my class makes me reflect on what I am doing...showed the chair by his own behavior how to be more open...

Figure 5.2 Skills needed by change agents (Source: Miles, Saxl and Lieberman, 1988)

as well to remember that apparently 'difficult' colleagues may not be simply 'pig-headed' in their resistance to change. They may, for example, distrust their own ability to change, have a preference for current, well-tried and tested practice and need to be approached in different ways. One way of planning for work that is more likely to involve controversy is to use a technique called 'force-field analysis'.

FORCE-FIELD ANALYSIS

Force-field analysis is a conceptually simple yet powerful method of planning programmes of action. It may be undertaken alone or, preferably,

Figure 5.3 Strategies for managing difficult people

with a critical friend. Its purpose is to identify facilitating and restraining forces associated with a particular planned task as a means of developing action strategies. Ultimately the balance between them might be adjusted so that it is shifted towards success or the achievement of a stated goal. Figure 5.4 shows the forces as arrows. The arrows can be made long or short, thick or thin to indicate the perceived strength of the forces.

Innovation and Change: The Human Factor 125

Restraining forces

Forces resisting change   Work to decrease these

Forces assisting change   Work to increase these

Facilitating forces

Figure 5.4 Force-field analysis (Source: Egan, 1982)

One partner in a pair assists the other to identify restraining and facilitating forces, which are then shown diagrammatically. The use of simple and open-questioning techniques enables that person to focus on those forces that seem critical in relation to success or the achievement of the goal. Finally, and again by appropriate questioning, one member of the pair supports the other in finding methods of minimizing the restraining forces and maximizing the facilitating forces. These methods form the basis of an action plan for the achievement of the stated goal. Roles are then reversed if both members of the pair are planning programmes jointly.

It is important, then, to move with care, particularly when new (innovative) practices are being suggested. Figure 5.5 illustrates the affective dimensions of leading change. It cannot be assumed that rational discussion will convince 'Stone Age obstructionists' (Doyle and Ponder, 1976), who neither accept the need for change nor respond to the invitation to be involved. However, there are a number of dimensions of morale in organizations that, when linked to assumptions that professionals wish to increase their effectiveness, may be used as guiding principles for motivation. Most teachers would wish to have (Miller and Fom, 1966)

1. intrinsic job satisfaction;
2. Involvement in the immediate work of the group that constitutes the school;
3. identification with the organization;
4. satisfying interpersonal relationships with 'superiors' and immediate colleagues in the organization; and
5. satisfaction from work status.

---

1. The staff need to perceive the needs for change, and feel a responsibility for implementing and sharing in change, under good leadership (i.e. a need must be apparent to all those involved before change can begin).

2. The cooperation of the staff needs to be gained, and there must be good comunication with staff who are directly and indirectly involved.

3. There is a need for the positive support of the headteacher.

4. There is a need for time to implement change.

5. There is a need for those involved to see benefits for themselves in addition to 'the school', for example.

Figure 5.5 Interpersonal relationships in change: motivation

THE MANAGEMENT TASK

Providing Learning Opportunities for Staff as well as Children

It is a prime management task to plan, support and monitor the innovation process but not necessarily to initiate it. The head should provide environments that minimize constraints on learning, and in which a variety of concrete personal experiences may be reflected upon, talked about and assimilated or accommodated − in short, to promote reflection on, as well as reflection in, practice (Schon, 1983). Teachers need time for planning and this may involve (temporary) changes in teaching or lesson organization only heads are in a position to support − by, for example, taking a class (or classes) in order to release a teacher (or teachers) who wish to visit other classrooms or schools.

In organizational terms, this implies that the headteacher will ensure that regular opportunities exist for individuals and groups of individuals to

1. reflect on practice;
2. share practice;
3. identify issues for change that may arise from 1 and 2;
4. generate alternative strategies for change;
5. acquire the appropriate help to achieve this (human and material);
6. apply the strategies; and
7. monitor and evaluate the processes and outcomes.

Equally, he or she must take into account factors that may constrain success, for example, the following:

Innovation overload Don't involve yourself or others in too many changes simultaneously. Change (the act) and changing (the process of implementing the act) take time and emotional as well as intellectual energy. Already complex management tasks can be compounded by the number of innovations that have to be handled simultaneously.

Multiple-role pressures Teachers play a variety of life roles. For example, a teacher may also carry the role of parent, partner, nurse (to an aged relative). It is necessary to consider the stress these may cause when promoting innovation.

Disclosure and feedback sensitivities All change involves disclosure (e.g. of present practice through review) and feedback − whether these occur privately or, as is more likely with school development planning, target-setting and appraisal/review, publicly. The act of disclosure will create initial turbulence for many teachers if only because it is not a part of the traditional professional culture that ensures many teachers plan, carry out and evaluate their work in the relative isolation of their own classrooms. For successful sharing, for self or peer confrontation, a school climate of trust, confidence and confidentiality is essential.

Transformation The most fundamental form of innovation involves the transformation of teachers' attitudes and values. Resistance to change imposed from the outside may be an act of strength rather than weakness by teachers who are reluctant to move out of their spheres of competences and confidences because they are not committed to the values of what is proposed. This is a particularly difficult dilemma for heads who wish to support teacher autonomy and ownership of change so that teachers will internalize rather than comply with it.

Time The amount of time needed to innovate successfully is frequently under-estimated (note the speed of many DES initiatives). Too many of those who determine policy assume, incorrectly, that teachers can assimilate and implement new ideas with a minimum of planning time. Temporary 'burdens of incompetence', and the discomfort and dismay that are the defining characteristics of innovation (MacDonald, 1973), are not always considered. Day-to-day 'system-maintenance' demands on a teacher's time and energy are often under-estimated.

There is a tendency among teachers themselves and those outside the profession to assume that teachers, as 'trained professionals', will be in possession of skills that might be called for. This assumption, if not tested, may hinder the implementation of innovation. On the one hand, teachers may be slow to admit they need help; on the other hand, innovation managers may resort to claiming that it is the responsibility of the individual teacher to use his or her professional judgment or skills at the implementation stage.

Skilbeck (1982) lists some of the factors likely to discourage curriculum innovation:

> A sense of inadequacy and low self esteem in staff;
> Lack of relevant skills;
> Failure of authorities to provide advisory and specialist consultancy service;
> Lack of interest or conviction in staff, particularly in sustaining change processes over a period of time;
> Inadequate allocation of resources (time and personnel as well as money);
> Failure to appreciate the subtleties of group interactons when the balance of power in an existing institution is threatened;
> Tendency for institutions to revert to earlier forms of organisation and control if the pressure for change is not continuous.

The emphasis so far has been on the teachers' felt needs, whether these involve them as individuals in classrooms, the wider needs of the school or a combination of both. Figure 5.6 illustrates the importance of these by suggesting reasons for participation in change.

This is not to suggest that the head's needs are any less legitimate but that, like children, teachers may be best motivated when following their own interests and where the work is based on their own experiences. Eraut (1977) suggests that 'The best way to promote teacher development may be to expect it, or at least be careful that one's actions do not implicitly suggest that one does not expect it'. These principles have clear links with problem-solving, client-centred models of innovation. These models place the client's needs at the centre of the learning process. The client is thus an active causal agent and participant at every stage of his or

> 1. Individuals like to have responsibility and be trusted (ownership).
> 2. To create a feeling of belonging in the school (collegiality).
> 3. Support and encouragement to staff boosts morale (colleagueship).
> 4. It eases one's workload (in the short term) (practicality)!
>
> (NB Where responsibility is given, so must authority be.)

Figure 5.6 Reasons for participation in change

her learning. Our point, then, is that where work is related to personal experience and perceived needs, and occurs in the context in which this experience and these needs occur (i.e. the classroom or school), the teacher will feel more involved and learn more.

It follows that the primary function of headteachers and 'leaders' in schools is not to identify need for others, *but to involve others in identifying needs*. This indicates a recognition that change based on the teachers' perceived need is of prime importance. The list of steps towards successful leadership given in Chapter 1 (p. 12–13) is relevant here.

Asking Questions

Whatever the starting point for change, the head will need to pose the following questions:

1. What challenge and support do individuals need from me? Can this be made available?
2. What help and support does the teacher/group of teachers need from

    (a) inside
    (b) outside the school?

    Can this be made available?
3. What are the priorities for action? (What is appropriate at this time, at this stage of development?)
4. Is the activity practical in terms of time, energy and resources?
5. What will the teachers gain from the activity? (Doyle and Ponder's (1976) 'pragmatic sceptics' will want to know what's in it for them and their pupils, and what the 'cost' will be.)

In effect, the asking of these questions is the beginning of the formulation of a process-orientated policy for staff development within which innovation may occur.

LEADERSHIP ROLES

The general leadership stance taken by headteachers who achieve success in promoting change is consultative rather than directive or prescriptive (Figure 5.7). A distinction is being drawn here between authoritative and authoritarian. The former is built on agreement through negotiation whereas the latter is built on the use of status alone.

Although writing in a different context — that of evaluation — MacDonald's (1974) description of three 'ideal types' of evaluation study might equally apply to styles of leadership and intervention in schools:

1. *Bureaucratic* In which the key concepts are service, utility and efficiency, and in which the key justificatory concept is 'the reality of power'.
2. *Autocratic* In which the key concepts are 'principle' and 'objectivity', and in which the key justificatory concept is 'the responsibility of office'.
3. *Democratic* In which the key concepts are confidentiality, negotiation and accessibility, and in which the key justificatory concept is 'the right to know'.

There are clearly in-built difficulties of role definition for the headteacher who embarks on a 'democratic' style of leadership. Schools are not democracies since, albeit through the governing body, the head and not the teachers has responsibility for the curriculum and standards of the school. The head writes references on the staff so that there will inevitably be a power and authority gap. In cases where the head is non-teaching, there may also be a 'credibility' problem. Without denying the existence of these problems it is, nevertheless, possible for them to be minimized rather than emphasized by the way in which heads approach their leadership role. Research suggests that the 'democratic' style of leadership is most effective in leading staff development (see Chapter 1). The role so far described is similar to that described by Havelock (1971) in a consideration of change agents' roles. It would involve the head in playing any one or a combination of the following three roles:

1. Is the change short term, with a quickly achieved goal?
2. Is the change long term, involving continuity and spread through the school?
3. What is your estimated timescale? If a lengthy period, then be aware of the need for continuity and progression through staff meetings, discussions, priorities and choices.
4. Do you lead by example?
5. Enthusiasm – are you aware of possible insecurity of staff?
6. Are you able to offer the support needed to all staff and especially to those who feel unsure? Is there a colleague on the staff who could do this?
7. Can you make sufficient resources available – are you aware whether additional resources will be needed next year, and whether this will mean a reduction in cash for other areas of the curriculum?
8. Will you offer the advantage of school time to allow staff to implement change (i.e. head teaches their class or takes a group/supply cover)?
9. Do you use external help where appropriate? For example,
    (a) visits – in pairs to other schools, workshops;
    (b) INSET days and 'directed time' as an integral part of a curriculum and staff-development programme; and
    (c) use of external consultants (from local university or college).

Figure 5.7 Thinking and planning questions

1. *Catalyst* Who prods and pressures the system to be less complacent and to start reviewing its work.
2. *Solution-giver* Who knows when and how to offer a solution appropriate to colleagues' needs.
3. *Process helper* Who can help colleagues in the 'how to' of change. (In a paper on in-service, Eraut (1982) asserts that much INSET '...seems to assume that...knowledge use or process skills already exist; so the focus is on ideas which it is hoped the teacher will feel inspired to implement, without providing assistance with the process of implementation itself...'.)

This last role is crucial if colleagues are to be given long-term support and appropriate moral and intellectual support in the implementation of strategies.

AFFECTIVE RELATIONSHIPS

Clearly, all those involved in promoting change must be concerned with the manner as well as the matter of change. Many programmes of professional development are based on what we believe to be a myth, that one can simply sit down with others, work out policies, aims, strategies, etc., and implement them according to rational procedures based on apparently rational agreements. This does not take account of the fact that there may be conflicts over, for example, values, power and practicalities, an increase in workload or a desire for old certainties.

In work concerned with questioning the teacher's self-image, the affective relationship is of prime importance if one is to take into account such concerns as anxiety, status and identity. For example, as mentioned in Chapter 1, changing one's teaching style may involve a temporary 'burden of incompetence' (MacDonald, 1973) so that there will be a considerable need for psychological and moral support (Day, 1981).

This affective area is rarely made explicit, yet the attitudes of teachers are clearly crucial to the success, not only of the process of innovation but also of the interventionist. How is the headteacher perceived? Is he or she an authority or a threat? Is he or she a process helper or a judge with alien values? During the process of devising a policy and carrying it through, it is likely that the head, far from being non-directive, will play a variety of supportive roles. After all, he or she is as committed to the professional-development enterprise as anyone, and so cannot hope to be a 'neutral' figure — except when playing a role of 'procedural neutrality' that '...expresses a teacher's commitment not to use his authority to promote judgments which go beyond impartial criteria of rationality' (Elliott, 1975).

While it is important to build mutually supportive relationships with their teachers based on the commitment of both to enhancing the quality of education in the school, headteachers must be prepared to donate their experience and responsibilities in ways that are both appropriate to their role as head (with accountability to LEA and parents, as well as teachers) and to their role as a member of a team (with accountability to children and teachers). There will be times when some teachers may need to be 'told' or have an expectation that they should be 'told' or 'directed'; others when they should have some say in what and how they learn. Their perceptions may be formed by such factors as role expectation, socialization or psychological needs. Indeed, when adults are participants in their own learning, problems may arise because their enquiry skills are either underdeveloped or undeveloped. Among adults as among children, then, the need and ability to be self-directing will vary, and depend on factors such as cognitive and personality development, motivation, social development and role expectation (Day and Baskett, 1982). It follows that *the head will need to be able to adopt a variety of roles*: he or she will at various times be acting as an appraiser (of staff and pupil work); an adviser/counsellor (to staff and pupils); an organizer (of timetable, curriculum, resources); a linking agent (between staff within the school, between staff and other teachers, between staff and pupils, and staff and parents); an expert (on curriculum content or teaching techniques); a promotor (of an idea, etc.); a legitimator; or a devil's advocate (to test out commitment to a process or the logic of an idea). In effect the one individual is expected to be an innovator, a change agent, an evaluator and a friend!

The two main principles that seem to be fundamental to the intervention practices of the headteacher are

1. the perceived needs of the teacher(s) are of paramount (though not sole) importance; and
2. the interventionist's role is collaborative and co-equal, but not necessarily neutral or non-directive.

Interdependence rather than dependence or independence is thus a central feature in this process regardless of whether the change is focused on classroom teaching and organization, curriculum content, or school management and organizational structures.

THE HELPING PROCESS: ENTITLEMENTS, CONTRACTING AND ACTION PLANNING

The implication throughout this chapter has been that for innovation and change to have long-term success, relationships between colleagues need to be open, there needs to be an ethos of trust and sharing in activities that involve disclosure and feedback and that those in leadership roles need to be sensitive to a variety of learning needs among colleagues. It is also important to recognize that

> it is not always easy to receive help;
> it is difficult to commit oneself to change;
> it is difficult to submit to the influence of a helper: help is a threat to esteem, integrity and independence;
> it is not easy to trust a stranger and be open with him or her;
> it is not easy to see one's problems clearly at first; and
> sometimes problems seem too large, too overwhelming, or too unique to share easily.
> (Egan, 1982)

The message for leaders is that it is not enough to propose or make organizational or other changes without taking into account the amount of support those involved in implementing the changes will need – for change of this kind 'will not persist if some individual changes do not occur; and changes in the way professionals think and work will soon regress without supporting organisational change' (Schmuck, 1980).

The notion of formal 'entitlements' and contracts for and between staff may appear to be alienating to the essentially non-legalistic tradition of primay schools. Yet there is a sense in which, in the same way that pupils are entitled to a National Curriculum, all LEAs to annual school-development plans and all teachers to appraisal, all teachers may be 'entitled' to support in the processes of change. Whilst some 'entitlements' may be context and task specific, there may be others that are more general and that, along with job specifications, should be made explicit, for example, the following:

- Consultation in the formulation of school-development planning.
- Time to reflect on and participate in the monitoring and evaluation of curriculum innovation.
- Quality support appropriate to training and development needs raised by the processes of change.
- Equal rights in judgments made of the outcomes of change.
- Ownership of the change process.

The curriculum reform movements of the 1960s and 1970s were largely unsuccessful because they were often initiated outside the school community, did not involve classroom teachers in the curriculum design and ignored the user context. Teachers were, by inference, passive receivers of curriculum packages. They had no sense of 'ownership' in what was largely a top-down process of innovation. The curriculum reform movement of the late 1980s is ensured of adoption at the initial stage of implementation because it is the product of legislation. External monitoring and evaluation will ensure that the letter (if not the spirit) of the law is enacted. Nevertheless, the fact remains that it is the individual teacher who still holds the key to the successful long-term impact of change within his or her own classroom. This chapter has suggested that, if the quality of teaching in the classroom is to be enhanced, then headteachers must provide practical as well as intellectual and moral support and promote a climate in which teachers themselves can take ownership of and responsibility for innovation in practice.

6
MANAGING THE CURRICULUM

The introduction of the National Curriculum has presented a challenging management task for schools. This chapter is not about the curriculum itself, but about the practical approaches schools can make to managing the teaching and learning processes. Like the other chapters in the book, this proceeds from the assumption that the process of managing is a collaborative activity in which all members of the teaching team work together as co-managers, each with their particular role to play and responsibilities to exercise, but united under a common purpose. Essentially, the chapter is about the ways in which the crucial interaction of teacher and pupils within a learning environment can be affected by the process of management. The emphasis is thus practical and a variety of participatory exercises that may be adapted to suit the reader's particular situation and purposes are included.

Learning experiences result both from the formal programmes of work initiated by teachers and from a wide variety of informal factors often referred to as the hidden or covert curriculum. In this chapter, 'curriculum' is used to refer to all planned activity involving teachers and pupils and to teaching methods and approaches.

It is not enough simply to think of a curriculum as a set of policy documents and guidelines. A wider concept of the curriculum was firmly established in the Schools Council working paper 70, *The Practical Curriculum* (Schools Council, 1981):

> there is a need for a visible structure for the curriculum. A useful starting point is to consider each pupil's right of access to different areas of human knowledge and experience. The heart of the matter is what each child takes

away from the school. For each of them, what he or she takes away is the effective curriculum.

This document thus emphasizes a view of the curriculum as the experience each child has at school and what each takes away.

Much of the activity undertaken in schools under the name of curriculum development over recent years has been about the formulation of desirable objectives. The classroom lives of learners have been little affected, as the study of Barker Lunn (1984) has demonstrated. In fact, this research into junior classrooms suggested that teaching methods and practices have changed far less significantly than has often been thought.

A WORKING MODEL

Managing the curriculum can be considered as a process consisting of three key stages:

1. *Planning* Working out the educational philosophy of the school.
2. *Operating* Defining, implementing and controlling the learning processes.
3. *Evaluating* Determining how well the philosophy has worked in practice.

Each of these three broad processes will be discussed in detail, but before this it is important to stress again that the chapter is about how the curriculum is managed, not about what that curriculum should be. For the first time in this country, the curriculum for schools is established in the form of a set of subject requirements. The emphasis will be placed on the way the staff as a whole can work together to provide a cohesive approach to classroom work, and the practical ways the National Curriculum can be brought to life in the classroom. It will also consider the ways in which they bring their collective hopes, expectations and experiences to bear in formulating and implementing decisions about the direction in which the school needs to go, and how they create a working climate conducive to professional growth and development.

Such working conditions are not easy to create and maintain. They are most likely where there is a happy balance between task and process. This requires the recognition of the three key factors described in Chapter 2 – the task itself, the needs of each individual and the needs of the team as a whole (Adair, 1983). Much will depend upon the headteacher's capacity to maintain a purposeful concentration on the tasks in hand while, at the same time, providing sensitive and encouraging support to individuals. Keeping the team as a whole informed and motivated is also necessary, especially if particular tasks only involve certain members of staff.

PLANNING

This stage of the curriculum-managing process is essentially one of making policy. While National Curriculum attainment targets and programmes of study determine the objectives for pupil learning it is vitally important for the staff to create agreements about the purposes of the school and the means of bringing them to reality. It is unlikely that effective learning will be achieved unless all staff have a clear sense of direction and share a common vision of what they wish to achieve.

In Figure 6.1 it is suggested that the process of curriculum management is a cyclic one in which the outcomes of previous plans and policies are used to inform the need for new ones. In most schools planning is an activity that is often very much a question of adaptation and development. Only those teachers fortunate enough to be given the somewhat rare privilege of setting up an entirely new school have the opportunity to plan without the limiting constraints of existing tradition and practice. The requirement for schools to produce National Curriculum development plans has firmly established planning as a key process in managing the educational activities of the school. This particular planning exercise is designed to identify the changes that need to be made in various subject areas to conform to the strictures of the national policy.

Before embarking on any policy-making activity it is important to be aware of the factors that influence and determine the way schools tend to go about the business of organizing learning. Four particular factors have been suggested as especially significant (Whitaker, 1983):

1. *Prescriptions* What we must do.
2. *Expectations* What we should do.
3. *Situations* What we have to take account of here.
4. *Predilections* What we would like to do.

Prescriptions for the curriculum are now clearly and comprehensively laid down in the statutory orders of the National Curriculum.

Expectations also exist in abundance. The way most schools go about their business is more determined by what they think they should do than

```
PLANNING ─────→ OPERATING ─────→ EVALUATING
    │                │                │
Managing the     Managing the     Managing the
 making of       learning process  monitoring of
policies and                      the learning process
   plans                          and providing
                                     feedback
                     Plans
         What the    ↑↕↔      What the
        teacher does  The      pupils do
                    learning
                   environment
```

Figure 6.1 Managing the curriculum — a working model

what they know they must. In other words, a wide range of influencing factors combine to channel schools in a particular direction. Some of the key determinants can be summarized as expectations deriving from

1. traditional educational practice;
2. assumptions about how children learn;
3. received wisdom about what schools should be like;
4. public experiences of the education system;
5. informed opinion;
6. public debate;
7. teacher training;
8. assumptions about what classrooms should be like; and
9. assumptions about how teachers teach.

Progressive trends in education are viewed with some suspicion and the affairs of the William Tyndale School in Islington in 1976 (Auld, 1976) and the subsequent public enquiry set in motion a 'back to the basics' movement that, despite receiving no official support or encouragement, continues to affect the policy-making of schools (Barker Lunn, 1984; DES, 1985).

The third set of factors influencing planning and development are those related to the particular circumstances of each school. These will include building design, previous curriculum history, the pattern of organization, the attitudes of parents and the community and the composition and attitudes of the teaching staff.

Many heads approach their first headship with grand plans in mind. Their predilections often stretch beyond mere curriculum development to a total transformation of the whole educational enterprise. Angela Anning (1983) has suggested that the management strategies of headteachers take a well-defined course. First comes an environmental impact. The head makes all sorts of improvements to the surroundings — plants appear in the entrance hall and drapes accompany displays of objects. The second stage involves the writing of curriculum guidelines. Mathematics and language are usually tackled first, those for dance, drama or art and craft rarely being accomplished. After this, Anning suggests, heads arrive at what she describes as Bechers Brook. This is the realization that despite all this effort, what goes on in the classroom between the teacher and the children has hardly changed at all. To affect this requires management activity designed to change fundamentally the way staff approach and conduct their professional business. In most cases Bechers Brook is too awesome even to attempt to jump.

This is not to disparage what heads find themselves doing, but it does emphasize the difficulties that face the agent of change in education. Individual predilections may have meaning for particular class teachers, but headteachers' predilections inevitably involve change in other people rather than themselves. In preparing for innovation in school there are four key factors likely to influence success (Whitaker, 1984):

1. An awareness of how individuals behave.
2. An awareness of the sources of power within the school, and how they operate.
3. An awareness of the values system of the school.
4. An awareness of how the proposed change will affect each of these factors.

(For a more detailed discussion of these factors, see Chapter 5.) This list suggests that in successful managing, awareness is everything. In terms of the planning stage of curriculum management there are some clear implications that relate back to the point about leadership being concerned with the task, the individual and the team. If policy-making is to be successful it needs to respond to individual needs as well as to those emanating from the staff as a whole. It is the staff itself, working together, that has to become the power source of policy and decision-making. The policies and decisions made need to reflect a value system forged by the working team through a process of questioning assumptions, challenging beliefs and synthesizing experience.

There may sometimes be a tendency to tackle curriculum development without first paying attention to the four factors listed above. A sense of direction is difficult to achieve when there is not only disagreement about the route but also arguments about whether the journey is necessary in the first place. The skill in management lies in harnessing the creative forces of those who in the end have to deliver the new policy. Therefore before planning the details of the learning process it is necessary to tackle the question of philosophy and values.

SCHOOL PHILOSOPHY AND VALUES

The following exercises are recommended as possible ways of approaching this issue. They are best undertaken as whole-staff activities after some work has been done to build a trusting and participative co-managing climate in the school.

Exercise 1

The first task attempts to deal with the four sets of determinants referred to above — prescriptions, expectations, situations and predilections. The printed sheet illustrated in Figure 6.2 should be given to all members of staff meeting together. It is important to undertake this activity as a collective experience since it is one of the ways in which cooperative and participatory skills can be developed.

Staff should be invited to complete the form individually, allowing about 10−15 minutes. When this has been done ask them to work in pairs to share each other's responses. Allow a good 20 minutes for this. It is likely that some fundamental issues will be raised by this questionnaire, issues that perhaps do not often get an airing in staff meetings. The next stage, numbers allowing, is to join pairs up into foursomes. Each group's task is to produce a further sheet listing responses on which there is broad agreement — factors each of the four can subscribe to. A small group of staff members can than be invited to take responsibility for producing a draft statement summarizing the factors affecting school philosophy and practice. Copies of this draft can be circulated for further discussion before being formally adopted.

The way in which this exercise is conducted is very important. As a task

Under the four headings below list the factors which you consider affect school policies and practices
1. Prescriptions – what we must do
2. Expectations – what we should do
3. Situations – what we have to take account of here
4. Predilections – what I should like to do

Figure 6.2 Factors affecting school policies and plans

it is designed to facilitate whole-staff interaction and cooperation. What goes on in the pairs and foursomes can help create a good climate for open and creative decision-making. For the head, who is likely to have responsibility for facilitating the activity, the question of pace and timing is crucial. It is vital not to inhibit free and open discussion by hurrying the stages of the exercise. On the other hand, providing some time constraints does help to generate a keen sense of purpose. A useful technique is to suggest a time limit of, say, 20 minutes for the paired discussion, and then to offer a 5-minute extension if the talk seems active and productive.

The exercise described above could well occupy a number of hour-long staff meetings. When much of the work is being conducted in pairs and small groups it is useful to allow 15 minutes or so at the end for an open session when all staff can share their thoughts and feelings about what has been going on. This should not be too rigorously 'chaired'. Reticence will soon be overcome if contributions are accepted and valued. This exercise will have aired the issue of the purposes of education.

Exercise 2

Curriculum planning will also need to be informed by a clear understanding of how the staff view the learning process. In particular it is essential to tease out what the various beliefs are about how children learn. This next exercise is designed to do this, by helping teachers get in touch with how they feel about the learning process and the pupils they teach. The questionnaire, illustrated in Figure 6.3, should be duplicated and a copy given to each member of staff. Working on their own the teachers should be invited to complete the sentences, not thinking too hard about them but responding fairly quickly and intuitively.

After allowing a reasonable time for completing the sentence stems, staff should then work in pairs. The talk should focus first on the process of answering the questions: which ones were difficult, or perhaps seemingly impossible, and whether any of them actually caused discomfort. The talk should then move on to sharing responses to the questions themselves. The same procedure as in the previous exercise can then be adopted, with staff working in pairs and then as a whole group, attempting to bring together the various value positions. Again a small group can be asked to prepare a summary draft for discussion.

1. Children learn best when . . .
2. The pupils I like best are those who . . .
3. It is important that children . . .
4. When I think about the children I teach . . .
5. The children I most worry about are . . .
6. I don't like children who . . .
7. What I want my pupils to acquire is . . .
8. What children really need is . . .
9. The qualities I most admire in pupils are . . .
10. What we should really be emphasizing in the curriculum is . . .

Figure 6.3 Questionnaire: values and beliefs about learners

Exercise 3

The third exercise is one to clarify philosophy and values. It attempts to synthesize the outcomes of the previous two activities. Following consideration and discussion of the draft summaries comes the task of forging these outcomes into a coherent form. This exercise is best carried out in a room where large sheets of paper can be stuck or pinned to the wall. Three large sheets of paper should be prepared for the meeting, headed, respectively, What we hope for our pupils; What we believe in about learning; What we believe in about teaching.

Working as a whole group, or smaller ones if the staff is larger than eight, the idea is to 'brainstorm' responses to each of the headings. It is important to sustain the rules of brainstorming — all responses are valid and are recorded and there is no discussion about items offered. When the lists are complete the staff should divide into three, each small group taking one of the lists. The next stage is to classify and categorize the responses, providing headings for each classification. The summary documents from the previous exercises should also be produced and items from these added to the lists. The classified lists should then be photocopied and distributed for further discussion and refinement.

These various summary documents should provide enough material to form the basis of a very thorough and comprehensive statement of the educational philosophy of the staff. This does not have to be a lengthy well-argued document but can be more a set of statements setting out the values and beliefs that underwrite school practices and procedures. It is a good idea to aim to produce a statement short enough to form the introduction for the school booklet for parents.

THE LEARNING PROCESS

Having considered some ways to reach agreement about basic school philosophy and values, the next stage is to consider how the daily work of the school can be planned. To facilitate this it is useful to adopt a conceptual model that closely reflects the ideas and values that have previously been agreed. Many such models exist and schools are faced with rather too many to choose from. Certainly one of the new pressures on schools in recent years has been the regular and sometimes concentrated publication of documents about the curriculum. These now form a central part of those determining factors summarized above under the heading of 'expectations'. For the head and staff of a school, one of the problems is what to believe. Although the plethora of curriculum documentation contains many common themes, it also represents variety and divergence of approach. It is also important to remember that the National Curriculum specifies objectives for learning — it does not deal with classroom methods and techniques. In planning its approach to implementing the National Curriculum the school has to decide which of the following courses to take:

1. Choose a particular approach and follow its suggestions.
2. Stick to a school-based approach and make adjustments where necessary in response to published evidence.
3. Look at available documentation and develop a flexible and pragmatic working model that has the capacity to respond to new challenges and changed situations.

Whichever approach is adopted it is important to underwrite it with some clear assumptions about the nature of curriculum change and development. Three particular assumptions seem necessary:

1. Curriculum development should not be regarded as a once-and-for-all event but as a natural process of dynamic growth.
2. In the changed and changing times we now work in, flexibility of management systems and structures is crucial. If the system is rigid and unbending the strains will be felt by all.
3. Change needs to be seen as the natural order of things. We should expect that it will become increasingly necessary to do things differently as circumstances change and as we learn more about the learning process in our school and about what works well for learners and what does not.

For the staff of the school involved in curriculum management, the implications are clear. It is vital to adopt a working model that reflects the school as it is now and takes account of current values. It is also necessary to resist the temptation to plan for a distant vision — a school in an ideal world. Above all, it is essential to see the management of the curriculum as a constant cycle of planning—operating—evaluating, a process closely linked to the roles and responsibilities teachers occupy and also to a clear policy for staff development.

The wide variety of approaches to curriculum management can be illustrated by reference to five key documents published in recent years (Figure 6.4). A comparison of these particular approaches to curriculum design demonstrates just how varied conceptual thought on the subject is.

Document	Approach	Example
Primary survey (DES, 1978)	Subject based	Aesthetic and physical education: 1. Art and crafts 2. Music 3. Physical education Language and literacy: 1. Reading 2. Writing Mathematics Science Social abilities: 1. Social, moral and religious education 2. Geography and history
Aims into Practice (Schools Council, 1975)	Personal growth	Development: Intellectual Physical Aesthetic Spiritual/religious Emotional/personal Social/moral
Primary Practice (Schools Council, 1983)	Subjects and approaches	Science Mathematics Language and literacy Past and present Imagination, feeling, sensory perception Personal and social Topic work Assessment and records Organization Staff development Evaluation
The Curriculum 5–16 (DES, 1985)	Issues and concerns	Breadth Balance Relevance Differentiation Progression
The National Curriculum (NCC, 1989)	Core subjects and foundation subjects	Programmes of study Attainment targets Four key stages Ten levels of attainment Assessment arrangements

Figure 6.4 Approaches to curriculum management

One of the most important functions of planning for learning is to create a clear and cohesive action plan for bringing school philosophy to life in the classrooms, a policy for organizing learning expericences to realize purposes and intentions. This takes the issue of curriculum planning into the classroom and into matters of teaching style and classroom organization.

Figure 6.5 suggests a framework that conceives of the learning process as a dynamic interaction of four key factors. By separating out these key ingredients it becomes possible to provide a simple yet comprehensive approach to planning. For each class teacher the task becomes one of making decisions about the relationship between learning intentions, teacher behaviour, pupil behaviour and the environmemt in which that relationship is developed. Such decisions have traditionally been left to individual class teachers, and the making of agreements about teaching methods and approaches has not traditionally been regarded as a significant part of curriculum planning and management. What is now being suggested is that such agreements are a central part of that key process and that effective learning cannot be planned for if the essential practical factors in that process are not part of school policy-making.

KNOWLEDGE ABOUT TEACHING AND LEARNING

Teachers must be encouraged to identify questions to ask of themselves and to devise procedures that will enable them to collect and record

Figure 6.5 The learning process

relevant information. The desire for particular changes in curricula, organization, teaching strategies or assessment procedures may emerge from this. Realistically, however, it cannot be expected that all teachers will be able to undertake the sort of comprehensive scheme of self-evaluation through programmes of action research outlined in Chapter 7. Indeed, it has been argued that such commitment to self-disclosure should occur only from time to time. Assuming that in practice only a relatively small part of teacher time can be made available for systematic practical reflection and analysis, it is most important that intellectual and moral support is provided throughout, and that opportunities to engage in appropriate in-service activities are provided.

The notion of 'leading professional' is often used to describe the head of a school, and one area in which this concept can be usefully applied is in assisting teachers to consider the implications in general terms for pupil learning of the use of different planning and teaching strategies. Clearly, particular uses will depend on particular purposes, and no one way is necessarily any better or worse than any other. However,

> Values are involved in education not so much as goals or end products but as principles implicit in different manners of proceeding and producing... in my view, many disputes about the aims of education are disputes about principles of procedure rather than 'aims' in the sense of objectives to be arrived at by taking appropriate means.
>
> (Peters, 1968)

It is worth while, therefore, highlighting briefly how some of these values are communicated through planning, pupil tasks and their negotiation, and teacher-pupil interaction.

Many teachers claim that they plan for 'discovery-learning' experiences for pupils, yet it is worth considering that within this term two distinct models may be identified, each with different planned processes and outcomes:

1. Learning by discovery (or 'guided discovery'), in which the teacher has pre-specified content objectives, e.g. certain knowledge and principles to be learned. Here the teacher will tend to use non-instructional means to achieve his or her ends, e.g. guessing or 'information' games.
2. Learning to discover (or 'enquiry based') where the emphasis is on the process of how to enquire rather than on the product of past enquiries. Here students are involved in learning procedures for critically evaluating knowledge and principles, leaving what is to be

learned as an open matter (Schulman and Keisler, 1966; Elliott, 1973).

The amount of teacher dominance over classroom events may be related to the characteristics of pupil-task activities rather than the personal characteristics of teachers. Depending on the degree of control exercised by the teacher over the subject matter, the pacing and the direction of the task, pupils will be discouraged or encouraged from

1. valuing their ability to make decisions, creating and shaping knowledge and becoming their own experts in thematic content;
2. forming and testing hypotheses about themselves and others and the signs and symbols used to create, express and communicate meaning;
3. viewing the teacher as a keeper and controller of knowledge; and
4. viewing themselves as uninformed acolytes, passive knowledge-receivers who are dependent on the teacher for their learning.

In the classroom itself teachers might observe how much time they spend talking in relation to pupil talk. Are their conversations one-way? What is the language they use? If it is mainly functional, what opportunities for learning about language are being denied to pupils? Does teacher 'busyness' in the classroom (Sharp and Green, 1975) mean that they are spending more time with those articulate pupils who demand attention than others who appear to be quietly 'getting on with it'? One of the questions asked by Bassey and Hatch (1979) concerns the differences between long and short interactions: 'Is it the case in your classroom that short interactions mainly serve to keep everyone busy, while long interactions are more valuable as teaching events? Would it be more desirable to have more long interactions?' Such issues as those above and others raised by Barnes (1976) and others, should be core reading for all engaged in managing the curriculum.

A useful way into the debate about teaching style and classroom management is to use some of the very interesting analysis from the ORACLE project (Galton and Simon, 1980). This examination of primary classrooms identified three basic teaching styles — instructing, enquiring and monitoring — that involve teachers working either with the class as a whole, or with small groups or individual pupils. A high proportion of teachers use a combination of all three approaches but often with an emphasis on one in particular. Before agreements can be made to adopt common approaches in the classroom it is necessary to conduct some wide-ranging discussions about how teachers are already carrying out their teaching. Much will depend on the confidence of individual teachers but the following strategies are possible approaches.

Describing Experience

A series of staff meetings can be held in each teacher's classroom in turn and the teacher can be invited to describe

1. how the classroom is organized;
2. how learning experiences are managed;
3. the range of learning experiences of the pupils;
4. the range and variety of teacher behaviour (perhaps using the ORACLE categories);
5. styles of presentation;
6. expectations about standards; and
7. basic approaches in particular curriculum areas.

Observing Practice

Although staffing constraints can make it difficult it is very helpful to create the possibility of teachers spending some time in colleagues' classrooms observing – not observing to evaluate but observing to inform. Following general discussions among the staff as a whole a programme of observation can be drawn up so that all teachers have the opportunity both to observe and to be observed. The purpose is very much to help the teacher who is observed, although it is likely that the observer will gain considerable insights into the learning process by observing it closely and in some detail. One of the best ways to conduct such a programme is to ask teachers to draw up a list of factors in their classroom work they would like more information about and to use the observer to gather evidence. The following examples serve to illustrate the range of possibilities of this strategy:

1. Observing an individual pupil and recording behaviour.
2. Observing a group of pupils undertaking a task.
3. Monitoring pupil interactions.
4. Observing in a particular area, e.g. the book corner or science bay.
5. Monitoring the teachers' interactions with specified pupils.

6. Monitoring the teachers' use of instructional language.
7. Monitoring use of resources by pupils.

An observation of an hour can provide considerable data for a most useful professional conversation as the observer provides feedback on what was observed and the observed teacher seeks clarification about it.

Generating Checklists

Working together in meetings, staff can build a variety of checklists to assist classroom analysis. These can be in the form either of questionnaires or of the sentence stems used in Figure 6.3. The lists could refer to a whole range of factors. Perhaps a good start could be made by inviting the staff to brainstorm factors under the following headings:

1. The classroom.
2. What the teacher does.
3. What the pupils do.

Staff could undertake to complete one checklist per day for a week. The next meeting could then be used to share information and to see how wide a divergence of practice there is between teachers. This will provide much material for discussion and planning. A technique similar to this one is referred to in Chapter 7.

A PRACTICAL APPROACH TO CURRICULUM MANAGEMENT

The activities and procedures that follow are designed to help the head and staff keep the curriculum under review. They constitute a practical approach that conceives of curriculum management in terms of five key factors. Attention to these ensures that the whole process of managing the learning is systematic. Each of these factors is dealt with separately in the form of a series of practical activities. Together the five sets of activities constitute a package that can be applied in whole or in part to the educational life of a school. The activities are offered as examples, and each is capable of considerable expansion and modification to suit particular circumstances, and as new ideas are developed and new needs identified. It is the general approach, rather than the specific contents, that is important. The activities can usefully be presented in a working folder, a copy of which is held by each member of staff. The five factors for consideration are

1. the teacher;
2. the pupils;
3. aims and objectives;
4. teaching style; and
5. classroom organization.

The Teacher

Activity 1: 'myself as a teacher'

This questionnaire (Figure 6.6) has been designed to help teachers get in touch with how they feel about their work in the classroom and to raise issues about the values they incorporate in their work. The exercise is best handled when the staff are meeting together as a group. Each member of staff should be invited to complete the sentences and then to talk them through with a colleague. In fact the approach is very similar to the one described earlier (p. 143).

It is useful if staff keep their questionnaires and their responses and make a note in their diaries to return to them in about six months. The questionnaires could then be completed again and responses compared with earlier ones. There will be much fruitful discussion arising from the changes that can be detected and from any new themes that have begun to emerge.

Activity 2: 'myself as a learner'

This is a similar exercise but is designed to focus on the nature of learning in the teachers' own lives. The procedure is the same as that in activity 1 (Figure 6.7).

Activity 3: effective teaching

This exercise provides an opportunity to consider the various factors that contribute to effective teaching. The activity should be conducted as follows:

1. What I most like about myself as a teacher is . . .
2. I am at my best in the classroom when . . .
3. My pupils like it when . . .
4. I would describe my teaching style as . . .
5. When I think about my classroom I . . .
6. I like it best in teaching when . . .
7. I should like to change the way I teach but . . .
8. The main change I should like to make in my classroom is . . .
9. What I have most to learn about teaching is . . .
10. What I most try and avoid in my teaching is . . .
11. I envy those teachers who . . .
12. I am the sort of teacher who . . .
13. When somebody criticizes my teaching I . . .
14. What I would really like to see happening in my classroom is . . .
15. What I most dislike about being a teacher is . . .
16. Children seem to learn best when I . . .
17. I wish I was better able to . . .
18. Most of my colleagues think I am . . .

Figure 6.6 'Myself as a teacher'

1. I have found learning most enjoyable when . . .
2. The teachers I have learnt best from have been . . .
3. When I succeed in my learning I feel . . .
4. Things I would like to have learnt but failed to do so . . .
5. One specific learning goal I have is . . .
6. I can learn on my own if . . .
7. My particular skills as a learner are . . .
8. I sometimes avoid learning because . . .
9. The most recent thing I have learnt is . . .
10. What I should most like to learn about myself is . . .

Figure 6.7 'Myself as a learner'

1. Provide each teacher with fifteen small index cards.
2. Ask the teachers to use five cards to write down the five areas of professional knowledge most important in teaching.
3. The next five cards should be used to list the most important skills in teaching.
4. The final five cards are for the most important qualities in teachers.
5. Spread out all the knowledge cards and invite staff to categorize them, putting similar cards in a pile. A new card can be written to incorporate a composite statement, which represents these.
6. These cards should then be pinned to a large sheet of paper in an arrangement agreed to by the staff. This pattern should reflect the relationship between the different categories of 'knowledge' statement accumulated.
7. Do the same for the 'skills' and 'qualities' cards.
8. The creation of these posters should provide considerable potential for staff discussion and negotiation. Certainly it will generate consideration of a wide range of issues associated with the learning process.
9. The outcomes of the discussions, both formal and informal, will have many implications for staff development, the allocation of roles and responsibilities, the process of change within the school and curriculum planning.

The Pupils

Activity 1: traditional assumptions

This activity is designed to help teachers consider the learning process from the pupils' point of view. This can be done by examining the sorts of assumptions that underlie the learning process in schools. Carl Rogers (1983) has suggested that the following assumptions about learners have become firmly rooted in the schooling system:

1. Pupils cannot be trusted to learn.
2. An ability to pass examinations is the best criterion for selection and judging potential.
3. Evaluation is education; education is evaluation.
4. What a teacher teaches is what a pupil learns.
5. Knowledge is the accumulation of content and information.

6. The truths of subjects are known and must be learnt.
7. The way a pupil has to work is more important than what is being studied.
8. Creative people develop from passive learners.
9. The 'weeding out' of the majority of pupils is the best way of producing the well educated.
10. Pupils are best regarded as manipulative objects, not as people.

Working in small groups (or as a whole staff if there are fewer than six), the teachers should be invited to take each assumption in turn and consider what evidence there is in the school of the presence of that assumption. Evidence that is accumulated will provide much food for thought, discussion and decision-making.

Activity 2: good learners

It is important for teachers to have clear ideas about the qualities to be encouraged in learners and for these to be shared and feature in the school's curriculum policies. The brainstorming of the characteristics of good learners can be followed by comparing it to this list compiled by Postman and Weingartner (1971). Good learners

1. enjoy solving problems;
2. know what is relevant for their survival;
3. rely on their own judgment;
4. are not afraid of being wrong and changing their minds;
5. are not fast at answering – they find out and think first;
6. are flexible in their learning;
7. have a high degree of respect for facts;
8. are skilled in enquiry;
9. do not need to have a final irrevocable solution to every problem; and
10. are not depressed by saying 'I don't know'.

Activity 3: pupil feedback

It is important for teachers to be sensitive to pupils' reactions to learning activities and experiences, and to take account of these in managing the curriculum. A useful staff exercise is to design the sort of sentence-stem questionnaires illustrated above for pupils to complete. These can focus on a wide range of school issues from arrangements for break times to the detailed responses to particular classroom experiences. Other sorts of pupil evaluation sheets can also be designed and tested in order to find effective ways to incorporate pupil views into the scheme of things.

Aims and Objectives

Activity 1: 'primary practice'

Unlike many of the documents issued in the wave of curriculum publishing in recent years, the Schools Council working paper 75, *Primary Practice* (Schools Council, 1983), offers a whole range of strategies for curriculum management. In particular there are many procedures for planning the nature and the shape of learning activities. Case-study material is offered to provide much useful discussion material and there are checklists and questions on specific issues. The document has much to recommend it as a practical resource for curriculum management.

Activity 2: flow charts

Most teachers in primary schools are familiar with flow charts as aids to planning in topic work. They also have considerable potential in planning the more detailed aspects of classroom management, particularly when there are time factors involved and the sequencing of events is important. Flow charts are essentially the working diagrams of the creative process and therefore have a valuable part to play in a wide range of management activities. They can be used in the initial stages of planning to develop ideas, and in the final stages to work out ways to conduct the implementation of new procedures.

Any issue of current concern to the staff can be used to conduct a trial run with flow charts. They make an imaginative alternative to written discussion papers, offering scope for originality of design and use.

Activity 3: planning change

When changes to the established order of things are being planned, it is very important that careful thought and consideration is given to each aspect of the innovation. The planning sheet illustrated in Figure 6.8 can be used on those occasions when it is necessary to be very clear about the steps to be taken in introducing an element of change, either in professional behaviour or in the management of the classroom.

My problem is . . .	
I hope to overcome it by . . .	
My particular aim is . . .	
My first objective is . . .	What:
	How:
	When:
Statement of intent: I shall . . .	

Figure 6.8 Planning change

Teaching Style

Activity 1: ORACLE

One of the most illuminating studies of the primary classroom has been that carried out by Maurice Galton and his colleagues at Leicester University (Galton *et al.*, 1980). Using close observational techniques the research has revealed a wealth of information about what goes on in primary classrooms. A study of the teaching styles revealed by the research and of the pupil types present in all classrooms should be high on the agenda for discussion in all primary schools. A whole range of management exercises can be built from the information produced by the project and a study of this research is highly recommended.

Activity 2: process factors

Curriculum management needs to give a high priority to various factors that affect the learning process. The key ones of these have been summarized in *The Curriculum from 5–16* (DES, 1985) as follows:

1. *Breadth* The extent to which pupils have access to the full range of learning experiences and opportunities.
2. *Balance* The extent to which each area of learning is given appropriate attention in relation to the others and the curriculum as a whole.
3. *Relevance* The extent to which the learning experiences provided by the school meet the present and prospective needs of the pupils.
4. *Differentiation* The extent to which the learning experiences cater for individual needs and differences.
5. *Progression* The extent to which the learning experiences relate to each other as part of a continuous process.

An important management activity for the head and the staff is to design ways in which these factors can be built into the three key managing processes — planning, operating and evaluating. As it stands, the list provides a useful check to apply both to the curriculum as a whole and to the detailed and practical plans teachers make to bring the curriculum to life in the classroom.

Activity 3: teacher behaviour

An important element of teaching style is the sort of interpersonal behaviour adopted by teachers in the classroom. Research has suggested that it is the way in which teachers relate to pupils that is particularly important in promoting effective learning in pupils. Three particular behavioural qualities have been found to be especially significant:

1. The teacher's ability to understand the meaning classroom experience is having for each pupil.
2. The respect the teacher has for each pupil as a unique and separate person.

3. The ability of the teacher to engage in a genuine person-to-person relationship with each pupil (Rogers, 1983).

Pastoral care of this kind is a key consideration in any school. Its importance in primary schools relates especially to the role of the class teacher and the ways in which pupils are helped to overcome any difficulties in their personal lives as well as in their learning. A key part of any staff-development programme should be a consideration of how the qualities listed above can be developed. Agreements about desirable strategies for teaching should give high priority to these key characteristics. The questionnaire in Figure 6.9 will help teachers to focus on this issue.

Classroom Organization

Activity 1: the learning environment

It is a useful exercise for teachers to consider why they arrange and organize their classrooms as they do. One way to focus on this issue is to ask each member of staff to draw a scale plan of their classroom and to show on it the disposition of furniture, the location and storage of resources and equipment and the presence of display. Used in conjunction with the activity on pp. 150 this activity can provide an opportunity to consider the following questions:

---

1. Upon which assumptions about my pupils do I base my teaching?
2. What are my criteria for effective learning?
3. What proportion of my teaching involves active learning by my pupils?
4. How well do I sense the meaning that classroom experience is having for my pupils?
5. How do I show my pupils that I respect them?
6. How much of myself do I disclose to my pupils?
7. How well do I listen to what my pupils have to say to me?
8. What sort of praise do I give, what sort of encouragement?
9. In what ways do I judge my pupils?
10. How well do I understand the self-concept and its importance in the learning process?

Figure 6.9 Person-centred teaching

1. Which particular criteria about learning have determined the layout of furniture?
2. Does the arrangement of furniture suit all learning activities?
3. How does the arrangement of furniture affect pupil interaction and movement?
4. How were the decisions made about where resources would be located and stored?
5. How are resources distributed, collected, checked and made available to pupils?
6. To what extent has the classroom been organized to create special areas, such as a book corner, facilities for imaginative play or an area for science and technology?
7. For what purposes are displays in the classroom arranged?
8. What are the criteria for displaying the work of pupils?

The more staff can discuss the answers to these sorts of questions with each other, the greater the opportunity for developing agreements about priorities and practices in the school.

Activity 2: visiting other schools

Most teachers enjoy visiting other schools and seeing how colleagues approach their work in a different setting. Visiting schools is an important part of good staff development but consideration needs to be given to procedure. Whenever possible staff should visit in pairs. The opportunity to discuss the visit and its particular implications is very important and should not be under-estimated. A key management activity for the staff when a programme of visits is being planned is to draw up a checklist of factors upon which information is sought. These are often best phrased as questions to which the visit will supply answers.

Activity 3: encouragement to learn

This activity focuses on the extent to which classroom organization is designed as a learning environment that can itself encourage learning. Staff can be invited to look at their classrooms and list responses to the following questions:

1. In what particular ways does the classroom and what is arranged in it provide opportunities for the curiosity of the pupils to be stimulated and satisfied?

Managing the Curriculum 161

2. In what ways does the classroom as an environment motivate children to learn?
3. How does the organization of the classroom facilitate the pupils' access to essential resources and equipment?
4. How does the classroom facilitate and encourage interactions between the pupils?
5. What back-up facilities are provided so that there is a range of alternative activities for pupils to choose from when set work is completed?
6. How does the classroom reflect the learning of the pupils?
7. How are the pupils involved in the management of the classroom?
8. How are the pupils involved in creating new ideas for developing the classroom as a learning environment?

Managing the curriculum of the primary school is essentially a practical activity. Far too often it is seen as a theoretical exercise divorced from the learning lives of the pupils and the practical activities of their teachers. This chapter has attempted to provide both a theoretical perspective on curriculum management and a practical guide to carrying it out. The activities and exercises are only examples of approaches and are offered as ways into the process of collective and participatory management that underpins each chapter in this book. As exercises they are designed to create and stimulate staff interaction and discussion. If nothing else they will produce a great deal of lively professional debate, which is a prerequisite of effective and dynamic curriculum management.

7
REVIEW, DEVELOPMENT AND APPRAISAL

This chapter places appraisal within the context of professional and institutional review and development, asserting that it represents more than an individual and school's accountability procedures. It provides the reader with a description of the principal elements within an appraisal system and discusses key design and implementation issues. It asserts that it is vital for managers to place teacher autonomy (and thus self-appraisal) at the heart of the system of review and development, and provides suggestions as to how this may be achieved. Finally, it provides practical examples to assist teachers and schools in processes of review, development and appraisal.

CONTEXTS OF APPRAISAL

The HMI survey of primary education (DES, 1978) asserted that it was important 'to make full use, on behalf of schools as a whole, of teachers' strengths to build on the existing knowledge of individual teachers.... However the requirements of society come to be formulated, teachers have the main responsibility for responding to them'. Certainly the opportunity for individuals and institutions to engage in appraisal must underpin any curriculum or professional development work that may be undertaken at school or classroom level. How, otherwise, may we proceed or make decisions about future work if we cannot judge where we are now, and how worth while our past endeavours have been? So the need for appraisal would appear to be self-evident. Indeed, it may be argued that most teachers and schools are already involved daily in appraisal processes through events such as staff meetings, curriculum workshops, pupil records, job specifications (see Chapter 4), in-service events and even informal conversations with colleagues. Nor should we forget the 'on-the-spot' appraisals carried out by teachers in their own classrooms. These may cause teachers to change the direction and even content of their teaching according to their perceptions of their own effectiveness or the response of their pupils.

Nevertheless, there is little doubt that the use of the term 'appraisal' often evokes negative responses by teachers. The reason for this is that it is perceived as something that is usually

1. initiated and carried out by someone else in an authority position;
2. something done to someone (passive), often without agreement as to the standards, criteria and processes being used;
3. for the purposes of making judgments in which weaknesses are highlighted; and
4. not providing support for long-term remedial work where required or requested.

So appraisal — even if we can understand the reason for it — is not always seen to be helpful. At the very least it means that we must disclose something more of ourselves to others than we would like or are used to. After all, teachers are trained to be 'professionals'. Once they qualify they are regarded as competent and, by implication, able to plan, teach and evaluate their work. They are immediately given responsibility for a class of children and, apart from any who undergo planned induction processes, are 'left to get on with it', with the occasional visit by outsiders and, in more enlightened schools, headteacher, colleagues and parents. So, although teachers are engaged daily in evaluating their pupils, by tradition it is rare for the teachers themselves to be evaluated by anyone other than themselves.

It is likely, then, that teachers will operate on a model of restricted professionality. Once they have developed a personal solution to any problems of teaching they perceive — and this is usually achieved without any systematic assistance from others — it is unlikely that this solution will again be significantly questioned. Argyris and Schon (1976) characterize this pattern of teacher development as 'single loop' learning, in which theory-making and theory-testing is private. In a world of restricted professionality, professionals protect themselves and colleagues by speaking in abstractions without reference to directly observed events. This has the effect of both controlling others and preventing others from influencing oneself by withholding access to valid information about oneself. These effects are manifested in the 'Stone Age obstructionists' (Doyle and Ponder, 1976) and other forms of resistance to change described in Chapter 5.

Formal appraisal, which involves others, clearly threatens this world of restricted professionality. Although writing in the context of programme evaluation, the American educator, Ernest House (1972) summed up neatly the ambivalent attitude most of us hold:

> The first observation I want to make is that there is no real demand among teachers and administrators for evaluating their own programs. To evaluate kids, yes, we cannot live without that; but to evaluate ourselves and our own programs – no. At times, in that strange ideology with which we disguise our motives and cover our tracks, we educators convince ourselves that we would be overjoyed to receive data about our teaching and educational programs. Well, try it sometime. Try evaluating a program. On simply asking teachers their goals, we have had them break into tears and throw chalk across the room. Rare events, but not unrepresentative of teachers' attitudes towards evaluation.
>
> After all, what does a teacher have to gain from having his work examined? As he sees it, absolutely nothing. He is exposing himself to administrators and parents. He risks damage to his ego by finding out he is not doing his job as well as he thinks he is. Perhaps worst of all he risks discovering that his students do not really care for him, something a teacher would rather not know. The culture of the school offers no rewards for examining one's behavior – only penalties. Since there are no punishments for not exposing one's behavior and many dangers in so doing, the prudent teacher gives lip service to the idea and drags both feet. And this is not so strange, is it? Do we have any serious evaluations of lawyers, or doctors, or cabdrivers? That there is no such demand is a corollary of a broader principle: No one wants to be evaluated by anybody at any time. Evaluate an evaluator's work and see how he reacts.

So where appraisal of teachers is not by teachers it is not surprising that it is often seen as an unhelpful activity. This perception has been exacerbated by the 'hostile' environment in which many teachers perceive themselves as living. With increasing government intervention in the curriculum (see Chapter 6), more parental involvement (see Chapter 8), diminishing resources, fewer opportunities for promotion, a plethora of HMI and DES documents and restrictive conditions of service linked to salary structure, it is understandable, then, that some teachers feel threatened.

ACCOUNTABILITY

As long ago as 1979 the East Sussex Accountability Project identified three kinds of accountability:

1. *Answerability* to one's clients, i.e. pupils and parents (moral accountability).
2. *Responsibility* to oneself and one's colleagues (professional responsibility).
3. *Accountability* in the strict sense to one's employers or political masters (contractual accountability).

Although the three overlap, we may say that in recent years the emphasis has moved from 'responsibility' to 'answerability' and 'accountability'. However, these need not always be mutually exclusive, and the exemplification of the facets of accountability provided in the East Sussex Accountability Project supplies a clue as to how professional development, evaluation and accountability may be linked in practice (Figure 7.1).

The prime means by which a school may demonstrate its accountability to parents and the LEA, whether in terms of 'preserving and enhancing general levels of performance' ('maintenance' procedures in Figure 7.1) or through, 'the detection and amelioration of individual points of weakness' ('problem-solving' mechanisms in Figure 7.1) are the domestic monitoring of standards and regular review of staffing, curricula and teaching arrangements (Box 3, Figure 7.1). While there is no doubt that these do occur, they must be seen to occur and be communicated. As has been observed, 'In the case of schools, the teaching profession might demonstrate that they had procedures, of which self-evaluation could be a major component, to keep the quality of education under review, and with enough teeth to ensure that changes were made when needed' (Nuttall, 1981). Thus leaders in schools have a professional, moral and contractual responsibility to ensure not only that appraisal occurs but that it is also seen to occur, and that the results of appraisal are communicated in appropriate ways to appropriate audiences. (The issue here concerns both the form(s) of the communication(s) and the kind of information communicated.) As part of this, a climate of trust, support and openness must be established in which innovation may be encouraged and in which the learning needs of teachers as well as children must be considered (see Chapters 1 and 4). The assumption is that the central purpose of appraisal is the professional development of teachers and that the central goal is

	Answerability (to parents)	Responsibility (to self and peers)	Strict Accountability (to LEA direct or via managers)
Maintenance	1: – Regular communication on individual children's progress (via written reports etc.); – Accounts of overall policy (via prospectus etc.). Explanation of curricular aims and methods; – Reports on general standards of performance, academic and other (via open days, speech days etc.); – Encouragement of better parental awareness of school's activities and endeavours (via ready access to classrooms and staff, atmosphere of open enquiries and discussion).	3: – Domestic monitoring of standards; – Regular review of staffing, curricula and teaching arrangements; – Promotion of good relationships with parents (via school social occasions etc.); – Promotion of good relationships with feeder and receiving (secondary) schools; – Promotion of good relationships with managers, advisers, and LEA as a whole.	5: – Observation of mandatory and constitutional procedures; – Meeting of centrally agreed specifications; – Openness to authorized visitation; – Readiness to justify curricular goals and methods and overall policies; – Readiness to account for pupil performance standards.
Problem-solving	2: – Notification to all parents of complaints procedures; – Prompt acknowledgement and investigation of parental complaints, confirmation of action taken; – Early disclosure to parents, where appropriate, of problems (i) relating to individual children (ii) involving wider issues.	4: – Screening of individual children at risk (via internal reporting, pupil records, tests, etc.); – Provision of remedial help to children in need; – Awareness of incipient points of weakness; – Anticipation of potential crises.	6: – Reporting of unresolved external complaints and grievances; – Reporting of unresolved internal difficulties; – Development of effective means to deal with problems arising.

NB: The entries above are not intended to be comprehensive. They are meant only to indicate possible expectations or demands in each category. They should *not* be taken as indicating policies which are necessarily feasible, desirable or deserving of priority at the school level.

Figure 7.1 Elements of school accountability (Source: McCormick, 1982 © The Open University) the enhancement of the quality of education for pupils in classrooms. We have discussed elsewhere in this book the skills necessary for leadership and the importance of consultation and collaboration of staff if they are to be committed to the enterprise.

REVIEW, DEVELOPMENT AND APPRAISAL

Headteachers must, by law, supervise and participate in any arrangements within an agreed national framework for the appraisal of the performance of teachers, ensure that they have access to advice and training appropriate to their needs and provide information about the work and performance of the staff where this is relevant to their future employment. Yet unless appraisal is a part of, rather than apart from, an agreed system of review and professional development it is unlikely to achieve its purposes of contributing to the professional growth of teachers, the management of the school or the quality of teaching and learning. Instead, it is likely to become a 'paper' exercise that may be used for strict accountability and public-relations purposes.

We have already asserted that appraisal is not new. Pupils, governors and parents – as well as members of the wider social and political community and teachers themselves – have been appraising teachers for years in largely informal ways. The difference in the 1990s is that appraisal is formalized, with purposes, processes and outcomes documented for professional development and external-accountability purposes. It is important, therefore, that this opportunity to celebrate professionalism in a more systematic and public way is grasped.

What kind of appraisal system, then, may contribute to a school's plans for INSET and staff development? What are the conditions necessary for establishing, implementing and monitoring the effectiveness of appraisal within review and development? Clearly, much may be learnt from the experiences of the six LEAs that piloted appraisal schemes between 1986 and 1989. These were summarized in the recommendations of the National Steering Group (NSG). Below are some extracts presented as a means of indicating the 'flavour'. First, the NSG affirmed the aims of appraisal as set out in the 1986 ACAS report:

AGREED PRINCIPLES

Nature and purpose. The Working Group understands appraisal not as a series of perfunctory periodic events, but as a continuous and systematic process intended to help individual teachers with their professional development and career planning, and to help ensure that the in-service training and deployment of teachers matches the complementary needs of individual teachers and the schools. An appraisal system will take into account the following matters:

i) Planning the induction of EG teachers and assessing their fitness to transfer to an MPG.

ii) Planning the participation of individual teachers in in-service training.

iii) Helping individual teachers, their head teachers and their employers to see when a new or modified assignment would help the professional development of individual teachers and improve their career prospects.

iv) Identifying the potential of teachers for career development, with an eye to their being helped by appropriate in-service training.

v) Recognition of teachers experiencing performance difficulty, the purpose being to provide help through appropriate guidance, counselling and training. Disciplinary procedures would remain quite separate, but might need to draw on relevant information from the appraisal records.

vi) Staff appointment procedures. The relevant elements of appraisal should be available to better inform those charged with the responsibility for providing references.

It will be seen that what the Working Group has in mind is a positive process, intended to raise the quality of education in schools by providing teachers with better job satisfaction, more appropriate in-service training and better planned career development based upon more informed decisions.

It would appear that negative associations (where appraisal is perceived as a means of 'weeding out' poor teachers) are ill-founded. Indeed, one of the pilot LEAs, Somerset, named its scheme 'Review and Development', and was clear about the resulting individual professional and institutional benefits (Figure 7.2).

Most readers will already know or have access to the detailed recommendations of the NSG and their own LEA responses to these. We will not, therefore, repeat them in detail. However, it may be useful to outline the key elements and stages of appraisal, the recommended appraisal cycle, and the benefits claimed for appraisal in order to proceed to an examination of these and suggestions for in-school review and development.

```
┌─────────────────────────────────────────────┐
│            WHAT ARE THE                     │
├─────────────────────────────────────────────┤
│          BENEFITS OF REVIEW                 │
├─────────────────────────────────────────────┤
│           & DEVELOPMENT?                    │
└─────────────────────────────────────────────┘
```

FOR THE TEACHER

- better understanding of the job
- improved feedback and recognition
- regular review of INSET needs
- increased accuracy of references
- greater awareness of career development factors
- support in work related issues
- greater job satisfaction

FOR THE SCHOOL

- school aims and individual staff aims coordinated
- priorities clarified and determined
- staff clarity about responsibilities
- professional development of management
- school needs met through target setting
- improved communication
- greater exchange of ideas
- a more supportive environment

Figure 7.2 What are the benefits of review and development? (Source: Somerset LEA, 1987)

KEY ELEMENTS

Who should Appraise?

The headteacher should decide who should appraise each teacher in a school. Normally, this will be the 'line manager'. Whilst this appears to be a managerial model of appraisal, it is perfectly possible within this to ensure, for example, a 'negative preference' system in which appraisees are able to exercise a choice of appraiser from within a panel. Additionally, the information or data discussed within an appraisal interview may consist of self-appraisal, peer observations of classroom action, etc.

What should be Appraised?

Appraisal should clearly be based upon a teacher's (or headteacher's) job description. However, the central focus of all teacher appraisals should be teaching performance in the classroom.

What are the Key Components in an Appraisal System?

1. *The initial meeting*   The initial meeting between the appraiser and the appraisee is to clarify the purposes and to identify areas of work on which the appraisal might concentrate; to consider the teacher's job description; agree arrangements for classroom observation, data-collection methods and timetable of events.
2. *Self-appraisal*   (By the appraisee.) All teachers will be expected to reflect systematically on their work.
3. *Classroom observation*   (For teachers.) There should be at least two sessions of classroom observation taking at least one and a half hours in total. The appraisee must give a full briefing to the appraiser before the observation and feedback by the appraiser must be given within two days of the observation.
4. *Information collection*   Appraisers should conduct a review of other relevant information, e.g. the work of pupils and information about duties outside the classroom and school.
5. *The appraisal interview*   This should provide an opportunity for genuine dialogue and should be interruption free. Its purpose is to identify successes ('catch them being good'), agree areas of work to be developed and targets for action.
6. *The appraisal record*   The record of the appraisal should be prepared by the appraiser in consultation with the appraisee. This should then be subject to a further discussion aimed at a final, agreed document. The records will be kept by the headteacher and appraisee, with access available to the chief education officer on request. *This clearly raises problems of confidentiality*. Despite a further recommendation

by NSG that separate records of targets for professional development and training should be kept, the problem of access remains. Under local management of schools (LMS), for example, who can legitimately deny rights of access to the school governing body?

Despite the clarity of these organizational sequences, in Figure 7.3 there can be no assumption that the two central elements — classroom observation and the appraisal interview — will necessarily be able to be conducted with skill.

Figure 7.3 Review and development cycle, including classroom observation (Source: Somerset LEA, 1987)

CLASSROOM OBSERVATION

There are innumerable checklists of 'good practice' available, and this chapter contains suggestions for looking at classroom action systematically. It is important to remember, however, that where classroom observation leads to changes in classroom planning and teaching, this in itself will not necessarily result in 'improved' learning of pupils. Research has demonstrated that there are simply too many variables to draw a direct cause-and-effect relationship.

Nevertheless, it is reasonable to infer that the clearer the teacher is about his or her values, purposes and practices (and their place within the agreed school-curriculum development plans) the greater will be the opportunities for achieving a match between them. Apart from the 'technical' skills of observing (in an appraisal context) 'human-relating' skills are needed so that a climate of trust and understanding is able to be established in what for some teachers will be a relatively new situation of disclosure of practice.

THE APPRAISAL INTERVIEW

Similar human-relating skills are needed here too, within the three main elements of preparation, process and follow-up. Essentially, the appraisal interview should be set against a background of trust, mutual respect and agreed purposes. It must allow the appraisee and appraiser to review the past and the present, and to set priorities or targets for the future. By the end of the interview, an action plan should be agreed. In preparing for the interview, consideration needs to be given to the following questions (Day, Whitaker and Wren, 1987):

1. What is the purpose of the interview?
2. When will it be held?
3. Where will it be held?
4. What form will the interview take?
5. What questions will the appraiser ask?
6. What questions will the appraisee ask?
7. What other information, documentation etc might be required?
8. What do both participants hope to gain from the experience?
9. How will the interview end?
10. How long will the interview take?
11. How will the interview be recorded and what will happen to the interview notes?
12. How will the interview be followed up?

Additionally, and crucially, it is right for the appraisee to ask (*ibid.*):

What's in it for me?
- I should have a clear understanding of my job and how well I am doing it and of what is expected of me.
- I should feel secure in the knowledge that my talents are known, appreciated and exploited and that my weaknesses have been identified and constructive help has been offered to improve them.
- I should have discussed my future, including my ambitions and my career prospects, and have received guidance in achieving those aspirations.
- I should feel satisfied that all aspects of my work in and around the school have been discussed in a professional way.
- I should feel happy that everything discussed will be treated in confidence.

The implications for time and training were recognized and addressed by the NSG, for it must be assumed that the appraisal process will occur within the 1265 hours of work enshrined in teachers' conditions of service, and that not all appraisers or appraisees possess the skills necessary to engage in and monitor the effectiveness of appraisal systems.

In respect of the frequency of and the elements within appraisal, first, it is recommended that appraisal of teachers and headteachers should be conducted on a two-year cycle, with each successive two-year period treated as one appraisal programme. The intention here is that in each second year of the programme there will be a formal follow-up interview with the appraiser to, for example, discuss to what extent targets agreed in the preceding year have been reached. The notion of even an annual appraisal interview for all has been criticized (Eraut, 1989) on the grounds that it

- is too infrequent for monitoring
- is unnecessary for identifying low performing teachers
- is so frequent that it is likely to lapse into an expensive piece of bureaucratic tokenism after the first couple of years
- is unlikely to address the fundamental issues that ought to be faced in a quinquennial review
- is likely to be divorced from curriculum evaluation
- will divert resources away from staff development

The point here is that not all staff will have the same needs at the same time and, by inference, a 'good' school will be one in which needs are constantly reviewed, practice constantly challenged and support planned accordingly. This implies particular kinds of leadership and leadership values as described in Chapter 1. It is unlikely, then, that review, development and appraisal will be effective in a school that does not already foster openness, trust and collegiality among staff (Figure 7.4).

The Consortium of Teacher Appraisal Pilot Schemes in a progress report in May 1989 (NDC/SMT, 1989) emphasized the importance in its experience of

- *Consultation* and school self-review in planning for appraisal;
- *Climate setting* – 'If the degree of mutual trust and understanding is less than perfect then awareness raising has to begin by creating it';
- *Training* – 'There is wide agreement that both appraisees and appraisers need preparing for appraisal...experience strongly suggests a need for 'on the job assistance';
- *Ownership* – 'We are advocating an organisational framework which gives space for individuality and freedom to develop a variety of approaches to suit the climate, style and stage of development of each school';

- There should be an atmosphere of trust.
- Those involved need to be open-minded.
- The teacher's self-image is regarded as important. Appraisal should not imply a situation that is unpleasant, possesses psychological threat, and typically culminates in unrewarding consequences.
- The organizational climate needs to be positive.
- Appraisal systems need to be an integrated part of school development planning.
- Appraisal systems need to be designed and implemented through negotiation rather than imposition.
- Appraisal systems must be fair and perceived to be fair by all the parties involved.
- Appraisal systems must be economic in their use of resources (including teacher time and energy).
- Appraisal systems must ensure that tangible support for learning after appraisal is provided.
- Appraisal must begin and end with self-appraisal.

Figure 7.4 Organizational preconditions for successful implementation of appraisal

- *Job description* – 'job descriptions are necessary for agreement; negotiation is a creative process, especially where responsibilities are shared or overlap';
- *Classroom observation* – 'Prompt lists of criteria for effective teacher appraisal were developed, which later became an agreed basis for planning and feedback in teaching analysis'; and
- *Outcomes* – 'Absolute clarity about the uses that will be made of the outcomes of the process is vital for a confident start'.

In terms of the management of primary schools, the most important of these findings is 'ownership', for if teachers do not experience the reality as well as the rhetoric of this, then they are unlikely to commit themselves to an appraisal scheme. 'Ownership' implies *autonomy*.

TEACHER AUTONOMY

If the assumption is made that appraisal is a form of accountability, then

> Any genuine accountability procedure presupposes that the accountable subjects are capable of acting responsibly and autonomously. The imposition of external constraints and controls through external monitoring is inconsistent with a genuine accountability procedure.... The association between 'external monitoring' and 'accountability' is...an attempt to legitimate social control over the teaching profession, and to influence it through power-coercive rather than rational procedures.
> (Elliott, 1978)

This statement remains as true in the 1990s as it was in the 1970s and, while at school level appraisal may be negotiated within national and LEA agreed frameworks, in essence teachers' capability of acting responsibly and autonomously will be eroded unless teacher autonomy is built into the planning, organization, processes and evaluations of the appraisal system itself. It should be noted at this point that a distinction is being made between 'licence' – allowing complete freedom for teachers to do what they want, how they want, when they want, regardless of pupil or society – and 'autonomy' – self-government within an ethical framework. There is no suggestion that teachers should not be accountable to society but rather that appraisal systems should be devices that enhance teachers' abilities to act responsibly and autonomously, thus empowering them to be more accountable. One way of achieving this is through the use of a 'process' rather than a 'product' model for appraisal. The *product* model has been described as one in which

> the main value of the appraisal process lies in the value of the product it will generate. This product is, in the first instance, ...a new comprehensive and up-to-date information base on teacher performance for the use of LEAs and governing bodies (Joseph 1986). This information base will then be used to achieve the purposes of appraisal, namely to improve professional standards through recommendations as promotion, remediation or training.
> (Winter, 1989)

The author contrasts this (*ibid.*) with a *process* model in which

> the value resides in the process of carrying it out. It is the process itself which will result in professional development. Any outcomes are unique to the individual practitioner and the specific content. Whereas the product model seeks to generate authoritative ('accurate') *assessment* of teacher performance (so that learning experiences can be prescribed, subsequently, for the teacher) the process model seeks, in itself, to stimulate effective *learning* by the teacher. It would not generate 'information' *about* teachers' work, but *insight* for those teachers themselves to use in improving their work.

Underpinning both of these models are particular conceptions of teaching that must be made explicit in the formulation of any appraisal scheme. In America, Wise *et al.* (1984), as a result of an investigation of teacher-appraisal practices in 32 cities, also associated the type of teacher appraisal with conceptions of teaching itself. They suggested the existence of four basic views of teaching (and thus teachers) that are relevant to any discussion on appraisal and teacher autonomy. Teaching was viewed as either labour, a craft, a profession or an art. As labour, the teachers' role is to implement schemes designed, directed and monitored by external authorities who supervise and inspect. It would not be difficult to associate the introduction of the National Curriculum and the move in LEAs towards increasing monitoring and inspection with this. As a craft, it is assumed that there are specific, generalizable skills or competences defined by external authorities who monitor by periodic inspection. The introduction of a national or local appraisal system that included prescribed lists of competences associated with 'the good teacher' could be one expression of this view. In teaching as a profession it is assumed that teachers require a repertoire of skills that may be differentially applied according to the teacher's judgment. These skills and judgments will be self and peer developed and monitored. In teaching as an art, evaluation by self or peers relies upon holistic judgments that recognize the unpredictable, personalized nature of teaching. Clearly, the process model is user friendly, emphasizing the professional culture in which most teachers work — teaching as a profession or an art rather than a craft or labour —

whereas the product model reflects the managerial culture of those who are responsible for resourcing education. Both cultures would claim responsibility for ensuring quality education for pupils.

Contract making through negotiation and 'entitlements' could be expected to be essential features of the landscape of any review, development and appraisal system that valued teacher autonomy. Entitlements are not defined in any legalistic way but rather are concerned with responsibilities and answerabilities to a variety of 'audiences'. For example, it may be that in an appraisal scheme there are six main 'audiences' who may justifiably have entitlements (i.e. the teacher, the school, the governors, the children, the parents and the LEA). The organization and process of appraisal should, therefore, be based upon a consideration of the entitlements of each of these groups. Much of the writing and most of the legislation on appraisal is focused upon the entitlements of the last five of the groups. In an attempt to redress this imbalance, this chapter concentrates on entitlements for teachers. Below is a list illustrating some possible teacher entitlements. It is not intended to be definitive or comprehensive, although it attempts to reflect the principles embodied in the process model described. *Teachers are entitled to*

- consultation in the design, monitoring and evaluation phases of appraisal;
- full participation in the collection of data;
- quality time for appraisal from colleagues and with colleagues;
- appropriate training and development resources in support of appraisal outcomes for professional development;
- equal rights in judgments of self, where others are involved in the appraisal;
- ownership of the appraisal process;
- time and support for training in and the implementation of self and peer-appraisal; and
- access to critical friends of their choice.

In order to operationalize such entitlements, it will be necessary for managers to engage in 'contracting'. 'Contracting', like 'entitlements', is not intended to be a legalistic process. 'Agreements' (a softer, more humane word than contracts) are, of course, often made informally between teachers and, increasingly now, more formally under 'school development plans'. Many teachers will have experienced the value of being able to share thoughts, practices and feelings with one or more trusted colleagues. The importance of agreeing entitlements is such, however, that it may be necessary to document them for use as *aides-mémoire*. Written or at least explicit verbal contracts can do much to clarify mutual expectations as to goals and methods. In other words, the contract needs to be explicit. Although writing in the context of interviewing, Cormier and Cormier (1979) outlined what could well serve as the basic features of such a contract:

- The contract should be negotiated, not proclaimed, by the partners involved — that is the head, staff and governors.
- The contract should be clear to all involved parties. They should know what appraisal is about.
- Some kind of oral or written commitment to the contract should be obtained.
- The contract should be reviewed as the parties progress, and revised if necessary.

One practical example of contracting is the use of action planning. Action planning is the process of helping a colleague or colleagues to think constructively about professional and curriculum concerns by supporting and challenging them through conversation. The helper's main task is to listen and question critically his or her colleagues whilst they

1. explore concerns;
2. focus on a specific aspect or problem;
3. consider a range of ways of looking at the problem;
4. construct a statement of intent;
5. identify and set goals;
6. generate and analyse ways of achieving those goals; and
7. plan a precise programme of action.

The task may be organized in a series of partnerships so that when the process is complete the partner is then in the position to

- implement the programme of action; and
- monitor and evaluate the programme and its outcome.

Figure 7.5 provides a framework for undertaking this.

WHOLE-SCHOOL REVIEW

The next section of this chapter describes briefly three approaches to whole-school review that provide frameworks for action that, in different

Task:			
Goal(s):			
Timescale:			
Start date:	Completion date:		
Action steps (including provisional times and timings)	Own strengths	Sources of resistance	Strategies
1.			
2.			
3.			
4.			
5.			
6.			
7.			
8.			

Figure 7.5 Action-planning contract

ways, may be seen as attempting to fulfil these criteria. These are as follows:

1. Local-authority self-evaluation/appraisal schemes.
2. *Guidelines for the Review and Internal Development of Schools* (McMahon, Bolam and Holly, 1984).
3. *Making School-Centred INSET Work* (Easen, 1985).

While none of these would claim to be perfect, each offers schools a practical means of establishing and implementing evaluation within the context of a professional development policy.

Local-Authority Schemes

The first thing to note here is that, though the set of guidelines or checklists that make up the schemes are often the result of negotiation between LEA and teacher representatives, the idea has come from the LEA itself. In some LEAs participation in the scheme is obligatory, in others voluntary. In the former case this usually entails formal report to the school governors and the LEA itself. While this holds out the possibility of LEA support in remedying needs identified as a result of the process, it is clear that both professional and contractual accountability are being served.

Given the number of schools in an LEA, and the finite human and financial resources available to provide appropriate support for them, the value of such self-review schemes must be limited. Additionally, the checklists themselves may not be appropriate to the needs of every school – more often than not teachers (other than headteachers) have not been involved in their design. On the other hand, some of these schemes do recognize implicitly that review that is purely by self is limited, and promote the use of advisers/inspectors or others as 'auditors' who discuss or check the validity of the findings and reports. This raises issues of confidentiality and control of information, and may lead to a rhetoric rather than a reality of evaluation. Perhaps a more 'neutral' auditor of reports may be a colleague from a nearby school, teachers' centre, university or institute of higher education. Many of these schemes have been surveyed (G. Elliott, 1981; 1982), and the list below (ILEA, 1983) provides an illustration of the main headings posed in one such scheme:

1. The children, their parents, the governors and the community.
2. Teaching organization – school staff – responsibility structure – non-teaching staff – staff development.
3. The curriculum – continuity – assessment – extending the curriculum.
4. Organization and management.
5. The building and the general environment.
6. Questions for the individual teacher to ask him or herself.
7. Questions for the headteacher to ask.
8. The future.
9. The acid test. (Would I recommend a colleague to apply for a post at this school? Would I recommend this school to friends for their children?)

Checklists as summarized by the headings above, though useful, are almost always value-laden and their sheer numbers and comprehensiveness can often be daunting for schools. First teachers have to read, digest and interpret meanings, and then select – and there is little, if any, guidance as to how to engage, as a staff, in the process of school self-review. The next two schemes to be described attempt to avoid these problems by concentrating on providing guidelines not only for the organization and content but also for the processes of self-review (see Fig. 7.6).

The GRIDS Scheme

This scheme is the result of a project established by the Schools Council (later reconstituted as the Schools Curriculum Development Committee) which 'concentrated on assisting whole staffs to carry out a systematic self-review of policy and practice at their school' (McMahon et al. 1984). It is important to note that the project involved collaboration between fifteen primary schools in five LEAs and a university school of education. The result is materials which contain detailed advice to heads and senior staff on how to conduct a school review and development exercise. One important distinguishing feature is that initially staff are recommended to take a broad rather than detailed look at the school, and 'on the basis of this identify one or two areas that they consider to be priorities for specific review and development, tackle these first, evaluate what they have achieved and then select another priority' (McMahon et al., 1984).

The following extract from GRIDS highlights the key principles underlying the scheme, the importance of the coordinator's role in managing the process of innovation and change and the outline stages of development:

(a) the aim is to achieve internal school development and not to produce a report for formal accountability purposes;
(b) the main purpose is to move beyond the review stage into development for school improvement;
(c) the staff of the school be consulted and involved in the review and development process as much as possible;
(d) decisions about what happens to any information or reports produced should rest with the teachers and others concerned;
(e) the head and teachers should decide whether and how to involve the other groups in the school, e.g. pupils, parents, advisers, governors;
(f) outsiders (e.g. external consultants) should be invited to provide help and advice when this seems appropriate;
(g) the demands made on key resources like time, money and skilled personnel should be realistic and feasible for schools and LEAs.

(Ibid.)

The authors of GRIDS recognize the problematic nature of review and development work by emphasizing the importance of the provision of a coordinator (whether it be the head or not) whose principal functions are

```
┌─────────────────────────────┐
│ Stage 1: getting started    │
│ 1. Decide whether this method│
│    is appropriate for your  │
│    needs.                   │
│ 2. Consult the staff.       │
│ 3. Appoint a school         │
│    coordinator.             │
└─────────────────────────────┘
```

Stage 5: overview and restart
1. Decide whether the changes should be made permanent.
2. Decide whether and how to restart.
3. Restart.

Stage 2: initial review
1. Plan the initial review.
2. Collect information.
3. Survey staff opinion.
4. Identify priority areas.

Stage 4: action for development
1. Check on the implications of the development plan.
2. Decide what INSET opportunities should be made available.
3. Action.

Stage 3: specific review
1. Plan the specific review.
2. Identify present policy/practice.
3. Check on its implementation and effectiveness.
4. Draw up recommendations for development.

Figure 7.6 The internal review and development process (Source: Skilbeck, 1982)

to provide moral and intellectual support as well as to be responsible for progression and continuity. Eight essential tasks are outlined. The coordinator should (*ibid.*)

1. try to ensure that the teachers and others involved feel that the review and development exercise is significant, that the consultation is genuine and that their recommendations will not be ignored;
2. explain the process clearly to the staff at the outset;
3. sustain pace and momentum by helping teachers to draw up realistic timetables at each stage and then checking that deadlines are kept;

4. provide strategic advice where necessary, e.g. how to collect information, what criteria might be used for assessment;
5. keep a check on what is happening at each stage and advise specific review and development teams if they meet difficulties, e.g. if they cannot decide on a focus for the specific review, fail to meet deadlines, find that some of their recommendations are not feasible;
6. contact 'outsiders', e.g. LEA advisers, teachers from other schools, college lecturers, who might be brought in to provide advice and help at different stages or to organize training courses;
7. try to ensure that the review and development exercise is both rigorous and systematic; and
8. make some evaluation of the effectiveness of the GRIDS method and whether it achieved what was wanted; the end of the first twelve months may be an appropriate moment.

As with some of the LEA schemes, the project points to the usefulness of outside assistance, but in this case outsiders are called in to assist at appropriate points in the process of the work itself. Oldham LEA, which adopted a GRIDS review policy for all its primary schools with a seconded headteacher acting as coordinator, began in 1988 to develop a model that represents one of the few documented attempts to link teacher appraisal to school-based review and development (Figure 7.7).

Making School-Centred INSET Work

A third approach to review is contained in materials entitled *Making School-Centred INSET Work* (Easen, 1985). These are intended 'to provide practical evidence and support for any teachers who wish to work together in their schools in order to review and develop their pupils' experience of the curriculum', and are aimed also at 'those who are expected to fulfil a "leadership" or "consultancy" function'. As with GRIDS, the ideas and materials were developed in collaboration with teachers in a number of LEAs. Here, however, the similarity ends. The aims are (*ibid.*) to

1. increase your understanding of your own feelings, thoughts and actions in relation to your activity as a teacher within your school;
2. develop your repertoire of choices for handling both the educational experience provided for the pupils in your school and your relationships with your colleagues;

184 *Managing Primary Schools in the 1990s*

Figure 7.7 A model for teacher appraisal linked to school-based review and development (Source: Oldham LEA, 1988)

3. try out for yourself some of these new ways of handling your professional life; and
4. make decisions about what 'works' and makes sense in relation to your particular school.

Through a series of writings and structured activities, the authors provide experiential and reflective frameworks for coping with the challenges of school life, curriculum change (cooperation and conflict), identifying and tackling school problems, collecting information in classrooms, and personal and interpersonal change. The materials are designed to enable each school to work at its own pace on the content it has chosen to take account of its own priorities. Head, senior staff (there is a guide for group leaders) and teachers can therefore 'dip in' as appropriate to particular parts. Each chapter is organized into reading and practical-activity sections. These activities focus on a range of issues concerned with, for example, counselling; creating a less critical atmosphere; classroom observation and analysis; breaking down a problem into manageable parts; problem-formulation; feelings engendered by change; humour to relieve tension; effective meetings; etc. While the materials are very different from those of GRIDS and apparently not so straightforward, they do provide uniquely documented insights into the intricate processes of change and changing in which all those engaged in review and development will be involved.

MANAGING THE PROCESS

Regardless of the particular scheme adopted, the head or deputy who is managing the process must lay firm foundations. Not only must the school climate be right but staff must also feel secure, and there must be practical support. Figure 7.8 provides a summary of some of the principal issues.

Even then, and regardless of which scheme is adopted, used or modified, success will depend on a number of 'human' factors. Although these have been discussed elsewhere in this book, it is worth restating some of them in the context of this chapter. Clearly it is important for head and staff to agree on the timing of the exercise (the organization of the school needs to be adaptive and the staff receptive). It is important to allocate human and other resources over an agreed time period to the project as a high priority (this may involve releasing some teachers from other commitments for the duration of the project). It is also necessary for the work to

Aims	Reasons
1. Familiarization with the notion of evaluation	To gain and share information To lower anxieties To generate commitment
2. Establishment of supportive evaluation environments	To facilitate changes in attitudes, values, role definitions and self-images. To foster cooperation
3. Provision of physical and psychological space	To demonstrate support To provide time and somewhere to meet, discuss and work.

Figure 7.8 Preparing for evaluation (Source: Davis, 1981)

be seen by the teachers as relevant to perceived need; feasible as well as desirable; uncomplicated but significant; and of ultimate if not immediate benefit to teaching and learning in the classroom. Without the commitment of the staff no amount of careful planning and organization, and monitoring and support, can ensure success. Such commitment is likely to arise in schools where there are a climate and an organizational structure that offer opportunities not only for inter-staff development that focuses on identified school needs but also for individual members of staff to reflect systematically on individual needs – aspects of the teaching and learning in their own classrooms. This too has implications for those in leadership roles, and the next part of this chapter discusses these.

CLASSROOM-BASED SELF-APPRAISAL

'[All] teachers need help in assessing their own professional preformance and in building on their strengths and working on the limitations so identified' (HMSO, 1985). This statement implies not only that teachers have a responsibility for evaluating their teaching but that they also need help in doing so. However, if school-based evaluation is perceived by some teachers as threatening, then evaluation of individual teachers is likely to be much more so. Even self-evaluation is potentially threatening since it inevitably involves self-disclosure, and this is not always welcomed.

The problems of increasing knowledge about practice have been highlighted by Keddie (1971) in her distinction between teacher as educationist and teacher as practitioner: 'while, therefore, some educational aims may be formulated by teachers as educationists, it will not be surprising if "doctrine" is contradicted by "commitments" which arise in the situation in which they must act as teachers'. And yet from time to time it is essential that life in classrooms is systematically evaluated in some or all of its aspects. Otherwise, curriculum and staff development will always be based on what people say about education and this may not always be the same as what actually occurs.

The justification for ensuring that teachers evaluate their own classroom practice systematically from time to time in order to increase professional effectiveness is based on three assumptions (Day, 1981):

1. That teachers cannot be developed (by others) but only given opportunities to develop (for themselves).
2. That effective learning arises in response to the identification and confrontation of 'real' questions by the learner.
3. That decisions about teaching should stem from reflection on the effects of previous actions.

The problem is often that, while teachers have the capacity to engage in self-appraisal, they are constrained in the extent to which they may do so by the following:

1. *Practical factors* Such as time, energy, skills and resources.
2. *Sociological factors* Teachers operate within a framework of norms, expectations and values that are often at an implicit level. For example, a new teacher very quickly develops assumptions about practice which allow him or her to cope with the complexities of teaching and being a member of staff. However, since it is relatively unusual for these to be made explicit or tested, the possibilities for evaluating those assumptions that underpin the planning and practice of his or her teaching are minimal.
3. *Psychological factors* It is natural to want to live in a world that is constant, that we can control and that does not threaten our self-esteem. It is not always in our best interests to 'probe' ourselves too much.

There may well be, therefore, a difference between what people say (their intentions or aspirations) and what they do (their practice). It is worth considering the possibility that exhaustive discussions designed to produce documents on the curriculum, aims and objectives, and even job descriptions, may produce a rhetoric that is, in varying degrees, inconsistent with the reality of what actually happens in classrooms and schools. It may be much more productive to base such discussions on shared observed and observable experiences of classroom teaching.

Let us assume that most teachers have 'a capacity for autonomous professional self-development through systematic self-study, through the study of the work of other teachers and through the testing of ideas by classroom research procedures' (Stenhouse, 1975), and that while many already engage in self-study this is not as systematic as it might be. We have considered briefly some of the reasons for this. While most teachers may be described as connoisseurs, able with experience to distinguish, for example, between the significance of different sets of teaching and learning practices, or to recognize and appreciate different facets of their teaching and pupils' learning, they may not find it so easy to be critics who 'disclose the qualities of events or objects that connoisseurship perceives' (Eisner, 1979).

The role of the head is crucial here, for it is he or she who must provide opportunities for the development of the connoisseur who is also a critic. Ways in which this may be achieved have been described throughout this book in relation to styles of leadership conducive to promoting curriculum and staff development. Although the ethos or climate of the school will go a long way to minimizing the psychological and sociological constraints described above, it is worth remembering that 'the road to educational critique' (MacDonald, 1978) may go through several stages and take many years to travel.

At some stage, however, the practical constraints must also be tackled — and it may be argued that this should come sooner rather than later. Heads must provide opportunities for deliberate reflection on classroom practice. The way in which they might provide these opportunities is through their own knowledge of

1. the procedures by which teachers may self-review;
2. techniques that may be used in monitoring classrooms; and
3. the means by which teachers may be provided with the moral and intellectual support necessary for self-review.

SELF-REVIEW PROCEDURES

The six questions in Figure 7.9 have been identified by teachers themselves as being essential for self-evaluation. While these are not listed in order of priority they do focus attention on the three central elements of classroom life — the pupils, the teacher and the task. It is worth noting that while these questions inevitably give rise to others (for example, 'How do I find out what the pupils were doing?' or 'What did I intend to do?'), they are designed also to ensure that the teacher moves through four distinct and necessary phases:

1. *Description* — identifying and selecting events.
2. *Interpretation* — assessing the consequences of these events.
3. *Judgment* — assessing how far these events were worth while.
4. *Decision* — accepting responsibility for 1–3 and planning for future action.

The importance of beginning with description cannot be over-emphasized since it ensures that any bias in interpretation, judgments and decisions can be checked against available observed action rather than assumptions or expectations or memories a teacher might have about the action.

The problems of potential bias will be considered later in the chapter, but before this it is worth while exploring evaluation procedures a little further.

Action Research

In order for the teacher to answer the questions posed in Figure 7.9, it will be necessary for him or her to become engaged in action research, which has been defined as the 'study of a social situation with a view to

```
THE PUPILS
What did they actually do?
What were they learning?
          ↕
How worth while was it?  ←——→  What do I intend to do now?
          ↕
THE TEACHER
What did I do?
What did I learn?
```

Figure 7.9 Six essential self-evaluation questions (Source: The Open University, 1980, Block 1)

improving the quality of action within it', and as providing 'the necessary link between self-evaluation and professional development' (J. Elliott, 1981). Its concern is to 'promote improvement in practice and improvement in understanding simultaneously' (McCormick and James, 1983). While this movement originated in America, it has grown in England in the last 25 years largely through the efforts of Lawrence Stenhouse (1975, 1979), John Elliott (1981; Ford Teaching Project, 1975) and in Australia through the work of Kemmis *et al.* (1981), who describe the process of action research as follows:

> In practice, the process begins with a *general idea* that some kind of improvement or change is desirable. In deciding just where to begin in making improvements, one decides on a *field of action*...where the battle (not the whole war) should be fought. It is a decision on where it is possible to have an impact. The general idea prompts a *'reconnaissance'* of the circumstances of the field, and fact-finding about them. Having decided on the field and made a preliminary reconnaissance, the action researcher decides on a *general plan* of action. Breaking the general plan down into achievable steps, the action researcher settles on *the first action step*. Before taking this first step the action researcher becomes more circumspect, and devises a way of *monitoring* the effects of the first action step. When it is possible to maintain fact-finding by monitoring the action, the first step is taken. As the step is implemented, new data starts coming in and the effects of the action can be described and *evaluated*. The general plan is then revised in the light of the new information about the field of action and the second action step can be planned along with the appropriate monitoring procedures. The second action step is then implemented, monitored and evaluated; and the spiral of action, monitoring, evaluation and replanning continues.

J. Elliott (1981) argues that the 'general idea' should be allowed to shift and that 'reconnaissance' should involve analysis in addition to fact-finding. The model he presents is too elaborate to present here, but – as with others introduced in this chapter – should form essential reading for all those with responsibility for promoting the professional development of staff. For the present purposes, however, and before moving on to discuss some of the techniques for collecting classroom observations (as a part of action research) that may be used, here is some practical advice on getting started:

The WHY of observation   Decide what is the purpose. Is it primarily to solve a problem or to check on the effectiveness of a particular strategy or aspect of curriculum content?

The WHAT of observation This will be determined by the teachers' own interests, needs or concerns.

The WHO of observation Teachers should beware of being over-ambitious. For example, it may be sensible, if pupils are the focus, to observe one pupil or a small group; or if observing self it may be wise to focus on one aspect of teacher talk (e.g. questioning). Figure 7.10 shows an example of a plan for investigating an aspect of teaching.

The WHEN of observation Observation must be built in as a part of the teaching plan, and short concentrated periods of time for this *standing outside* actual contact with pupils may be more practical than long periods when the teacher is likely to be distracted.

The HOW of observation Examples of techniques for collecting observations will be given later in the chapter. It is equally important, however, to find ways of organizing the activity itself so that time and energy can be focused in support of the commitment; and frameworks for recording the information gained from classroom observations must also be devised.

While knowledge of evaluation procedures is important, so also is knowledge of monitoring techniques that will enable teachers to collect, process and reflect upon classroom action.

CLASSROOM MONITORING TECHNIQUES

J. Elliott (1981) has summarized many of the monitoring techniques that are easily available to most teachers, and makes the point that they need to be sufficiently flexible to cater for evidence of the unintended as well as the intended. The list below is our own summary, and while the headings are similar to those used by J. Elliott, the descriptions are our own unless otherwise indicated.

Document analysis Teaching plans, syllabi, written work may be analysed.

Impressionistic diaries Of 'observations, feelings, reactions, interpretations, reflections, hunches, hypotheses, and explanations' (Kemmis *et al.*, 1981).

Analytic memos These are short periodic analyses which consist of 'one's systematic thinking about the evidence one has collected' (J. Elliott, 1981).

> Step 1: Choosing the investigation.
> Step 2: Asking 'What learning opportunities am I trying to provide?'
> Step 3: Deciding on the questions you want to ask.
> Step 4: Designing the investigation.
>   (a) What data do I need to collect?
>   (b) What should be the timing and circumstances of the investigation?
>   (c) What techniques should I use?
> Step 5: Carrying out the investigation.
> Step 6: Analysing the data.
> Step 7: Reflecting on the analysis.

Figure 7.10 Investigating an aspect of teaching (Source: The Open University, 1980, Block 3)

Lesson profiles For example, to record teacher and pupil activity at ten-minute intervals (Walker and Adelman, 1975).

Checklists, questionnaires, inventories These 'allow one to quantify people's observations, interpretations and attitudes' (J. Elliott, 1981) and should be used, if at all, as a means of checking against qualitative judgments.

The running commentary Here the teacher who is observing an individual or group should write down as much of what he or she hears and observes as possible. This is useful for short periods of observation of at least five minutes.

The shadow study This is as above, but the recorder is an observer from outside the classroom.

Audio/video-recordings and transcripts Potentially videotape is a most useful means of collecting verbal and non-verbal information. Almost certainly, however, it requires another person to be present and may, initially, cause a distraction in the classroom. However, used sympathetically and over a period of time it can provide by far the richest mine of information (Day, 1981). Audio-tape, on the other hand, is easy to use and, though transcription is time-consuming and care has to be taken in attempting to record a group of more than three or four children at work, it provides extremely valuable information.

Interviewing It is very useful to interview pupils for their responses to a lesson and even more so to have a sympathetic outsider or 'critical friend' (Habermas, 1972) do this. The power and authority of a teacher figure must be taken into account when judging the authenticity of pupils' responses, and it is worth while for any outsider to be able to assure them that while general feedback of information to the teacher is necessary, individual comments will remain confidential.

Use of an outside observer (who may be a colleague) A brief example of this is provided later in this chapter. Given a trusting and sympathetic relationship, this outside resource or 'third eye' can be invaluable.

Case studies These essentially provide a set of reflections on the processes of investigation, the results specific to it and general issues that arise from it. In the context of the individual and the school, such documents may provide reference points for future as well as past work.

As far as possible the techniques used ought to enable one to look at what is going on from a variety of angles or points of view. This is particularly important to those engaged in what is for the most part a qualitative enterprise; for while there is no notion of achieving 'objective' views of classrooms in the narrow, quasi-scientific sense, it is important to provide a subjectively reasoned picture that is internally valid. One means of achieving this is to check 'results' with a colleague and/or pupils, or invite a colleague into the classroom to help decide whether teaching intentions are matched by teaching practices. Another more complicated but potentially more satisfactory and satisfying technique is that of *triangulation*. This is essentially the collecting of 'observations or accounts of a situation (or some aspect of it) from a variety of angles or perspectives and then comparing and contrasting them' (J. Elliott, 1981). So pupils, observer and teacher may comment on the same piece of teacher talk, for example, and these comments may be checked for match and mismatch. An added dimension is that these accounts themselves may be checked against the recording of the teacher talk.

PROVIDING MORAL AND INTELLECTUAL SUPPORT THROUGH 'CRITICAL FRIENDSHIP'

It has been implicit throughout this chapter that teachers who are engaged in review, development and appraisal need support, not only at the beginning but also throughout the process. Self-disclosure may involve considerable anxiety for the teacher and the sympathetic support of colleague(s) must be built in from the beginning. It may also be that the teacher will require practical support (assistance in processing data, use of resources, time, etc.) and intellectual support (advice on the design of an observation schedule, the interpretation of a transcript, etc.). The likelihood is that the teacher will also need further support in acquiring new skills and knowledge or modifying current skills.

While in-service and consultancy support may be available from the LEA, and this must not be under-estimated, it is likely that colleagues in the school will ultimately be the most important single factor in providing mutual support.

'Critical friendships' may be defined as practical partnerships entered voluntarily, based upon a relationship between equals and rooted in a common task or shared concern. They can be a means of establishing links with one or more colleagues to assist in processes of learning and change so that ideas, perceptions, values and understandings may be shared through the mutual disclosures of feelings, hopes and fears. Critical friendships can serve to decrease isolation and increase the possibilities of moving through stages of reflection to confrontation of thinking and practice. Reflection in itself will not necessarily lead to self-confrontation, and self-confrontation may need skilled support to be translated into new action. If one is on one's own, 'one will only see what one is ready to see; one will only learn what is on the edge of the consciousness of what one already knows' (Thompson, 1984). In terms of the appraisal of classroom practice, for example, a critical friend may establish and sustain a responsive, mutually acceptable dialogue about classroom events and their context. Through this, situations will be created in which the teacher is obliged to reflect systematically on practice.

The results of this kind of interaction, if successful, will be more effective teaching standards. But the process will also generate documented information that may be used by teachers as part of an appraisal interview and as a means of helping the representatives of their employers (whether LEA advisers/inspectors or HMI) who might be visiting the school for the purpose of evaluation or inspection to gain an informed view and context for their own interpretations and judgments. Below is a summary of some of the advantages and disadvantages of the use of a critical friend:

Advantages of Critical Friends (from Inside or Outside the School)

Providing they are skilled and trusted, they can

1. lighten the energy and time loads for observation (enable teacher to

carry on teaching, maintain his or her duties), often relieving the teacher of the burden of collecting and analysing his or her own data;
2. be used to check against bias in self-reporting and to assist in more lengthy processes of self-evaluation;
3. offer, where appropriate, comparisons with classroom practice elsewhere;
4. move freely and see the children working in different situations;
5. focus in on an agreed issue or area of concern, e.g. small-group task work;
6. provide post-lesson critical dialogues;
7. act as a resource the teacher may use at times appropriate to the needs he or she perceives.
8. In addition, children may be more open with outsiders (e.g. in interviews).

Disadvantages

If they are unskilled and not trusted, then (Day, Whitaker and Wren, 1987)

1. unless a regular visitor, their interpretations may be out of context (observers will have their own biases!);
2. children may be less open with outsider (e.g. in interviews); and
3. unless they become a regular part of the classroom over time, then children and teacher may react to their presence in such a way as to cause untypical behaviour.

In addition,

4. the exercise is time consuming − observer and teacher must spend time together before and after the work observed to negotiate and fulfil the contract; and
5. skilled observers are difficult to find!

Whether teachers invite colleagues from in school or someone from outside (e.g. from a local higher-education institution) will be a matter for their discretion. However, it may be worth noting that some research (Hopkins, 1986) suggests that

> It is preferable from the user's point of view to learn from a peer far enough from home so that: (1) asking for help can't be interpreted as a

self-indictment; (2) invidious competition and comparison is reduced; (3) the ideas can be changed with impunity; (4) they can be credited to their new user.

Whatever the choice, elements in successful sharing will be

1. a willingness to share;
2. a recognition that sharing involves

    (a) disclosure, and
    (b) opening oneself to the possibility of feedback;

3. a recognition that disclosure and feedback imply being prepared to consider changing;
4. a recognition that changing is sometimes

    (a) threatening (to self-esteem and current practice),
    (b) difficult (it requires time, energy, new skills), and
    (c) satisfying;

5. a recognition that the degree to which people are willing to share may, therefore, be restricted.

Collegiality, contract-making, entitlements and critical friendships are all elements within review, development and appraisal schemes that support rather than erode teacher autonomy and that encourage staff to respond to new demands. They reinforce a sense of responsibility by affirming confidence in teachers' professionalism.

8
DEVELOPING RELATIONSHIPS WITH PARENTS AND GOVERNORS

Our final chapter provides some suggestions on how the head can communicate with those people who are external to the school but likely to have some form of relationship with, and increasingly influence upon, the people working in it. It can no longer be assumed that the public will support a school simply because the building exists. Today, schools must gain support through good performance and a well-thought-out information service. The head cannot be the sole spokesperson for the school. The entire staff, pupils and the school itself must all become vehicles of information to all groups associated with supporting the life of the school. The successful primary head is the one who knows how to capitalize on the interest of all those involved with the school and to turn their involvement into a positive force in the school. Developing relationships is all about the head and staff understanding the roles, expectations and needs of all those who make up the wider community associated with any single school community.

While it is true that the head must take into account both the resources available, and the expressed needs of others in the home–school partnership, it is also true that effective management requires not only a knowledge and understanding of what 'is' but also a clear and acute vision of what 'might' be – of what is desired. Without such a vision, school management is likely to degenerate into little more than a set of techniques designed to minimize difficulties and lead to a less hectic life. An essential ingredient for the effective development of relationships with parents, therefore, is a clear and articulate philosophy of education with respect to the desired relations between the home and the school, for without this the head has no criteria by which to decide between opposing possibilities.

For this reason, it is important that both heads and teachers identify possible philosophies of home–school relationships, and make conscious choices between these on the basis of some clear and coherent set of values. Unless primary heads know where they stand and can communicate their ideas successfully, it is unlikely that they will do more than confuse others.

There is no set of clear and unequivocal 'answers' to major questions on how to work effectively with parents and governors because the solution to a problem has to be found in that situation and not imported from outside that school's environment. It is a skill required by the head, as leader, to have the insight to be able to identify the most important factors in a situation and to be able to relate these factors in such a way that an answer is found for that situation.

THE ROLE OF THE PRIMARY HEAD

The position of the primary head in the UK remains a powerful one, in spite of the many social, political and economic changes that have taken place during the last two decades. The changes have made the role of the present-day head a more demanding and complex one than ever before, and have highlighted the head's need to form and develop a whole range of relationships. Managing any relationship successfully requires considerable ability and a wide range of personal skills, particularly the ability to listen carefully and be sensitive to the needs of others.

The head is, in fact, at the centre of a web of relationships. Each member of the head's role set – governors, parents, teachers – has expectations as to how the head should perform the role. It is essential, therefore, that he or she should not only have thought through issues very carefully but also be efficient at communicating those thoughts to others and listening to their opinions and questions.

Since the late 1970s, primary heads have been led as a result of reports and circulars from the DES to question the nature of their role in relation to maintaining external relationships. The Great Debate initiated by the Prime Minister in 1976 gave rise to the notion that schools should be organized so as to provide a framework of consent and accountability. The message is clear – a head cannot run an effective school without taking into consideration the views of teachers, governors and parents. This demands a serious consideration of the role heads must play if they wish to retain the support of those with whom they have to work. To some heads this may seem a threat to their professional territory, and they may worry that influential minorities will begin to dominate schools and undermine their efforts. Heads who have traditionally regarded themselves as the only influence over the curriculum and relationships with parents may well feel very threatened by the events of recent years. To ignore the consequences of the Education (No.2) Act 1986 and the Education Reform Act 1988 would be a major folly.

Heads ought to ask themselves, 'How can I gain the full support of the local community, parents and governors whose understanding of primary education may be outdated and ill informed?' and 'How can all those people who are in any way associated with this school share with me the responsibility of providing the best possible education for the children?' Primary schools in the final decade of the twentieth century have to be more open, accountable to and cooperative with the wide community, which may require some heads to change their attitudes towards the patterns of authority and influence that have long been established. The change has, in fact, been willed by the government and, although it may be difficult for some heads to accept in practice, there can be no avoiding the need for the head to examine methods of managing the school in order to discharge effectively all the responsibilities towards the parents and governors.

RELATIONSHIPS WITH PARENTS: SOME INITIAL CONSIDERATIONS

In formulating any policy concerning the relationship of the school to the parents of its pupils, and in implementing such a policy, heads and all staff must bear in mind a number of considerations, especially an awareness of the needs of others and possible resource implications.

Needs

Central to any consideration of home–school relations is the question of the needs of pupils, teachers and the community itself. These needs are important in at least two main ways. On the one hand, many of these needs are of considerable importance in providing objectives for the school – the school exists partly in order to go some way towards meeting the needs of pupils. On the other hand, the needs people have act as powerful motivators for them, influencing what they consider to be important, what is considered worth striving for and ways in which people react to various ideas. Without some understanding of how people are motivated it is difficult for the head to identify what are likely to be successful strategies and programmes in relating the school and the home.

An awareness of needs supplies, in a specific situation, a sort of checklist of questions that can be asked, with the purpose of sensitizing the head to what may be important dynamics of a situation. Thus, when faced with a 'difficult' parent, it is worth stopping to consider such questions as the following:

1. What need is this parent meeting in acting this way?
2. What needs am I meeting in acting as I am?
3. Has this parent needs in this situation that are obviously legitimate, and that I can assist in meeting?
4. Am I working with this parent in such a way that the parent is reassured about the school, and will be welcome on future occasions? Is the parent only likely to be welcome if certain approved behaviours are exhibited?

Any consideration of the needs and interests of children, parents, teachers and the community must take account of potential conflicts. Not all parents want the same things and some of them want conflicting things, e.g. different styles of classroom discipline. Within a single staffroom teachers will have different needs, interests and concerns. This is often expressed by heads as a worry about the motivation of staff. Whatever the cause, and whatever the form any differences may take, such potential conflicts make considerable demands on the skills, patience and sympathy of the head.

In planning to identify and meet the needs of parents it must be recognized that quite often teachers themselves, and the profession as a whole, have had a vested interest in establishing certain kinds of relationships with parents. This is often expressed by teachers as a fear of 'parent power'. So when there are discussions about the partnership between parents and teachers, there is not always the assumption that what is being talked about is an equal partnership.

It is important, in practice, to sort the various needs into an order of priority. Given that time is always a limited resource, it is essential that priorities be clearly established. Upon what basis can this reasonably be done? The great temptation is that heads will accept all needs as legitimate, but actually do what they would have done anyway – on the grounds that while all needs are legitimate, a certain set are either the most important, or the most readily met, or the most urgent. So, in practice, the good can indeed be the enemy of the best.

Resources

Any proposal to develop relationships with parents is likely to have resource implications — to involve the expenditure of some sort of resource. Typically, in schools, when we hear the word 'resource' we think first of money; but when considering home–school relationships there are more likely to be other resources of greater importance, for example, as follows:

Time A most valuable and very scarce resource. How much time is available? Where? Will they want to spend it in that way?

Goodwill Again a valuable resource, often not noticed until it is missing. This is related to the following:

Reputation If the head has a good reputation for meeting important needs, for being efficient and effective, then it is most likely that some innovation can take place. Innovation often involves asking other people to trust you as together you venture into the unknown. A reputation for usually being 'right' is a valuable start to people trusting you, although under some circumstances this can also work against the head!

People The most important resource of all. All who are to be involved must be seen very positively as resources that can be organized and developed, resources without which the programme cannot happen, and without which no leader can be effective. Careful consideration must be given not only to their needs but also to their relationships, hopes and aspirations. The success of a programme of home–school relationships will depend on the skill of the head to develop such a programme so that all the people involved continue to be willing participants.

ACTION STRATEGIES FOR DEVELOPING RELATIONSHIPS WITH PARENTS

Informing the Parents

Since the publication of the Plowden Report in 1967 (Central Advisory Council for Education (England)), primary schools have made great efforts to follow the recommendations by keeping parents better informed. After all, the advice from the DES over many years as to what schools ought to inform parents about, and how this may be attempted, it is indicative of present trends that it is now a statutory obligation for detailed written information about the school and each child's achievements in relation to the National Curriculum to be published annually. The East Sussex Accountability Project (Cleave, Jowett and Bate, 1982) suggests that many parents' views of school are based on misunderstanding, ignorance, fears and fantasies that can easily be increased rather than decreased by what teachers say and do! The researchers point out that most parents in their survey had no means of reassuring themselves that gloomy rumours about present-day education did not apply to their local school, while such false accusations only made teachers more defensive. The study emphasizes that what parents really want is more information on their child, the methods of teaching and classroom organization.

How does the head know the information provided by the school matches the needs of parents — tells them what they want to know? The head and staff must be conscious of the need to question parents on issues that affect the children's education. As well as the personal contact it may be appropriate for the school to produce a questionnaire for parents to complete about the practices employed within the school. Perhaps the parent governor could assist with the compilation of such a document. Only when genuine attempts have been introduced to investigate parental opinion thoroughly can the head begin to develop real and lasting home—school relationships. Some of the main strategies for informing parents are likely to be as follows:

The school brochure Don't just provide the minimum information that by law must be presented. Tell parents about such things as school finance, the powers of the governing body, the role of the parent governor, the National Curriculum, how children and work are organized, what is kept in children's records, and the full yearly programme of school events. The brochure should be available to all parents and the wider community. Heads should make it available in local libraries, clinics, churches and community centres.

The newsletter A monthly newsletter can help the parents make sense of what the children may tell them about various class or school activities. In addition it can provide up-to-date announcements about meetings, courses staff are attending, parents' functions and particular achievements. It can also contain children's poems, imaginative stories and accounts of recent happenings. An advertisement column may add to its interest.

The noticeboard This will probably serve many of the functions of the newsletter but be big enough to contain examples of children's original art and story work. There may be enough space to give greater details on classroom organization and teaching methods. Some space can be left for parents to use to advertise local events.

Parents' meetings Relate these to the children's education but before beginning find out what the parents would like to discuss. Don't make the meetings too large. An informal atmosphere gives parents and teachers time to talk about individual children. Avoid outside speakers – plan workshop sessions when parents have an opportunity to participate in practical learning situations similar to those undertaken by the children. Involve the children where appropriate – they can be a great help with necessary explanations. Try to provide some written statement for parents to take away to read at leisure. If morning or afternoon meetings are held, provide a crèche for pre-school children in order to maximize the parent response.

Visits to the classroom Most parents are keen to understand the teachers' methods. Parents can be invited in small groups at predetermined times to see the children at work – these may be termly, fortnightly or weekly, depending on local circumstances. Experience suggests that parents will make a special effort to see the 'class assembly'.

Consultations Individual consultations between parent and teacher probably provide the single most important opportunity for parents to find out about their children's progress and how best to help them. Give parents a choice of appointment times and make sure the time allowed is long enough to discuss the child in detail – be a good listener. Ensure that such consultations are in private. The children's work should be available on the day before the consultation for parents to collect and browse through at home – this will provide a firm basis for discussion.

Unless the consultation time is used wisely by teachers and heads, the parent may be more alienated than helped by such meetings. To help teachers prepare for such consultations, ask them to observe these *don'ts*:

1. Don't let your desk form a barricade between you and the parent. Encourage the parent to join you sitting around a table or on easy chairs in the head's office.
2. Don't confuse parents with too many suggestions at any one time. Concentrate on one or two things they can do to help their child at home. Emphasize important points.

3. Don't display disapproval. Any sign that you disapprove of what a parent is saying or doing may make him or her stop talking and listening.
4. Don't pry or ask questions if the parent appears reluctant to discuss personal matters.
5. Don't assume that parents want your advice. Many come to school only because they think it is their duty. If you give the impression that they need help, they will see it as disapproval and criticism.
6. Don't generalize or sound vague. Always try to be concrete in your suggestions and specific about the areas of weakness.

There are ways in which the head can also help parents prepare for a parent–teacher consultation in advance, especially by producing some guidelines for parents. These suggestions can appear in the school brochure or may be sent home a few days prior to a meeting:

1. Ask your child if there is anything he or she would like you to discuss with the teacher.
2. Decide in advance the questions you want to ask the teacher. It is a good idea to write them down.
3. Be ready to tell the teacher a little bit about your child's home life. The school wants to know about your child's hobbies, interests and feelings. Knowing these things will be helpful in the teaching approach to your child in school.
4. If you are concerned about a rumour you have heard, or something your child has told you about his or her class or teacher, then ask about it at the consultation.
5. Be reasonable in what you expect the teacher to do and the amount of special attention your child can receive. Ask how you can meet some of the child's needs at home.
6. A phone call or visit to your child's teacher will set up an appointment at a time convenient to both of you.

Programmes designed to involve parents are only worth while if put into practice, and may be negated by one seemingly insignificant oversight by a well-intentioned member of staff or even by the head! The list of suggestions below may help the head reflect upon current parent relationships:

1. Be aware of your manner when greeting parents as they enter the school. Do you greet them with the words, 'Can I help you?' in a

tone of voice indicating something akin to, 'What are you doing here?'
2. Provide comfortable chairs for those who have to wait. Ensure that the waiting area is aesthetically pleasing, with plants and flowers a regular feature. A school brochure and examples of children's imaginative stories can also be on display.
3. Show new parents around the building and introduce them to their child's teacher. Talk with them in private about the school and encourage them to talk with you about their child without constantly bombarding them with questions.
4. Reporting bad news to parents is never easy but is far better received if done personally. So try not to resort to the typewriter before the telephone to initiate contact and, where at all possible, encourage a meeting to talk things over. It may be that the school is not the best place for this.
5. When parent's evenings/days are being held, circulate amongst the parents and chat to as many as you possibly can. Those parents who really wish to talk with you will soon search you out!
6. When a family moves from your area, present them with a farewell questionnaire about the school. The parting comments of parents can be very revealing.

Heads often assume that every parent knows of their availability. Because a few parents come into school frequently it is assumed that every parent knows just how to contact them. Parents do not automatically know how to contact the head; they do not know whether he or she welcomes phone calls from them on routine matters and, if they are new to the school, they don't know the many kinds of activities in which they are welcome to get involved. Early in the school year the head should urge parents to do the following:

1. Contact the school when a problem arises or when a crisis occurs at home that may affect the child.
2. Bring any special talent or skill they may have to the knowledge of their child's teacher.
3. Let you know when a child is enthusiastic about a class project or seems to be having particular difficulty with one.
4. Contact the school to check out the facts when they hear a rumour from their child or from a neighbour.
5. Offer their services as a volunteer helper.

Involving the Parents

The NFER Survey, *Parental Involvement in the Primary School* (Cyster, Clift and Battle, 1980), which examined the practice in primary schools ten years after the Plowden Report (Central Advisory Council for Education (England), 1967), suggests that any progress towards involving parents during the working day must be treated cautiously. Parents helping in the school are not the key method of building good home–school relationships, not only because the proportion of parents likely to be involved in this way is small but also because of the pressures placed on heads and teachers. However, the implications of the early intervention studies (Armstrong and Brown, 1979) are that there are likely to be beneficial long-term effects on parents' views of education and of their role in relation to their children's development when the school, parents and children work together. Parents should be viewed as educators, with a role to play in their child's development – their participation should be active, working directly with children, whether at home or in school.

There are three good reasons why it is important to involve parents as working partners. First, when parents work in the school they gain first-hand experience and a degree of insight into how the school functions, and therefore a firmer basis on which to discuss their child's education. Second, parents working in the school are able to offer a wide range of skills and interests that otherwise might not be available. Third, it is likely that the parents will become good 'public relations' officers for the school. This was borne out in the East Sussex Accountability Project (Cleave, Jowett and Bate, 1982), which reported that those mothers who were allowed to help in the classroom were noticeably better informed than others and often radically changed their opinions to become strong supporters of the school's activities.

Parents can be an important resource in the life of the school and are often under-utilized. However, not all parents can, or want, to work in the school and not all schools would find it easy to accommodate large numbers of parents during the day. Organizing parents as partners is no easy matter, and there is a need to consider a series of planned developments before a programme can become effective. The head is likely to play four different yet essential roles:

1. *Initiator* The head must set up staff discussion in order that the needs, interests and concerns of the teachers can be identified. There is little point in parents becoming involved unless the teachers have a

clear perception of the role of parents, recognize their possible needs and are willing to recognize the potential benefits to the school. A number of key questions need to be answered. How can the parents' contributions best be utilized throughout the school and in individual classrooms? How many parents can be accommodated? What times of day are most suitable? How regular a commitment is required, or can reasonably be expected? Do all the teachers have to be involved initially?

2. *Promoter* The head must give all parents the opportunity to offer regular help to the school. An invitation should be sent to the parents asking them to respond if at all possible, requesting information about what they would be interested in doing and inviting them to an intitial meeting with the head and class teacher. It is important that a list of activities is drawn up by the teacher and publicized so that there can be a matching of teachers' needs and parents' skills or interests.

3. *Controller* The head must make it clear whether regular or occasional help is wanted and whether or not parents may come to help without prior notice. It is preferable to work towards planned regular help so that the teacher can communicate to parents the aim of the activity and how to deal with any difficulties over either the task or matters of discipline.

4. *Maintainer* The head must ensure through frequent discussion with teachers and parents that the partnership is able to develop. Parents must feel welcome in the school and should be provided with refreshments at break times, when they can meet either with the other parents or informally with the staff for discussion. The teacher's first task is to attend to the children. It may be that the involvement in the classroom of certain parents could present difficulties to the teacher, or to the children of those parents, and therefore this should be carefully explained to such parents. Some teachers will be unhappy with parents as partners in the classroom, but may be amenable to accepting other kinds of help, for example, in the preparation of teaching resources in an area away from the parent's own children. Experience suggests that the assistance of some parents in the classroom can be a valuable asset, but only at the teacher's instigation. If there are teachers who lack the confidence or experience to be involved with parents, then it is important not to rush into any partnership, but to build up a new situation gradually.

RELATIONSHIPS WITH GOVERNORS

It is understandable, given the educational climate that existed in the mid-1970s, and the conflict about the teaching methods to be used, that there was at that time a need for improved communication between the primary school and the home, if parents were to maintain confidence in the education system. The demise of the 11-plus examination, and the introduction of the 'learning by discovery' methods rather than 'rote', both of which were given ample media coverage, led to a demand amongst parents for wider participation in the life of the school. This pressure led in 1975 to the setting up of the Taylor Committee to consider the role of the school managers and governors. The view seemed to be that the power held by the school over the curriculum should be subject to the consent of those affected by the consequences of the decisions taken by the school.

The Taylor Report, *A New Partnership for Our Schools* (DES, 1977a) fully investigated parental involvement and the role the school should play. Parents were recognized as having a need for adequate communication: 'The Governing body should satisfy itself that adequate arrangements are made to inform parents, to involve them in their children's progress and welfare, to enlist their support, and to ensure their access to the school and teachers by reasonable arrangement'. In addition to their general responsibility for the wellbeing of the school and for good relationships, the governors, said the report, should establish the school's aims, share in the formation of a programme for achieving them, keep the school's progress towards them under continuous review and make periodic and more formal appraisals of that progress.

For many heads the recommendations of the Taylor Report were far-reaching and not all have found them either acceptable or easy to operate. However, since the publication of the report, some of the recommendations have been enforced by statutory measures that should, as a result, have led heads to review existing practices and the relationships between the governors, parents and the community at large.

All primary schools have a formally constituted governing body that needs to be kept well informed by the head on all matters relating to the school's organization, curriculum, allocation of resources, progress and general activities. The school governors are likely to meet at least once each term, when the head should present a written report outlining all the details of school life that will help the governors to have a clear insight into the workings of the school. In order that each governor can come to the meeting fully aware of recent school developments it is very important that the head's written report is circulated to governors at least 7–10 days before a formal meeting. In this way people can think in some detail about issues they may wish to comment upon, thus enabling the meetings to be more purposeful and relevant to the needs and interests of those associated with the local community.

The Headteacher's Report to the Governors

There are a variety of styles that can be adopted by the head in presenting a written report – the outline suggested below sets out the school's development under eleven main headings. The headings can be used as a basis for each report although certain items listed under them may only require comment at specific times during the school year:

1. *Pupils* Number on roll; class organization and size (in some schools this may only be necessary at the start of each school year); comparison with numbers on roll over the last 2–3 years at a similar stage in the school year; future numbers – falling/rising roll implications; a general statement of attendance; a general statement of lunches/sandwiches where it varies from the norm.
2. *Staffing: teaching and non-teaching* The teaching complement at the start of the academic year with any relevant details on teachers with posts of special responsibility; new appointments; resignation, with reasons; absence, with reasons.
3. *Curriculum/organizational developments* Comments on the National Curriculum and religious-education implementation and other specific projects or new approaches; assessment and testing; changes in teaching/class organization; educational visits; courses attended by staff; the development of schemes of work for each curriculum area.
4. *Extracurricular activities* Special events such as plays and concerts; news of clubs and societies; information on any inter-school activities.
5. *Parental involvement* Activities organized by the school and any form of parent association.
6. *Finance* An update of expenditure matched to budgeted targets.
7. *Buildings* Repairs; improvements; furnishing and equipment; the general appearance of the school building and surrounds; anticipated future needs.

8. *Health and safety* Visits of school nurse, dentist, doctor, etc.; a report on termly fire drill; any matter relating to general health and safety.
9. *Visitors* Details of any special visitors to the school.
10. *Special items* Requests for leave of absence; requests for secondment; requests for occasional holidays; a review of special needs that cannot be met within the school allowance.
11. *Future events* Dates of activities that are taking place in the school in the months before the next governors' meeting.

It is always wise for the head to have talked prior to the meeting with the chair of governors about any item in the head's report on the agenda that may need clarification, or points it is thought may give rise to debate amongst the governing body.

KEEPING GOVERNORS INFORMED

One of the most important responsibilities for primary-school governors under the Education Reform Act 1988 is the duty 'to secure that the national curriculum is followed in their schools' (DES, 1988). Each headteacher must make it a high priority to ensure that all govenors are fully helped and supported in this task. There are some governors who feel inhibited in the face of professional educators and who don't trust their own judgment or instincts; and there are others who swing to the other extreme and want to question in minute detail what goes on in the school. The Education Reform Act places governors in a position where the 'need to know' is essential and, however the need arises or in whatever form this presents itself, if ought to be fulfilled. The governors are faced with more sharply defined management responsibilities for the curriculum policy of the school, including specific responsibilities for providing religious education and collective worship, and will be partners with the head and staff in a new way. Fundamentally, governors represent the community – local and individual – of a particular school, and those who earn their living within the school need to be able to rely on governors to hold up a mirror of the world outside school.

Everything that goes on in a school contributes to the pupils' education and development. Before governors can evaluate that experience they need to know what changes the school is trying to bring about in their pupils; how it will help them to develop emotionally and socially; and what values and attitudes it seeks to encourage and support. A statement of aims need to be agreed between head, staff and governors, and is a working task for everybody involved in the school. It helps decision-making and enables people to know what they are there for and to make sense of their experience. Against this background, heads should encourage governors to raise questions about the curriculum, both in terms of what is being planned and what is being experienced by the pupils, which are not necessarily the same thing. Some key questions governors ought to be asking the head and staff based on visits to classrooms, preferably while the pupils are in session, are as follows:

- What are the links between the subjects of the National Curriculum?
- Where subjects are integrated, how is coherence maintained?
- How does the curriculum make sense to children in the context of this school?
- How are children challenged to think for themselves?
- Does the curriculum carry through to the home in activities supported and understood by parents?
- How does the school cope with children who are exempt from the National Curriculum?
- How does the school link assessment and curriculum plans?
- Are the children happy with their experiences? How do we know?
- What provision is made for children with special educational needs?

Governors may be helped to assess needs realistically if challenged to think about objectives for the school curriculum in three stages. In the long term, there is the complete curriculum package children will have received by the age of 11 years. In the medium term, there are the aims and objectives for each year group and how they relate is the whole. Then, in the short term, there is the detailed planning of the term's work for each class, and consideration of how individual children's varied needs can be catered for. Finally, there is the assessment of children at 7 and 11 years respectively. Governors should be encouraged to join with teachers to ensure that the assessment procedures do not become too time consuming or that they begin to restrict the development of a broad, balanced, differentiated and relevant curriculum. It is the responsibility of governors to see that the results of assessments are used wisely to inform parents about their children's progress and to help parents form a broad picture of the school's achievements.

Alongside the governors responsibility for securing the National Curriculum is the task of dealing with delegated budgets as part of local management of schools. As with the curriculum issues, it will be necessary for heads to encourage governors to ask questions regarding expenditure relating to the planned budget targets. Above all it will probably be necessary to form a smaller governors' sub-group to examine the detailed financial arrangements. At governors meetings the head should report on the visit of LEA officers/inspectors when any form of 'auditing' has taken place, whether it be of finances, the curriculum or school management. The governors need to recognize the LEA strategic role in monitoring and evaluating the work of schools and play an active part in responding to the information received.

There will be times during the year when it may be appropriate to give the governors the opportunity to be fully informed in depth on specific aspects of curriculum development when, by invitation, other members of staff can join a governors' meeting either to talk to the governors or to run a short workshop session. It is important that such sessions are planned well in advance by the head and staff so that every attempt is made to involve all governors actively in the learning process. Although all governors' meetings have an air of formality about them the head should make every effort to help people feel comfortable and relaxed in the school setting. Each governor should be greeted on arrival, when tea or coffee can be available for those who require refreshment. The arrangement of furniture should allow for relaxed seating with no large tables as barriers between various groups within the room. Some spare pencils and paper could be at hand for those who come without them so that they can keep notes of any particular points of interest.

The chair of governors should be kept regularly informed between meetings of developments within the school that fall within the jurisdiction of the governing body. Indeed, keeping in frequent contact with the chair throughout the school year is a most important and necessary role the head must play to ensure that decisions and information affecting the school are fully shared. There should also be many opportunities for the governors to be involved with the school in a whole range of activities that will provide them with the chance to see pupils at work, talk to the staff and meet the parents. The five points below will act as a reminder of some of the times when governors may wish to visit the school:

1. At any time during the school day to gain some experience of the processes by which children learn and teachers teach.
2. At specific times when aspects of curriculum policy are being developed that may add a new dimension to the work of the school.

3. All parents' evenings or open days when children's work will be on display and parents will be visiting the school.
4. When any curriculum activity is held to inform parents of the methods used to teach the children.
5. All concerts or special productions when the children will be demonstrating their various talents.

It may be that not all governors accept such invitations, but it is essential that they are invited to play their part in the integral life of the school so that they can have the chance to carry out their assigned responsibilities with as much information about the school as possible. Whilst all governors may not be fully versed in all that is involved in good primary practice there will be many who are likely to have considerable knowledge about education in general, and whose level of interest is very high indeed. The head must always be seeking to keep the channels of communication with the governors completely open, thus avoiding the criticism that the 'professionals' are not prepared to share working ideas and practices.

REFERENCES AND BIBLIOGRAPHY

ACAS (1986) Teachers' Dispute: ACAS Independent Panel Report of the Appraisal and Training Working Group, in DES (1989) *School Teacher Appraisal: A National Framework*, HMSO, London.
Adair, J. (1983) *Effective Leadership*, Pan Books, London.
Anning, A. (1983) The three year itch, *The Times Educational Supplement*, 24 June.
Argyris, C. and Schon, D. A. (1976) *Theory in Practice: Increasing Professional Effectiveness*, Jossey-Bass, San Francisco, Calif.
Armstrong, G. and Brown, F. (1979) *Five Years On: A Follow Up Study of the Long Term Effects on Parents and Children of an Early Learning Programme in the Home*, Social Evaluation Unit, Oxford.
Ashton, P. et al. (1975) *Aims into Practice in the Primary School*, Hodder & Stoughton, London.
Auld, R. (1976) *William Tyndale Junior and Infant Schools Public Enquiry*, ILEA, London.
Barker Lunn, J. (1984) Junior school teachers: their methods and practices, *Educational Research*, Vol. 26, no. 3.
Barnes, D. (1976) *From Communication to Curriculum*, Penguin Books, Harmondsworth.
Barnes, D. (1982) *Practical Curriculum Study*, Routledge & Kegan Paul, London.
Bassey, M. and Hatch, N. (1979) A seven-category interaction and analysis for infant teachers to use themselves, *Education Research*, Vol. 21, no. 2.
Becher, A., Eraut, M. and Knight, J. (1981) *Policies for Educational Accountability*, Heinemann, London.
Birchenough, M. (1985) *Making School Based Review Work*, NDC, School of Education, University of Bristol.
Central Advisory Council for Education (England) (1967) *Children and Their*

Primary Schools (the Plowden Report), Vol. 1, HMSO, London.
Cleave, S., Jowett, S. and Bate, M. (1982) *And So to School*, NFER/Nelson, Slough.
Consortium of Teacher Appraisal Pilot Schemes Newsletter (1989) National Development Centre for School Management Training, May.
Cormier, W. H. and Cormier, L. S. (1979) *Interviewing Strategies for Helpers: A Guide to Assessment, Treatment and Evaluation*, Brooks/Cole, Monterey, Calif.
Coulson, A. (1986) *The Managerial Work of Primary School Headteachers*, Department of Education Management, Sheffield City Polytechnic.
Coulson, A. (1987) Recruitment and management development for primary headship, in G. Southworth (ed.) *Readings in Primary School Management*, Falmer Press, Lewes.
Cyster, R., Clift, P. S. and Battle, S. (1980) *Parental Involvement in the Primary School*, NFER, Slough.
Davis, E. (1981) *Teachers as Curriculum Evaluators*, Allen & Unwin, London.
Day, C. W. (1981) *Classroom Based In-Service Teacher Education: The Development and Evaluation of a Client-Centred Model*, University of Sussex Education Area, Occasional Paper no. 9.
Day, C. (1989) *Promoting School-Focused Professional Learning and Change through LEA Devolved Ownership and Decision Making* (paper presented to International Conference of the Classroom Action Research Network), University of East Anglia, 15–17 September.
Day, C. W. and Baskett, H. K. (1982) Discrepancies between intentions and practice: re-examining some basic assumptions about adult and continuing professional education, *International Journal of Lifelong Education*, Vol. 1, no 2.
Day, C., Whitaker, P. and Wren, D. (1987) *Appraisal and Professional Development in Primary Schools*, Open University Press, Milton Keynes.
Dean, J. (1987) *Managing the Primary School*, Croom Helm, Beckenham.
DES (1975) *Report of the Committee of Inquiry appointed by the Secretary of State for Education and Science under the chairmanship of Sir Alan Bullock (A Language for Life)*, HMSO, London.
DES (1977a) *A New Partnership for our Schools* (the Taylor Report), HMSO, London.
DES (1977b) *Information for Parents* (circular 15/77), HMSO, London.
DES (1978) *Primary Education in England*, HMSO, London.
DES (1981) *The School Curriculum* (circular 6/81), HMSO, London.
DES (1982) *Report of the Committee of Inquiry into the Teaching of Mathematics in Schools under the Chairmanship of Dr W. H. Cockcroft (Mathematics Counts)*, HMSO, London.
DES (1983) *Teaching Quarterly*, HMSO, London.
DES (1984) *Education Observed – A Review of Published Reports by HM Inspectors*, HMSO, London.
DES (1985) *The Curriculum from 5–16: Curriculum Matters 2*, HMSO, London.

DES (1986) *Education (No.2) Act*, HMSO, London.
DES (1988) *Circular 7/88: Education Reform Act 1988: Local Management of Schools*, HMSO, London.
DES (1989a) *Circular 14/89: School Curriculum and Related Information Regulations*, HMSO, London.
DES (1989b) *The Implementation of the Local Education Authority Training Grants Scheme (LEATGS): Report on First Year of the Scheme 1987–88*, HMSO, London.
Doyle, W. and Ponder, C. A. (1976) The practicality ethic in teacher decision making, *Interchange*, Vol. 8, 1977.
Easen, P. (1985) *Making School-Centred INSET Work*, Croom Helm in association with the Open University Press, London.
East Sussex Accountability Project (1979) *Accountability in the Middle Years of Schooling: An Analysis of Policy Options*, University of Sussex (mimeo.) in R. McCormick (ed.) (1982) op. cit.
Egan, G. (1982) *The Skilled Helper*, Brooks/Cole, Monterey, Calif.
Eisner, E. W. (1979) *The Educational Imagination*, Collier Macmillan, West Drayton.
Elliott, G. (1981) *Self Evaluation and The Teacher*, parts 1–4, Schools Council, London.
Elliott, G. (1982) *Self Evaluation and the Teacher*, parts 1–3, Schools Council, London.
Elliott, J. (1973) Is instruction outmoded?, *Cambridge Journal of Education*, Vol. 3, no. 3.
Elliott, J. (1975) The values of the neutral teacher, in D. Bridges and P. Scrimshaw (eds.) *Values and Authority in Schools*, Hodder & Stoughton, London.
Elliott, J. (1976) Preparing teachers for classroom accountability, *Education for Teaching (Journal of the National Association of Teachers in Further and Higher Education)*, no 100.
Elliott, J. (1978) *Who Should Monitor Performance in Schools?*(mimeo.), Cambridge Institute of Education.
Elliott, J. (1981) Action-research: a framework for self-evaluation in school, Schools Council programme 2, *Teacher–Pupil Interaction and the Quality of Learning Project*, Cambridge Institute of Education working paper no. 1, in J. Elliott and D. Ebbutt, op. cit.
Elliott, J. (1982) Institutionalizing action research in schools, in J. Elliott and D. Whitehead (eds.) *Action Research for Professional Development and Improvement in Schools 5*, CARN Publications, Cambridge.
Elliott, J. and Ebbutt, D. (eds.) (forthcoming) *Facilitating Action Research in Schools*, Falmer Press, Lewes.
Elliott-Kemp, J. and Rogers, C. (1982) *The Effective Teacher*, Sheffield City Polytechnic.
Eraut, M. E. (1977) Strategies for promoting teacher development, *British Journal of In-Service Education*, Vol. 4, nos. 1–2.

Eraut, M. E. (1982) What is learned in in-service education and how, *British Journal of In-Service Education*, Vol. 9, no. 1.

Eraut, M. E. (1988) Learning about management: the role of the management course, in C. Poster and C. Day (eds.) *Partnership in Education Management*, Routledge, London.

Eraut, M. E. (1989) Teacher appraisal and/or teacher development: friends or foes?, in H. Simons and J. Elliott (eds.) *Rethinking Appraisal and Assessment*, Open University Press, Milton Keynes.

Ford Teaching Project (1975) *Unit 2: Research Methods: Ways of Doing Research in one's own Classroom*, CARE, University of East Anglia.

Friesen, J. W. (1987) *Reforming the Schools for Teachers*, University Press of America, Lanham.

Galton, M. and Simon, B. (1980) *Progress and Performance in the Primary Classroom*, Routledge & Kegan Paul, London.

Galton, M. et al. (1980) *Inside the Primary Classroom*, Routledge & Kegan Paul, London.

Gray, H. and Coulson, A. A. (1982) Teacher education, management and the facilitation of change, *Educational Change and Development*, Vol. 4, no.1.

Habermas, J. (1972) *Knowledge and Human Interest*, Heinemann, London.

Hand, G. (1981) First catch your adviser: The INSET role of advisers, in C. Donoughue et al. (eds.) *In-Service: The Teacher and The School*, Kogan Page, London.

Havelock, R. G. (1971) The utilization of educational research and development, *British Journal of Educational Technology*, Vol. 2, no. 2.

Havelock, R. G. (1973) *The Change Agent's Guide to Innovation*, Educational Technology Publications, Englewood Cliffs, NJ.

Herzberg, F. (1966) *Work and the Nature of Man*, World Publishing, Cleveland, Ohio.

HMSO (1985) *Better Schools* (white paper), London.

Hopkins, D. (1986) *Inservice Training and Educational Development: An International Survey*, Croom Helm, Beckenham.

House, E. (1972) The conscience of educational evaluation, *Teachers College Record*, Vol. 73, no. 3.

House of Commons, Education, Science and Arts Committee (1986) *Achievement in Primary Schools*, Vol. 1, HMSO, London.

Hughes, M. (1976) The professional-as-administrator: the case of the secondary school head, in R. S. Peters (ed.) *The Role of the Head*, Routledge & Kegan Paul, London.

Hughes, M. (1988) Leadership in professionally staffed organisations, in R. Glatter et al. (eds.) *Understanding School Management*, Open University Press, Milton Keynes.

ILEA (1983) *Keeping the School Under Review*, ILEA, London.

ILEA (1985) *Improving Primary Schools, Report of the Committee on Primary Education*, ILEA, London.

ILEA (1986) *The Junior Schools Project*, ILEA, London.
The Industrial Society (1983) *Action-Centred Leadership*, Education for the Industrial Society, London.
Keddie, N. (1971) Classroom knowledge, in M. E. D. Young (ed.) *Knowledge and Control*, Collier Macmillan, London.
Kelman, H. (1961) Three processes of social influence, *Public Opinion Quarterly*, Vol. 25.
Kemmis, S. *et al.* (1981) *The Action Research Planner*, Deakin University Press, Geelong, Victoria, Open Campus Program.
Lacey, C. (1977) *The Socialisation of Teachers*, Methuen, London.
Lewis, M. E. (1987) *Continuation of a Curriculum Innovation: Salient and Alterable Variables* (paper presented to the Annual Meeting of the American Educational Research Association), Washington, DC, April.
Lippitt, R. and White, R. K. (1943) The social climate of children's groups, in R. Barker *et al.* (eds.) *Child Behavior and Development*, McGraw Hill, New York, NY.
MacDonald, B. (1973) Innovation and competence, in D. Hammingson (ed.) *Towards Judgement: The Publications of the Evaluation Unit of Humanities Curriculum Project 1970–2*, Centre for Applied Research in Education, Nottingham, occasional publication no. 1, pp. 88–92.
MacDonald, B. (1974) quoted in Walker, R. (1980) The conduct of educational case studies: ethics, theory and procedures, in W. B. Dockrell and D. Hamilton (eds.) (1980) *Rethinking Educational Research*, Hodder & Stoughton Educational, London.
MacDonald, B. (1978) Accountability, standards and the process of schooling, in A. Becher and S. Maclure (eds.) *Accountability in Education*, NFER, Windsor.
Machiavelli (1513) in A. Harris *et al.* (eds.) (1979) *Curriculum Innovation*, Croom Helm in association with the Open University Press, London.
Maritain, J. (1960) *Education at the Crossroads*, Yale University Press, New Haven, Conn.
Maslow, A. (1968) *Towards a Psychology of Being* (2nd ed.), Van Nostrand-Reinhold, New York, NY.
Maslow, A. (1970) *Motivation and Personality* (2nd ed.) Harper & Row, New York, NY.
McCormick, R. (ed.) (1982) *Calling Education to Account*, Open University/Heinemann Educational, London.
McCormick, R. and James, M. (1983) *Curriculum Evaluation in Schools*, Croom Helm, Beckenham.
McGregor, D. (1960) *The Human Side of Enterprise*, McGraw-Hill, New York, NY.
McMahon, A., Bolam, R. and Holly, P. (1984) *Guidelines for the Review and Internal Development of Schools: Primary School Handbook*, SCDC/Longman, York.

Meighan, R. (1981) *A Sociology of Educating*, Holt, Rinehart & Winston, London.
Miles, M. B., Saxl, E. R. and Lieberman, A. (1988) What skills do educational 'change agents' need? An empirical view, *Curriculum Inquiry 18*, no. 2, Ontario Institute for Studies in Education.
Miller, D. C. and Fom, F. H. (1966) *Industrial Sociology*, Harper & Row, New York, NY.
Morris, B. (1972) *Objectives and Perspectives in Education*, Routledge & Kegan Paul, London.
NDC/SMT (1989) *Consortium of Teacher Appraisal Pilot Schemes*, Newsletter, May, NDC/SMT, Bristol.
Nias, D. J. (1987a) *The Culture of Collaboration* (summary of paper given at BERA Conference), Manchester, September.
Nias, D. J. (1987b) The Primary School Staff Relationships Project: origins, aims and methods, *Cambridge Journal of Education*, Vol. 17, no. 2.
Nias, D. J., Southworth, G. W. and Yeomans, R. (1989) *Staff Relationships in the Primary School: A Study of School Culture*, Cassell, London.
Nuttall, D. (1981) *School Self-Evaluation: Accountability with a Human Face?*, Schools Council/Longman, London.
Oldham LEA (1988) *A Model for Teacher Appraisal Linked to School Based Review and Development*, Advisers' Office, Byron Street Teachers' Centre, Oldham.
Open University (1980) *Curriculum in Action: An Approach to Evaluation* (P234, Blocks 1 and 3) Open University Press, Milton Keynes.
Peters, R. S. (1968) Must an educator have an aim?, in R. S. Peters (ed.) *Concepts of Teaching*, Macmillan & Nelson, London and Windsor.
Postman, N. and Weingartner, C. (1971) *Teaching as a Subversive Activity*, Penguin Books, London.
Rogers, C. (1983) *Freedom to Learn for the 80's*, Charles Merrill, Columbus, OH.
Rosenholtz, S. J. (1989) *Schools, Social Organization and the Building of a Technical Culture*, Longman, New York, NY.
Schmuck, R. A. (1980) Interventions for strengthening the school's creativity, in T. Bush *et al.* (eds.) *Approaches to School Management*, Harper & Row, London.
Schon, D. A. (1983) *The Reflective Practitioner: How Professionals Think in Action*, Temple Smith, London.
Schools Council (1981) *The Practical Curriculum – Schools Council Working Paper 70*, Methuen Educational, London.
Schools Council (1983) *Primary Practice – Schools Council Working Paper 75*, Methuen Educational, London.
Schulman, L. S. and Keisler, E. R. (eds.) (1966) *Learning by Discovery: A Critical Appraisal*, Rand McNally, Chicago, Ill.
Seligman, M. E. P. (1975) *Helplessness: On Depression, Development and Death*, W. H. Freeman, San Francisco, Calif.

Sharp, R. and Green, A. (1975) *Education and Social Control*, Routledge & Kegan Paul, London.

Simons, H. and Elliott, J. V. (eds.) (1989) *Rethinking Appraisal and Assessment*, Open University Press, Milton Keynes.

Skilbeck, M. (1982) School based curriculum development: a functionalist/environmentalist approach to curriculum change, in D. Barnes, op. cit.

Somerset LEA (1987) *Review and Development: An Introduction to Appraisal* (introductory pamphlet), Taunton.

Southworth, G. (1988) Vision and visibility, *Education*, Vol. 172, no. 10, September.

Southworth, G. (1990) Leadership, headship and effective primary schools, *School Organisation*, Vol 10, no 1.

Stake, R. E. (1967) The countenance of educational evaluation, *Teacher's College Record*, Vol. 68.

Stake, R. E. (1975) Language, rationality and assessment, in W. H. Beatty (ed.) *Improving Educational Assessment and an Inventory of Measures for Affective Behavior*, Association For Supervision and Curriculum Development, Washington, DC.

Steele, F. (1975) *Consulting for Organizational Change*, University of Massachusetts Press, Amherst, Mass.

Stenhouse, L. (1975) *An Introduction to Curriculum Research and Development*, Heinemann Educational, London.

Stenhouse, L. (1979) *What is Action-Research?* (mimeo.), CARE, University of East Anglia.

Sutcliffe, J. and Whitfield, R. (1976) Decison making in the classroom; an initial report, *Research Intelligence*, Vol. 2, no. 1.

Thompson, A. (1984) The use of video as an observation tool, in L. Thompson and A. Thompson, *What Learning Looks Like: Helping Individual Teachers to Become More Effective*, Schools Council (Program 2) Longman, London.

Walker, R. and Adelman, C. (1975) *Guide to Classroom Observation*, Methuen, London.

Whitaker, P. (1983) *The Primary Head*, Heinemann Educational, London.

Whitaker, P. (1984) *The Process of Change*, Personal Learning Associates, Leicester.

Winter, R. (1989) Problems in teacher appraisal – an action-research solution, in H. Simons and J. Elliott (eds.) op. cit.

Wise, A. E., Darling-Hammond, L., McLaughan, M. W. and Bernstein, H. T. (1984) *Teacher Evaluation: A Study of Effective Practice*, Rand Corporation, June.

Yeomans, G. (1986) A different way of dancing? An alternative perspective on leading and belonging to a primary school staff, *Cambridge Journal of Education*, Vol. 16, no. 3.

AUTHOR INDEX

Adair, J 39, 137
Adelman, C 192
Anning, A 140
Argyris, C 163
Armstrong, G 206
Auld, R 139

Barker Lunn, J 137, 139
Barnes, D 116, 149
Baskett, H 133
Bassey, M 149
Bate, M 202, 206
Battle, S 206
Bolam, R 179, 181
Brown, F 206

Cleave, S 202, 206
Clift, P 206
Cormier, W 178
Cormier, L 178
Coulson, A 3, 7, 10, 11, 37
Cyster, R 206

Davis, E 186
Day, C 19, 42, 132, 133, 172, 187, 192, 195
Dean, J 7
Doyle, W 117, 125, 129, 164

Easen, P 179, 183

Egan, G 125, 134
Eisner, E 188
Elliott, G 180
Elliott, J 114, 132, 149, 175, 190, 191, 192
Elliott-Kemp, J 40
Eraut, M 12, 22, 128, 131, 173, 190, 191, 192

Fom, F 125
Friesen, J x

Galton, M 149, 157
Gray, H 37
Green, A 149

Habermas, J 192
Hand, G 119
Hatch, N 149
Havelock, R 22-23, 130
Herzberg, F 107
Holly, P 179, 181
Hopkins, D 195
House, E 164
Hughes, M 9

James, M 190
Jowett, S 202, 206

Keddie, N 115, 187

Author Index

Keisler, E 149
Kelman, H 16
Kemmis, S 190, 191

Lacey, C 115
Lewis, M 116
Lieberman, A 117, 120, 121
Lippitt, R 14

MacDonald, B 19, 128, 130, 132, 188
Machiavelli, N 114
Maslow, A 108, 111
McCormick, R 166, 190
McGregor, D 13
McMahon, A 179, 181
Meighan, R 14–15
Miles, M 117, 120, 121
Miller, D 125
Morris, B xii

Nias, D, J 3, 5, 6
Nutall, D 165

Peters, R 148
Ponder, C 117, 125, 164
Postman, N 155

Rogers, C 40, 60, 154, 159
Rosenholtz, S 6

Saxl, E 117, 120, 121
Schmuck, R 134
Schon, D 126, 163
Schulman, L 149
Seligman, M 16
Sharp, R 149
Simon, B 149
Skilbeck, M 128, 182
Southworth, G 3, 4, 6
Stake, R 12
Steele, F 7
Stenhouse, L 188, 190
Sutcliffe, J 114

Thompson, A 194

Walker, R 192
Weingartner, C 155
Whitaker, P 42, 138, 140, 195
White, R 14
Whitfield, R 114
Winter, R 176
Wise, A 176
Wren, D 42, 172, 195

Yeomans, R 4, 5

SUBJECT INDEX

accountability 165–167, 198
achievement 108
action planning 178
action research 189–191
action-centred leadership 9–14
affiliation 108
agendas 84, 85
allowances 32, 33, 105
annual plan 45, 48
answerability 165
appraisal 1, 9, 37, 42, 51, 52, 54, 69, 81, 103–105, 118, 134, 162–196; ACAS Report 167; appraisal interview 172–175; National Steering Group on Appraisal 167, 171, 173; appraisal record 170; peer group appraisal 52, self appraisal 60, 170; teacher entitlements 177
appreciation 108
assessing candidates 79
assessment 27, 30, 37, 211
attainment targets 45
attainment targets 45, 138
authority 106, 107
autonomy 175–178

Bechers Brook 140
budget 45
Bullock Report, The 32
"burden of incompetence" 128, 132

Callaghan, James 1
catalyst 131
change 19, 36, 37, 38, 39, 185; change agent 114, 130; promoting change 116–117; resistance to change 117–123
classroom observation 150, 170, 172, 175, 190–193
climate 28
cliques 101, 102
co-management 33, 42, 51, 54, 55
Cockroft Report, The 32
collaboration 136
colleagueship 129
collegial management 34, 129
communication 17, 27, 46, 49, 81, 82, 108, 118, 165, 197, 198, 208; non-verbal communication 77, 87–89
communications network 8
complaints 99–101
conflict 6, 47, 60, 132, 185, 200
confrontation 26
congruence 41
consultancy 1–31
contracting 177
creating 46, 49
"critical friend" 21, 53, 124, 192–195
culture 2, 4, 6
curriculum management 38, 136–161; curriculum balance 158; curriculum

breadth 158; curriculum consultants 32; curriculum development 36, 37, 212; curriculum differentiation 158; curriculum guidelines 38; curriculum planning 138–141; curriculum progression 158; curriculum relevance 158; curriculum review 37

decision making 16
delegation 3, 27, 102–107, 108
delegation 108
"details on request" 58, 62
difficult people 123, 124
DION 42
directed time 1

Education No 2 Act (1986) 199
Education Reform Act (1988) 113, 199, 210
empathy 17, 41
encouragement 41
equal opportunities 65, 68
ethos 28
evaluating 46, 50, 137
expectations 138, 141, 142

feedback 102–103
flow charts 156
Fom 125
force field analysis 123–126

goals 91, 92, 93, 107
governors 8, 48, 56, 59, 82, 130, 167, 177–180, 197–213
"grapevine" 86
"great debate" 198
GRIDS 42, 179, 181–183

heads report to governors 209
human resources 35

ILEA 2, 3, 180
induction 80
influence 108
information for candidates 61–65
innovation and change 113–135
innovation overload 127
INSET days 116

interdependence 6, 133
interpersonal skills 104, 111, 112, 158
interviewing 71–73

job description 64, 175, 187
job outline 47
job rotation 34
job specification 163

leadership 1–31, 35, 39–41, 46, 47, 50, 114, 130–132, 167–173; authoritarian leadership 14–15; democratic leadership 14–15; leadership intervention 20–24; leadership skills 25; leadership style 14, 81; leading by example 17; leading professional 148
"learned helplessness" 16
learning enriched school 6
learning environment 159
learning impoverished school 6
learning process 144–147
LEATGS 116
listening 5, 75, 90, 91, 99, 118, 198, 203
Local Management of Schools 116, 119, 171, 211

"management by wandering about" 5
management functions 46, 49; management review exercise 43; management style 2; group focused management 41; management partnership 55
marketing 1
meetings 81, 82, 83–85, 86, 92, 151, 163, 203, 204
motivation 16–20, 21–25, 29, 46, 68, 81–83, 103, 128, 161, 200
"myself as a learner" 152
"myself as a teacher" 152

National Curriculum Development Plans 138
National Curriculum 1, 2, 6, 30, 37, 38, 43, 115, 119, 134, 136, 137, 138, 145, 146, 176, 202, 209, 211
needs and motivation 107–112; individual needs 25–26, institutional

Subject Index

needs 25–26; needs identification exercise 58
negotiation 5, 24, 25
notice boards 48, 86, 203

Oldham LEA 183, 184
Open University 189, 192
optimism 41
ORACLE 149, 157
organisational health 28
organizing 46, 49
"ownership" 129, 134

parents 197–213; parent/teacher consultations 203–205; parent power 200
participation 24, 27, 33, 57, 85–87, 133–135, 136, 141; participatory management 36, 37, 60, 161
person centred teaching 159
person specification 64
planning 3, 12, 13, 16, 19, 27, 43, 44, 46, 48, 55, 91, 92, 118, 126, 137, 211
Plowden Report, The i, 2, 37, 201, 206
policy group 47, 82
positive regard 41
power and authority 2
predilections 138, 141, 142
prescriptions 138, 141, 142
presenting image 76, 78
priorities and procedures 91, 92, 93, 200
process helper 131, 132
professional development 22, 38, 46, 48, 50, 58, 80, 115, 130, 132, 145, 160, 162, 165, 187, 190; professional development policy 80
professional learning 22, 114–116
professional qualities checklist 59
programmes of study 138
pupil feedback 155

questioning 73

record keeping 3, 202
references 69–71

reflection 20, 114, 115, 126, 127, 194
relationships 16–20, 28, 132, 133
responsibility 165
restricted professionality 163
reviewing 34, 48, 52, 53, 151, 162–196; whole school review 178–185
risks 39
role definition 50, 53
role plan 50, 51, 52
roles and responsibilities 33–55, 108; development approach 48–53; functional approach 42–48

school brochure 62
school development plan 1, 50, 134, 177
school philosophy and values 141–144
selection of staff 56–80
self awareness 40
self concept 40, 60, 74, 75, 109
self image 19, 106, 132
single loop learning 163
situations 138, 141, 142
solution giver 131
Somerset LEA 168, 169, 171
staff development 34
staff mobility 34
"stone age obstructionists" 164
summarising 78
supporting staff 18, 31

teamwork 32, 34, 39, 40, 41, 45, 50, 55, 57, 58, 60, 80, 82, 136; team leadership 24–27
term plans 48
"theory X" 13–14, 22
"theory Y" 13–14
time 127, 201; time management 92–98; timing 16; containable time 26
triangulation 193
trust 41
"twelve sixty five hours" 116, 173

vision 8
visiting other schools 160
visits and visiting 65–69

ways and means group 47
will to achieve 41

year plans 48